THE LEFT'S JEWISH PROBLEM

THE LEFT'S JEWISH PROBLEM

JEREMY CORBYN, ISRAEL AND ANTISEMITISM

DAVE RICH

Biteback Publishing

This new edition published in Great Britain in 2018 by
Biteback Publishing Ltd
Westminster Tower
3 Albert Embankment
London SE1 7SP
Copyright © Dave Rich 2016, 2018

ISBN 978-1-78590-427-1

10 9 8 7 6 5 4 3 2 1

A CIP catalogue record for this book is available from the British Library.

Set in Arno Pro by Adrian McLaughlin

Printed and bound in Great Britain by
CPI Group (UK) Ltd, Croydon CR0 4YY

In memory of

Yoel Kohen Ülçer z"l

1 January 1984 – 15 November 2003

and

Dan Uzan z"l

2 June 1977 – 15 February 2015

Who gave their lives protecting their communities

CONTENTS

PREFACE TO THE NEW EDITION

In 2011, I began work on a history PhD about the growth of left-wing anti-Zionism in Britain from the 1960s until the 1980s and how it affected relations between Jews and the left. It looked mainly at a narrow part of left-wing politics over a relatively short period of time and, like most PhD theses, I assumed it would be of interest only to a limited audience. Yet, by the time I graduated in 2016, the subject of my research was no longer a matter of history and had returned to the front pages of Britain's newspapers. The election of Jeremy Corbyn as Labour Party leader had, for one reason or another, made antisemitism and left-wing attitudes to Jews, Israel and Zionism a subject of national debate. It left me in the position of having something new to say about an old subject, and I set about converting my thesis into a political book explaining why this had happened. I expected it to have a short shelf-life: in the period between completing the first edition of this book at the end of June 2016 and its publication in early September of that year, most of the shadow Cabinet resigned,

Labour MPs overwhelmingly backed a motion of no confidence in Corbyn and he was fighting a second leadership election in twelve months, having been forced to take legal action just to get onto the ballot paper. Yet, two years later, Corbyn is not only still leader of the Labour Party; his control of the party is stronger than ever, its problems with antisemitism have become more, not less, entrenched, and his relationship with the mainstream Jewish community in Britain ranges from non-existent to hostile. The day may still come when antisemitism can be left to historians, but for now, sadly, it seems as topical as ever.

This updated second edition tells the story of why this is the case. It has two new chapters covering the period from Corbyn's election as Labour leader in September 2015 to Ken Livingstone's resignation from the party in May 2018, in addition to the original six chapters of the first edition, which remain unchanged. Taken together, they explain the origin and growth of these political trends on the British left, where they came from, how they ended up in the Labour Party, and the impact they have had on Labour's relations with British Jews. The early chapters draw on my original PhD thesis, but this book is quite different in both content and style and is hopefully more readable as a result. While my thesis ended in the 1980s, this book brings the story up to date, with new research covering the period since the 9/11 terrorist attacks, the war in Iraq and the profound change in the leadership and membership of the Labour Party.

When this book was first published in September 2016, I was grateful that most reviews were positive, but writing a second edition gives me the opportunity to consider criticisms that were made by some reviewers. One was that its primary focus should have been the alleged Israeli mistreatment of Palestinians and enduring occupation of Palestinian land, which, so these critics argued, is sufficient explanation of why relations between British Jews and the left have deteriorated so much. This misses the point: as I explain in the Introduction, this is not another book is about the Israeli–Palestinian conflict, but rather about attitudes and responses to that conflict on the British left that at times, however unwittingly, have incorporated or invigorated traditional antisemitic stereotypes and tropes. Another criticism was that I did not state whether I believe Jeremy Corbyn to be personally antisemitic, or whether anti-Zionism is invariably a form of antisemitism. The first question is one I address in the new material in this edition. On the second point, I argue throughout the book that while in theory a non-antisemitic form of anti-Zionism is possible and in the past has been quite common, in practice the dominant forms of anti-Zionism found on the left nowadays are usually antisemitic, whether by motivation, language or impact.

The most negative reviews and comments about this book came largely from anti-Zionist left-wing Jews. They paid it much more attention than any Palestinians did. It was as if they saw it as a threat to their own politics and to the position they have carved out for themselves as valued Jewish voices in parts of the left that are largely hostile to, or uninterested in, the concerns of the rest of the Jewish community. If that is the case, they will dislike this second edition even more than the first. The new chapters in this edition argue that Jewish anti-Zionists, in defending their own small patch of political ground, have done a great deal of damage to the left's relations with the wider Jewish community. They are central to the story of Labour antisemitism under Corbyn's leadership.

One challenge in writing about political history as it happens is that it can quickly go out of date, but, as this book explains, the political trends on the left that brought the problem of antisemitism into the Labour Party long predate Corbyn's leadership and are unlikely to disappear any time soon. Corbyn's rise is a symbol of the problem; whatever happens to him and his party in the near future, the issue of antisemitism on the left of British politics is unlikely to go away. Another challenge is that political language changes over time. In the 1960s and 1970s, large parts of the world were collectively described as the 'Third World'. This generally included those parts of Africa, Asia and Latin America that had been colonised by European powers and were seeking and gaining independence during the post-war period. The term feels anachronistic and rather crass nowadays and has been superseded by 'Global South'. Despite this, I have chosen to use 'Third World' where appropriate in this book, mainly for consistency. At that time there was a form of left-wing internationalism known as 'Third Worldism' that championed the rights and interests of those countries. It plays an important role in this book and had no other name. However, I appreciate the term may jar for some readers, for which I apologise.

The other problem with writing about left-wing politics is that the smaller groups on the Marxist and Trotskyist left have a habit of splitting and creating new groups, or just changing their own names, every few years. I have tried to follow and explain these changes as simply as possible whenever it is essential to do so, without overcomplicating the story. I expect some devotees of political esotericism may feel I have been too loose with my organisational attributions at different points in the text, but this book is not supposed to be a catalogue of British Marxism. It is an explanation of the different ideas and ways of thinking about Jews, Israel and Zionism that circulate on the British left. As such, the precise divisions between the left's component parts are less relevant.

There are several people who supported me throughout my academic research and who helped me turn it into this book. The Community Security Trust funded my studies and, as my employer, allowed me the time to pursue my research alongside my regular work. I particularly value Mark Gardner's support, advice and friendship over many years. Professor David Feldman at the Pears Institute for the Study

of Antisemitism, Birkbeck, University of London, has been
a source of wisdom and good humour during and since my
studies. Dean Godson, Andrew Roberts and Robert Hardman
helped to plot the path from academic to political writing.
Philip Spencer offered some astute observations on one of my
chapters. Simon Gallant's legal advice was as reassuring as ever.
Mike Day at the National Union of Students and Martin Frey
at the Board of Deputies of British Jews facilitated access to the
archives of those two organisations.

Many of the people who were involved in the events
described in my thesis, and in this book, volunteered their time
so that I could interview them for my research. Some extended
their assistance further by providing me with documents or
putting me in contact with other potential interviewees. It
would be impractical to list all of them and unfair to single
any out, not least because some asked to remain anonymous:
I am indebted to each and every one for the thoughts, memories and opinions they shared with me. Since the first edition
of this book was published there have been several other people in the Labour Party, Jewish and not, who have shared their
experiences of antisemitism with me. I am especially grateful
to them.

The idea for my PhD thesis, and some of its preliminary
research, originated in a chapter I contributed to *Antisemitism
on the Campus: Past and Present* (Boston: Academic Studies
Press, 2011), edited by Eunice G. Pollack. I am grateful to

Eunice for giving me that original opportunity and for granting permission to reuse some of the research in this book. Iain Dale, James Stephens, Olivia Beattie and all their colleagues at Biteback Publishing have been a pleasure to work with and I appreciate all they have done in making both editions of this book a reality.

Finally, I owe the biggest debt of all at home to Miriam and our children, who put up with this project intruding on our family life for years and who supported me throughout. When I finished the first edition, our children made me promise I would never write another book. Writing a second edition keeps the letter of that promise but, I concede, not its spirit. They have been very forgiving; my love and gratitude for them is limitless.

INTRODUCTION TO
THE NEW EDITION

'Tomorrow evening it will be my pleasure and my honour to host an event in Parliament where our friends from Hezbollah will be speaking. I've also invited friends from Hamas to come and speak as well ... the idea that an organisation that is dedicated towards the good of the Palestinian people and bringing about long-term peace and social justice and political justice in the whole region should be labelled as a terrorist organisation by the British government is really a big, big historical mistake.'

JEREMY CORBYN, LONDON, 30 MARCH 2009

'The JC rarely claims to speak for anyone other than ourselves. We are just a newspaper. But in this rare instance we are certain that we speak for the vast majority of British Jews in expressing deep foreboding at the prospect of Mr Corbyn's election as Labour leader ... If Mr Corbyn is not to be regarded from the day of his election as an enemy of Britain's Jewish community, he has a number of questions which he must answer in full and immediately.'

JEWISH CHRONICLE EDITORIAL, 12 AUGUST 2015

Since 2016, antisemitism has become a national political issue in Britain for the first time in decades. Stories about antisemitism lead the news and it is the subject of sharp exchanges in Parliament. This hasn't come about because of a surge in support for neo-Nazism or a spate of jihadist terrorism against Jews. It has happened because of a crisis in Britain's party of the left, a party that defines itself by its opposition to racism and which has enjoyed Jewish support for most of its history. Antisemitism is a headline story because of the Labour Party. It is important to acknowledge just how strange this is. The left has always seen itself as a movement that opposes antisemitism, opposes fascism and defends Jews and other minorities from bigotry and prejudice. This is a proud history that has always attracted Jewish support. Yet, in the first six months of 2016, the Labour Party felt the need to hold three different inquiries into antisemitism and found itself abandoned by Jewish voters. In March 2018, the leadership bodies of the British Jewish community took the extraordinary and unprecedented step of holding a demonstration outside Parliament to protest about antisemitism in Labour. The decline in the relationship between the Labour Party and Britain's Jewish community has intensified since Jeremy Corbyn's election as Labour Party leader, but it is fuelled by trends on the wider left that have been building for many years. There are socio-economic reasons for the long-term drift of Jewish voters from Labour to the Conservatives, but these reasons alone do not explain the scale of the change, nor its recent acceleration. A long-standing supporter of the Palestinians and opponent of Israel, Corbyn came into post facing a list of questions about alleged associations with people accused of Holocaust denial, antisemitism and terrorism. Beyond these immediate questions about Corbyn's personal associations and views, his rise to the Labour leadership personifies a widespread left-wing hostility to Israel that alienates many Jews. It is symbolic that while the last two Labour Prime Ministers, Tony Blair and Gordon Brown, were both patrons of the Jewish National Fund (an Israeli body that was instrumental in buying land for the new Jewish state before and after its independence in 1948), Corbyn is patron of the Palestine Solidarity Campaign. However, this is not just a story about the left's disenchantment with Israel. It is also a story about the growth of antisemitism on the left, the failure of many on the left to recognise and oppose antisemitism when it appears, and the extent to which people on the left and in the Labour Party even endorse and express antisemitic attitudes themselves.

Most British Jews feel a personal, emotional or spiritual connection to Israel. Most have visited the country and have family and friends there. According to a 2010 survey by the Institute for Jewish Policy Research, 95 per cent of British Jews said Israel plays some role in their Jewish identity, 82 per cent said it plays a central or important role and 90 per cent said they see Israel as the ancestral homeland of the Jewish people. A similar survey by City University London in 2015 found that 90 per cent of British Jews support Israel's right to exist as a Jewish state, while 93 per cent said it plays a role in their Jewish identity. For most Jews, this is what Zionism is: the idea that the Jews are a people whose homeland is Israel (wherever they actually live); that the Jewish people have the right to a state; and that Israel's existence is an important part of what it means to be Jewish today. This deep, instinctive bond doesn't necessarily translate into political support for Israeli governments or their policies: both surveys found strong support for a two-state solution and opposition to expansion of Jewish settlements in the West Bank. For many Jews, their relationship to Israel is not a political statement at all. The idea that Israel shouldn't exist, or that Zionism – the political movement that created Israel – was a racist, colonial endeavour rather than a legitimate expression of Jewish nationhood, cuts to the heart of British Jews' sense of who they are. Whether it is in arts, culture, education, religion, politics or cuisine, Israel is at the heart of global Jewish life, and British Jews are part of that world.

Meanwhile, sympathy for the Palestinians and opposition to Israel has become the default position for many on the left: a defining marker of what it means to be progressive. Find out what somebody on the left thinks about Israel and Zionism and you can usually divine their positions on terrorism, Islamist extremism, military interventions overseas and the historic wisdom of allying Britain to American power. Many who oppose Israel blame it for, amongst other things, the 2003 invasion of Iraq, the grievances that lead to jihadist terrorism, and the growth of prejudice towards Muslims in North America and Western Europe. The Israeli–Palestinian conflict has come to symbolise much more than a struggle between two peoples for the same small strip of land on the eastern Mediterranean. It is the epitome of Western domination, racism and colonialism, and the Palestinians have come to represent all victims of Western power and militarism. 'In our thousands, in our millions, we are all Palestinians,' Corbyn told a rally in 2010. Or, as Seumas Milne – then a *Guardian* journalist, now Labour's executive director of strategy and communications – put it, Palestine has become 'the great international cause of our time'.

One way to appreciate the gulf that has opened up between British Jews and Corbyn's part of the left came via two significant anniversaries in 2017. That year marked fifty years since the Six Day War, when Israel defeated the combined armed forces of its Arab neighbours, swept through the Sinai Peninsula, the Golan Heights, the Gaza Strip and the West Bank, and began its military rule over the Palestinian population of the latter territory that continues to this day. It was also the centenary of what many consider to be the starting gun for the entire conflict: the Balfour Declaration, when the British government promised to 'view with favour the establishment in Palestine of a national home for the Jewish people', and to 'use their best endeavours to facilitate the achievement of this object'. Whether someone considered these to be anniversaries worthy of celebration or occasions for deep remorse depends on where their political sympathies lie. The Balfour Declaration either began the process of redemption of the Jewish people via the sovereignty of national independence, or it was an act of immense colonial dispossession and betrayal of the Palestinians by Britain. The Six Day War was either a miraculous military victory that ensured the survival of the young Jewish state, or a campaign of aggressive conquest that began the occupation of Palestinian territory that has endured for half a century. Jeremy Corbyn has made his view of both clear. The Balfour Declaration, he wrote in 2008,

> became an iconic symbol for the Zionist movement and led to
> the establishment of the state of Israel in 1948 and the expul-
> sion of Palestinians ... Britain's history of colonial interference
> in the region during the dying days of the Ottoman Empire
> and its role as the mandate power from the end of the First
> World War to 1948 leaves it with much to answer for.

Corbyn turned down an invitation to attend an official dinner in London to celebrate the centenary of the Balfour Declaration in November 2017, sending shadow Foreign Secretary Emily Thornberry in his place. As for the Six Day War, it is one of several events in the history of the Israeli–Palestinian conflict that Corbyn once included in what he called 'the macabre list of inhumanity' inflicted by Israel on the Palestinians since Israel's creation.

Britain has played an important role in this history and continues to do so. The Balfour Declaration was issued by the British government in part due to the activism of a group of Zionists in Manchester that included Chaim Weizmann, who went on to become Israel's first President. Britain was the colonial power in Palestine from 1922 until Israel's creation in 1948 and the influence of this period can still be felt in Israel. Yet, by the 1980s, according to historian Colin Shindler, London had become 'the European centre of opposition to Israel's policies – and in a growing number of cases opposition to Israel as a nation-state'. British left-wing anti-Zionism grew out of international networks and continues to have global resonance. In 2010, the Reut Institute in Israel, a think tank that undertook a large research project into anti-Israel political activism, argued that London's role as a centre for international media, NGOs, academia and culture, all operating in the English language, made it 'a leading hub of delegitimization [of Israel] with significant global influence'. Furthermore, Reut claimed, 'London is the capital of the One-State idea – the concept of the One-State Solution is discussed and advanced in London more than anywhere else, and disseminated throughout the world.' What happens in Britain, and on the British left, matters well beyond its shores.

Disagreements over where the boundaries lie between anti-semitism, anti-Zionism and criticism of Israel underpin much of this problem. This is not just a disagreement about Israel and Palestine. There are also profound differences about what antisemitism is, where it is found and how it manifests. This book is an effort to explain how and why antisemitism appears on the left, and an appeal to the left to recognise and expel antisemitism from its politics. It is a truism that criticism of Israel – even harsh or inaccurate criticism – does not consti-tute antisemitism. This book is not intended to be a defence of Israel or an objection to criticisms of its behaviour. Criticisms of Israeli policies and practices that use the same kind of lan-guage used to criticise similar policies and practices of other governments are highly unlikely to be antisemitic. This lan-guage might involve discussion of human rights, or inequality and discrimination, or occupation and war crimes. Criticisms of Israel become suspect when they use language and ideas that draw on older antisemitic myths about Jews. These may include conspiracy theories about Jewish wealth and secret influence, or nods to the medieval 'blood libel' allegation that bloodthirsty Jews delight in killing children. Alarm bells should ring if Israel's Jewish character is enlisted as an expla-nation for its alleged wrongdoing. Comparisons of Israel to Nazi Germany are a new and insidious form of antisemitism, which exploit the lasting pain of the Holocaust – the Jewish people's greatest modern trauma – to attack the world's only

Jewish state. However, normal political criticisms of Israeli policies, or sympathy and support for Palestinian rights, are not
antisemitic, and, crucially, they are not anti-Zionist either. If
Zionism is simply the belief that the Jews are a people deserving of a state and that Israel is that dream made real, this allows
for a wide range of views about what the policies, citizenship
and borders of Israel should be. It is possible to be a Zionist, to
criticise Israeli policies and to support Palestinian statehood,
all at the same time – and many people, Jewish and not, do all
three with no contradiction at all.

Just to confuse matters further, there are different types of
anti-Zionism. In its basic form, anti-Zionism is an ideological position based on the belief that the State of Israel should
not exist and, for some, denial of the very concept of Jewish
peoplehood. When political Zionism first emerged in the late
nineteenth century to call for the creation of a Jewish home in
what is now Israel, many Jews rejected it as an unrealistic and
dangerous proposal. Orthodox Jews had theological reasons to
oppose the creation of a secular Jewish state. More assimilated,
secular Jews in the Diaspora feared that Zionism endangered
their status because it might encourage their non-Jewish fellow
citizens to view them as belonging to an alien nation, rather
than being loyal to the countries of their birth. Marxists argued
that Jews should seek emancipation via socialist revolution
rather than through their own national movement. Over time
Zionism won the struggle for the loyalty of most Jews, largely

due to the cataclysmic shock of the Holocaust and the redemptive hope found in the creation of Israel, and it is now by far the dominant view amongst Jewish people worldwide; but that does not mean the argument is over. Jewish anti-Zionists continue to pursue their own brand of Jewish politics, but, having lost the ability to appeal to the mass of Jews, instead seek support and solidarity from Israel's other opponents – some of whom are motivated by more sinister instincts. In addition, from the 1950s onwards, the Soviet Union developed a line in overtly antisemitic anti-Zionism that portrays Zionism as a global conspiracy with Israel as its tool, powered by the wealth of Jewish capitalists and responsible for war and economic exploitation. This antisemitic anti-Zionism has little to do with how Jews define Zionism and employs strikingly similar language to that used by antisemites when they defame Jews. It can now be found in far-right, Islamist and far-left circles. Its appeal to these different political extremes is a testament to the power and durability of conspiracy theories, especially when they involve the conspiracy theorists' favourite demon: the Jews. The pro-Palestinian movement in Britain includes anti-Zionists who object to Israel's existence through reasoned argument, those who do so as part of a conspiracy theory of global Zionist domination, and critics of Israel who want to see a Palestinian state created alongside, rather than instead of, Israel.

These differences can sometimes feel quite academic and

unrelated to the practical realities of how left-wing attitudes to Israel and Zionism actually work. Whenever violence flares between Israel and Hamas in Gaza, or with Hezbollah in Lebanon, tens of thousands of people march through the streets of British cities in protest. Left-wing leaders and commentators condemn Israel's actions, often accusing it of committing massacres or even genocide. Jeremy Corbyn, before he became Labour leader, would usually be found at the head of the march or speaking from the platform at these demonstrations. The issue generates more anger and activism on the left than any other overseas conflict. This anger and intense focus on Israel makes many Jews feel uneasy. It doesn't help that whenever such wars take place, the amount of antisemitic hate crime recorded in Britain usually goes up. Yet, just next door to Israel, the number of people killed in the Syrian civil war dwarfs the total number of dead in all of Israel's conflicts. There are no large left-wing demonstrations in Britain to protest against massacres of Syrians by its own government. Nobody chants: 'In our thousands, in our millions, we are all Syrians.' This begs the question: why Israel?

There are various simplistic answers to this question, none of which are satisfactory. Israel's opponents would say that Israel, quite simply, is one of the worst human rights abusers on earth and is a uniquely racist, violent and oppressive state. Even worse, it does all of this as a Western ally. According to this view, the reason that the left opposes Israel is because of what Israel does, and because of the West's complicity as Israel's political backer and armourer. There are a few problems with this explanation. Firstly, people on the left have viewed the same events in radically different ways at different times in Israel's seventy-year history. For example, Israel's creation in 1948 was once viewed by most of the British left as a necessary and welcome act; now it is lamented by many as a dreadful mistake. These shifts have as much to do with political changes in the British left over that period as with the nature of those events themselves. Secondly, criticism of what Israel does often becomes criticism of what Israel is – and from there to an argument that it shouldn't have been created and shouldn't continue to exist in the future. Thirdly, there are other countries, also closely allied to the West, whose human rights abuses do not provoke anything like the same reaction from the British left. Turkey is a NATO ally and has been occupying the territory of an EU member state in Cyprus for almost as long as Israel has occupied the West Bank. It buys substantially more arms from Britain than Israel does. Its conflict with its Kurdish minority over many years has involved terrorism, heavy loss of life, repression of Kurdish national identity and restrictions of basic freedoms, yet this elicits little activism from the British left.

Another simplistic explanation is that the left's hostility to Israel is nothing other than a modern expression of the same old antisemitism that Jews have faced for centuries. According to this argument, Israel is the world's only Jewish state and the left's disproportionate focus on its behaviour is a modern re-enactment of Europe's long history of anti-Jewish prejudice. Instead of persecuting individual Jews, now it is Israel that is always held to a higher standard and never forgiven for its (real and imagined) wrongdoing. This also fails to pass muster. Sympathy for the Palestinians and opposition to Israeli policies needn't involve antisemitism. Many of Israel's left-wing critics do not oppose its existence and would support a two-state solution to the conflict. The criticisms of Israeli policies found on the British left are also heard within Israel – indeed, many of them originate there. Most of Israel's left-wing critics are avowedly anti-racist and explicitly opposed to antisemitism. Many are Jews and say they act in the name of what they believe to be Jewish values. Even if these promises to oppose antisemitism remain unfulfilled and the mobilisation of Jewish identity to criticise Israel is cynically done, this still makes opposition to Israel different from the antisemitism that affected European Jewry in past centuries. Antisemitism does play a role in this story, but for the most part it does not involve people who are consciously antisemitic. Rather, it is a problem of antisemitic ideas and ways of thinking about Jews, Zionism and Israel that have spread, mostly unwittingly and often unchallenged, in what is supposed to be an anti-racist movement. It is possible to believe antisemitic stereotypes about Jews while not feeling any visceral hostility towards them and to still think of yourself as an anti-racist. This apparently contradictory phenomenon is found across British society. In September 2017, the largest ever opinion survey of British attitudes towards Jews and Israel was published by the Institute for Jewish Policy Research and the Community Security Trust (full disclosure: I worked on this project for CST). It found that only a small proportion of people in Britain are consciously antisemitic (between 3 and 10 per cent, depending on how the question is asked), but 30 per cent believe at least one negative stereotype or attitude about Jews. In other words, antisemitic attitudes are much more common than antisemitic people. This survey also found that the more anti-Israel a person is, the more likely they are to have antisemitic attitudes: 74 per cent of people with strongly anti-Israel views held at least one antisemitic viewpoint, compared to 30 per cent of the general population. Yet the same survey found other people who are just as strongly anti-Israel but have no antisemitic attitudes at all. This all suggests that the relationship between antisemitism, opposition to Israel and anti-Zionism is complex and differs from individual to individual. For some, anti-Israel activism is a socially acceptable way to express their anti-Jewish prejudice; for others, it is simply another political issue to campaign on and has nothing to do with antisemitism at all.

This book is an attempt to answer this question in a different way, by looking at how these ideas first emerged and have spread through activist groups and networks, from grassroots campaigners into the Labour Party; and how they have informed the thinking of Britain's left and Corbyn's Labour Party on the subject. This inevitably means that some parts of the left are given more attention than others in these pages. This book does not include a complete history of Labour Party Middle East policy, for example, or every twist and turn of Britain's myriad Marxist and Trotskyist organisations. These do feature in this book, but only when they are relevant to the main story. This book is also not about the Israeli–Palestinian conflict itself. There are already plenty of books that tell the histories of Israel's creation, Palestinian and Jewish refugees, wars, terrorism, occupation, current politics and colonial legacies. They are written from a variety of viewpoints, some more obviously politicised than others. That history and the ongoing conflict provide the backdrop to this book, but they aren't its subject. Nor does this book look in detail at the appeal of the Conservative Party to British Jews and the broader socioeconomic reasons why many Jewish voters have drifted rightwards since the 1980s. This book is specifically about the British left: how people on the left have tried to make sense of the Israeli–Palestinian conflict, why the political ideas and campaigns they came up with in response to it have sometimes involved antisemitic methods, language and ideas, and how this explains the problem of antisemitism in today's Labour Party.

To understand how Israel, of all the countries and conflicts in the world, has come to be a touchstone issue for the left, it is necessary to go back to the beginning. How did this left-wing anti-Zionism begin, what are its founding values and influences and what is its political vision? This change didn't happen by chance. It took activists, organisations and ideas to make it happen. To find an answer, this book begins by shining its light mainly at what was called the New Left – the 1960s, radical, youthful left – that played a decisive role in flipping left-wing opinion from being overwhelmingly pro-Israel to its current pro-Palestinian consensus. This political world was the seedbed for the ideas and activist groups that created the kind of left-wing anti-Zionism that is familiar today. The allegations that Israel is a product of Western colonialism, that Zionism is a racist ideology, and that both deserve the same opprobrium previously directed at apartheid South Africa came from that world. It is the part of the left that explains the politics of Jeremy Corbyn, Ken Livingstone, George Galloway, the Stop the War Coalition, the Palestine Solidarity Campaign and similar groups and people. Our story begins in the 1960s, a decade when left-wing attitudes to everything – including Israel – were turned upside down.

CHAPTER ONE

WHEN THE LEFT STOPPED LOVING ISRAEL

However permanent it feels today, the idea that being on the left means being opposed to Israel and Zionism is, politically speaking, a relatively recent development. It is true that opposition to Israeli policies, sympathy for the Palestinian cause and to a lesser extent outright anti-Zionism are now commonplace, although not unchallenged, across all parts of the British left. However, this only began to take shape in the 1960s, when some New Left thinkers and movements in Europe and North America came to view Israel as a part of Western colonialism rather than a progressive expression of Jewish nationhood. Having emerged on the radical fringes, this central idea gained momentum in the 1970s and burst into mainstream left-wing thinking in the 1980s. Prior to this development, left-wing opinion was broadly sympathetic to Israel and the political

movement that founded it – Zionism – for most of the twentieth century, while left-wing parties and organisations attracted
the support of many Jews.

The creation of the State of Israel in 1948 enjoyed the support of the Soviet Union and was welcomed across the British
left. Israel was created by Jews from within the European left
tradition, so most European leftists saw Zionism as a socialist project worthy of support. It was born out of a violent
insurgency against the British forces that occupied Palestine
under a United Nations mandate from 1922 to 1948. This insurgency during the final years of the British mandate period gave
Zionism grounds to claim an anti-colonial aspect, which helped
attract Soviet approval. In the years immediately following
the Second World War, Stalin sought to weaken and divide the
Western imperial powers, and this Zionist insurgency represented the strongest active threat to the British presence in the
region. In contrast, much of the Arab leadership at that time
comprised monarchies and hereditary sheikhdoms that were
hostile to communism.

Soviet support for Israel came in weapons and votes. When
the United Nations proposed in November 1947 to divide
Palestine into two states, one Jewish and one Arab (with Jerusalem under international administration), the Soviet bloc
at the UN supported the plan, effectively voting in favour
of the creation of a Jewish state. The weapons came from
Czechoslovakia, which was a vital source of arms and aircraft

for Israel in 1947 and 1948. Shortly after five Arab armies had invaded their new Jewish neighbour in May 1948, the Soviet representative at the United Nations, Andrei Gromyko, criticised them for trying to suppress 'the national liberation movement in Palestine' – a striking choice of words, given that so much left-wing opposition to Israel today is based on the idea that Zionism is a product of Western colonialism rather than a liberation movement against it. However, Soviet backing for Israel was always more pragmatic than ideological and turned out to be both superficial and temporary. It began to ebb as early as mid-1948 and the arms supplies came to a complete halt the following year. The two countries broke off diplomatic relations for a short period in 1953 following a series of antisemitic show trials in the Soviet Union and Czechoslovakia. In 1955, Egypt signed its own arms deal with Czechoslovakia, becoming a client state of the Soviet bloc, and relations between Israel and the Soviet Union were hostile thereafter.[1]

Significantly, even when the Soviet Union gave diplomatic backing to Israel in 1947 and 1948, it never endorsed Zionism as an ideology. Soviet support for Israel was based on sound foreign policy reasons but the thought it might lead to support for Zionism amongst Soviet Jews alarmed the Soviet authorities. Their fears crystallised when thousands turned out to welcome the new Israeli ambassador, Golda Meyerson (who later became Israeli Prime Minister Golda Meir), at Moscow's

Grand Synagogue for the festival of Yom Kippur in 1948. A predictable crackdown on Jewish cultural and political activity in the Soviet Union followed. Official Soviet policy had always disapproved of Zionism as a bourgeois political movement amongst Soviet Jews, even while helping the Zionist movement to achieve its ultimate goal of a Jewish state. Thus, when Gromyko and others explained their support for the partition of Palestine in 1947, they spoke only of the 'Jewish people' or the 'Jewish population' in Palestine, thereby observing a careful but crucial distinction between the national rights of Jews living in Palestine, and Zionism as an ideology or political movement. It was an important choice of words, given the historic (and future) hostility of Marxist–Leninism to Zionism, and the conspiratorial role Zionism was accorded in post-war antisemitic propaganda spread by the Soviet Union and its satellite states in Eastern Europe. Nevertheless, support for Israel in 1948 brought the USSR into line, at least temporarily, with the political sympathies of the wider British left, where admiration for Zionist efforts to build a new society in Palestine along socialist lines merged with sympathy at the plight of Holocaust survivors marooned in post-war Europe, and pragmatic recognition that nowhere other than the new Jewish state was willing to take in large numbers of Jewish refugees.

The Labour Party consistently supported the creation of a Jewish national home in Palestine from the Balfour Declaration of 1917 until the end of the Second World War. The socialist

Zionist organisation Poale Zion affiliated to the Labour Party in 1920 and in 1944 the party even endorsed a proposal to transfer Arabs out of Palestine to make way for Jewish immigration. This enthusiasm was tempered by Labour's post-war Foreign Secretary Ernest Bevin, who was more sympathetic to Arab claims on Palestine and feared that a socialist Israel might be pro-Soviet. He also had a habit of making antisemitic remarks about Jews. Under Bevin's watch, Britain abstained in the 1947 UN vote to partition Palestine, but generally speaking the ties between the Labour Party and Israel remained overwhelmingly friendly and supportive. There were strong links between the British and Israeli Labour Parties, both directly and as sister parties in the Socialist International. Labour Friends of Israel was formed in 1957 and at the time of the Six Day War, support for Israel remained consistent throughout the parliamentary party, constituency Labour parties and the trade union movement. During the 1960s, the TUC gave funding to its Israeli equivalent, the Histadrut, to train African trade unionists at its Afro-Asian Institute in Tel Aviv. Even *Tribune*, the newspaper of the Labour left, was firmly pro-Israel until the 1960s. 'The cause of Israel is the cause of democratic Socialism,' it wrote in 1955.[2]

This relationship between Jews and the left worked both ways: Jews were found in disproportionately large numbers in Socialist, Social Democratic and Communist parties across Europe and North America in the latter part of the nineteenth and early to mid-twentieth centuries. It is estimated that in the late 1940s and early 1950s, 10 per cent of activists in the Communist Party of Great Britain were Jewish, when Jews formed less than 1 per cent of the UK population. For much of this time, Jews and the left were intimately involved in each other's stories. Australian academic Philip Mendes went so far as to claim: 'It can, in fact, be argued that from approximately 1830 until 1970, an informal political alliance existed between Jews and the political left.' If this is perhaps stretching things too far, it does attest to the familiarity between the left and European Jews in the nineteenth and twentieth centuries. 'The history of the socialist movement since the 1930s', Belgian Trotskyist Nathan Weinstock wrote in 1969, 'shows that many of the decisive issues the working class has had to face have involved the Jewish question.'[3]

This all began to change in the 1960s. The Six Day War of June 1967 was greeted by an outburst of radical left-wing criticism of Israel, although – as we shall see – the roots of this critique were visible before that date. By the end of the decade, Britain's radical New Left had begun to actively campaign for Palestine, and in the 1970s the first grassroots activist groups dedicated specifically to the Palestinian cause were launched. This swelling support for Palestine started to have an impact on Labour Party policy in the 1980s, a decade when relations between the party and British Jews began to noticeably sour. Since then, the view that emerged from the New Left of Israel as a colonial, militaristic and racist state preventing the Palestinians from achieving self-determination has spread widely across the left in general. It is easy to overstate the extent of this change. Israel retains support within the Labour Party, notably from its last two Prime Ministers. However, opposition to (at the very least) aspects of Israeli policies in relation to the West Bank and Gaza Strip, and sympathy for the Palestinian national cause, now dominate British left-wing opinion on the subject, while anti-Zionism is axiomatic for much of the Marxist left.

To understand these changes, it is necessary first of all to appreciate how the left as a whole changed during that period. The New Left that formed in Britain in the 1950s and 1960s was quite different from the Old Left of trade unions, Communist Party branches and – ironically, given its current leadership – the Labour Party. The world that had defined the left since the 1880s, in which socialist labour movements, in both trade union and parliamentary forms, campaigned for the rights of working-class communities formed by mass industrialisation, was beginning to crumble by the 1950s. Its political foundations were increasingly eroded on one side by rising post-war prosperity across Western societies, and on the other by radical, left-wing causes that did not fit within the old class politics. Society was changing in other ways, too. The combination of the post-war population boom and sustained economic growth in Western Europe in the 1950s created a new phenomenon of young people with money to spend, who would provide the foot soldiers of the 1960s New Left.

This new political generation was marked by a lack of deference for authority and an organisational fluidity that spawned a bewildering array of single-issue pressure groups and campaigns. The old left-wing politics of mass labour mobilisation and class struggle were directly challenged, and at times replaced, by race, gender, sexuality, peace and the environment as the causes that shaped the New Left and continue to animate many left-wing activists today. It has spawned many well-known campaign groups: from the Campaign for Nuclear Disarmament and the Anti-Apartheid Movement in the 1960s, to the Stop the War Coalition and the Palestine Solidarity Campaign today. As New Left superseded Old, so identity politics replaced class politics as its primary mobilising idea. It was all very different from the Old Left that was forged in the hardships of the 1930s and the sacrifice of the wartime struggle against fascism. Instead, the New Left effectively represented a new social class, rooted in intellectual and cultural professions, populated by public sector workers, and whose political agenda would come to be dominated by identity and iconoclasm. It is no coincidence that anti-Israel sentiment and activism is prominent in the cultural, intellectual and academic parts of modern Britain, given that these are precisely the sectors where New Left politics has always found the greatest support.

As well as a new set of political ideas, the New Left also represented a new political attitude. While the 1950s New Left in Britain had been largely an intellectual movement, the 1968 version was much more activist, militant and confrontational. It forced its way into the national consciousness with large (and sometimes violent) demonstrations in central London against the Vietnam War. Direct action tactics, sit-ins and cultural change were as much a part of the New Left as marches and rallies, while it was the beginning of a connection between youth culture and political radicalism that remains to this day. Britain saw a wave of protests at university campuses in the late 1960s, while France experienced a much larger student insurrection against the state itself.

There is, admittedly, an element of mythology about all of this. While many of those who were present like to think that they were part of a global uprising of revolutionary youth, the reality was often rather more mundane. In Britain, most student protests related to parochial issues like night-time curfews, dress codes and exclusion from university decision-making bodies rather than more glamorous international campaigns. Shirley Williams, who was Minister of State with responsibility for higher education at the time, felt that 'the student revolution was pretty artificial … it was exciting all right, but pointless'. Nevertheless, student protests were part of a wider erosion of deference to generational authority, both within the left and in society as a whole. By the late 1960s, the split between Old and New Left was as much a case of mutual incomprehension across generations as any kind of political schism. The Old Left, defined by its collective ethos and economic deprivations, had little time for the student left, with its sense of individualism, cultural experimentation and consumer aspirations.[4]

The New Left is Jeremy Corbyn's political home. Born shortly after the war, he joined the Campaign for Nuclear Disarmament in the early 1960s, demonstrated against the Vietnam War in the late 1960s and did voluntary work in post-colonial Jamaica before travelling around Latin America. He is a patron of the Palestine Solidarity Campaign and has been chair of the Stop the War Coalition for most of its existence. Coming from a relatively comfortable background and working for two trade unions before becoming a Labour MP, Corbyn is a typical product of the 1960s New Left. His journey to the Labour Party leadership symbolises the New Left's gradual reshaping of the cultural sensibilities of left-wing politics: the ultimate New Left triumph, rather than a return to Old Labour. The disregard for NATO shown by Corbyn, Ken Livingstone and others on the left of the Labour Party fits perfectly with this New Left tradition and highlights how much it is a departure from Labour's own history. Corbyn has criticised NATO for expanding into Eastern Europe and said that it should have been wound up in 1990, at the end of the Cold War. Livingstone has questioned whether Britain should remain a member. Yet NATO owes its existence in large part to the same Labour government that created the National Health Service. It was a Labour Foreign Secretary, Ernest Bevin, who insisted that a post-war West European defence pact required American involvement. Efforts to rebuild a shattered Europe along social democratic lines would only succeed, so the thinking went, if further Soviet expansion could be deterred. But while Labour's creation of the NHS has become a sacred part of the left's own history, NATO is viewed with suspicion as a manifestation of American militarism.

Anti-Zionism and hostility to Israel are also part of this New Left worldview. The idea that Zionism is a racist, colonialist ideology, and Israel an illegitimate remnant of Western colonialism in the Middle East, came directly from the New Left of the 1960s. Anti-colonialism, race and the Cold War were formative in the New Left's development and created a framework that left Israel and Zionism on the wrong side of its political thinking. The British New Left was born in November 1956, when the Hungarian and Suez crises occurred in the same week. In Hungary, an uprising of students and workers demanding democratic freedoms and an end to Soviet domination was crushed by a Soviet invasion. Meanwhile, Britain, France and Israel secretly arranged a three-pronged invasion of Egypt that would allow Britain and France to seize the Suez Canal that had been nationalised by Egyptian President Gamal Abdel Nasser in July. The day after Soviet forces attacked

Budapest, British and French troops landed in Egypt, ostensibly as a peacekeeping move in response to the Israeli invasion of the Sinai Peninsula the week before, but in fact to seize control of the Suez Canal. The cynicism and violence of events in Hungary and Egypt, with Communism and the Western democracies both involved, caused huge disillusionment across the left. Communist parties across Europe had already been shaken that year by Soviet leader Nikita Khrushchev's 'secret speech' to the 20th Congress of the Soviet Communist Party, in which he denounced crimes committed under Stalin's leadership. Some 10,000 members left the Communist Party of Great Britain in protest at its support for the Soviet invasion, most of whom also departed organised Marxist politics for good. Many sought a new type of left-wing politics with an independent position beyond the two Cold War blocs, combining opposition to Western imperialism with freedom from the ideological constraints demanded by Stalinism. A series of dissenting publications emerged from academic and intellectual circles inside and outside the Communist Party, the most important of which, the *New Left Review*, was launched in 1960 and remains the house journal of the intellectual left in Britain today.

These crises, and the formation of the New Left, happened against a political backdrop in which decolonisation and race were increasingly prominent and urgent issues. The Algerian war of independence had begun in 1954, the same year in which

Labour MP Fenner Brockway founded the Movement for Colonial Freedom; 1955 saw the first Afro-Asian Conference in Bandung, where a bloc of newly independent, post-colonial states began to take shape; and in May 1956 Ghana became the first black African nation to gain independence from Britain. The Anti-Apartheid Movement was formed in London in 1960 and would go on to be the most successful of all New Left single-issue campaigns. The civil rights movement in America and the impact of commonwealth immigration to Britain in the 1950s and 1960s added to the sense that race would play an increasingly pivotal role in both domestic and foreign affairs. Anti-colonialism began as a campaign for European colonies to gain their independence, and morphed into a general political support for those new states after they had become independent. The sheer scale of change as decolonisation gathered pace and European empires were dismantled was reflected in the membership of the United Nations, which grew from fifty-one members at its formation in 1945 to ninety-nine members by 1960 and 142 by 1975. The new states that emerged from this process formed an ostensibly neutral bloc in international relations that was formalised into the Non-Aligned Movement at successive conferences in Cairo and Belgrade in 1961. As might be inferred from these two locations, although the Non-Aligned Movement was theoretically neutral in the Cold War, it was usually more closely aligned with Soviet interests than with Western ones. It provided fertile soil for the idea, now commonplace on the mainstream left, that Zionism is a European colonial movement and Israel is a bastion of white European settlers rather than a legitimate nation state in its own right. This is the basic intellectual and political framework through which Zionism and Israel are explained in New Left politics. It didn't happen by chance, and its development was a product of the radical anti-colonial politics of the 1960s.

This was a decade when some on the left gave up on the revolutionary potential of the Western working class and looked overseas for radical inspiration. By this way of thinking, the bloc of post-colonial states (and the national liberation movements that were fighting for decolonisation elsewhere) held the promise that the part of the world then known as the Third World might supplant the Western proletariat as the global engine of revolutionary change. The weakening of left-wing institutions and growing prosperity at home made socialist revolution in the West an ever more remote prospect. In contrast, the Maoist vision of workers' and peasants' revolutions overthrowing colonial rule, thereby weakening the power of capitalism at home, offered a new focus for the dreams of Western radicals. America's military troubles in Vietnam seemed to show what was possible. Some took this logic a step further and argued that the Western working class was not only incapable of revolution, but was even complicit in the colonial crimes of its own countries. Where the Old Left dreamed of class solidarity across nations, the New Left argued that colonialism created an insurmountable framework of conflict between occupiers and occupied. In this way of thinking, all of Europe was permanently cursed with the sin of colonialism, transferred since the Second World War to its imperialist offspring, the United States.

Supporting the violence of anti-colonial movements was part of this new politics. One of the more influential authors of this era was Frantz Fanon, an Algerian psychotherapist who fought for France in the Second World War before becoming an ambassador for the new Algerian Revolutionary Provisional Government. He viewed colonisers and colonised as absolutes. 'The colonial world is a Manichaean world,' he wrote, in which violence against the colonisers is 'a cleansing force' that 'frees the native from his inferiority complex'. A 'given society is racist or it is not', he argued, and differentiations within that society according to class or region are of secondary importance. Fanon was an early advocate of the idea that Third World peasantries were more progressive and revolutionary than First World working classes. European workers, he argued, bore their share of colonial guilt, 'for the workers believe, too, that they are part of the prodigious adventure of the European spirit'. Europe, Fanon wrote, 'has a racist structure' and has nothing to offer progressive politics; 'the European game has finally ended' and it is for the Third World to start 'a new history of Man' that does not imitate or replicate European values or behaviour. Fanon had great influence on radical left-wing thought in Europe and North America. His two best-known books, *Black Skin, White Masks* (published in 1952) and *The Wretched of the Earth* (published with a preface by Jean-Paul Sartre in 1961), became key texts for European and North American radicals in the 1960s and 1970s. Sartre was particularly taken with Fanon's ideas. 'Europeans, you must open this book and enter into it,' he wrote in his preface to *The Wretched of the Earth*. 'Europe is at death's door,' and while Europeans may think that they oppose colonialism, 'It is true, you are not settlers, but you are no better. For the pioneers belonged to you; you sent them overseas, and it was you they enriched.'[5]

Some on the left resisted this way of thinking, but Third World forms of Marxism, with their radical rejection of Western values and championing of revolutionary violence, were simply more in keeping with the Sixties mood than the old-fashioned Labour movements of the Old Left. By the mid-1960s, the Trotskyist Fourth International, represented in the UK by the International Marxist Group, had become the leading advocates of the idea that Third World struggles were the new focus of world revolution. Palestine was one of several causes that benefited. The Palestinian *fedayeen* (irregular guerrilla fighters), which gained the world's attention after 1967 through hijackings and other violent actions, were celebrated alongside the North Vietnamese and other national liberation movements, all of which were invested with the New Left's hope that a revolutionary wave would build in the Third

World and break onto Western societies. *The Observer's* Paris correspondents, reporting on the student uprising there in 1968, commented that for many left-wing student groups, 'Vietnam is the class struggle writ large: it is an integral part of the world-wide socialist revolution they work for.'[6]

This was an important step on the path that has led modern-day leftists to support movements like Hamas or Hezbollah that are socially reactionary, religiously conservative and not at all left-wing. Because 1960s liberation movements were anti-colonial – or, nowadays, because modern-day resistance movements are anti-American – and because they claim to act in the name and the interests of the downtrodden in their countries, any concerns about whether they are themselves socialist are overridden. The political logic is simple: any movement that is fighting against America or one of its allies is treated as progressive and on the right side of the global struggle against imperialism, irrespective of its actual character. This idea was apparent in New Left thinking from its earliest days. An article about the 'Arab national movement' in the *New Reasoner* journal in 1958 put it this way:

> ...despite its disorderliness, its confusion of objectives, its
> superficially farcical features, its exaggerated xenophobia,
> its apparent resemblance, in certain of its aspects, to Fascism
> or Nazism, and – most serious of all – its vitriolic hatred of the
> State of Israel, it is fundamentally and essentially a progressive

movement, with which we ought to be ready, as socialists, to express solidarity, even when it does things which run counter to Britain's real or supposed interests in the Middle East.[7]

Given the New Left's influence in shifting left-wing sympathy away from Israel and towards the Palestinian cause, and bearing in mind Israel's role in the Suez crisis, it may be surprising that the first journals of the New Left showed little antagonism to Israel in their early years. Writers disapproved of Israel's involvement at Suez but this did not translate into a wholesale dismissal of Israeli concerns, much less a fundamental rejection of its legitimacy as a state. New Left intellectual Stuart Hall criticised British Middle Eastern policy in 1957 for conniving 'both against the welfare of the Arab peoples and the stability of the state of Israel'. The following year, Claude Bourdet, editor of the French newspaper *France Observateur* and one of the leading intellectuals of the French New Left, called for 'the fixing and guaranteeing of the Israeli–Arab frontiers'. However, the centrality of anti-colonialism to the New Left's understanding of the world meant that, eventually, the constant description of Israel as a colonial entity in Arab and Soviet propaganda was bound to have an effect. Egypt, under the leadership of Gamal Abdel Nasser, was particularly determined to portray Israel as an agent of Western imperialism, and to depict Zionism as a conspiracy against Arab independence. Egypt pushed the question of Israel at every Afro-Asian

conference, arguing that Israel was a conduit for Western imperialism to regain its foothold in Africa. This bore fruit with the
1961 African Charter of Casablanca, signed by a minority of
African states, which denounced Israel as 'an instrument in
the service of imperialism and neo-colonialism not only in the
Middle East but also in Africa and Asia'. The Charter did not
have much practical impact on the actions of the sub-Saharan
states involved, all of which maintained friendly relations with
Israel at the time, but Egypt's repeated efforts left an impression on broader anti-colonial political thinking. Israel was
refused an invitation to the Belgrade Conference of the Non-
Aligned Movement in 1961, and the following year Indonesia
refused to invite Israel (and Taiwan) to take part in the 4th
Asian Games in Jakarta, resulting in Indonesia's suspension by
the International Olympic Committee.[8]

The idea that Israel was implanted in the Middle East by
Western colonialism was also a common theme in the propaganda of the Palestine Liberation Organization (PLO),
which was founded in 1964. The PLO's 1965 booklet *Zionist
Colonialism in Palestine* described the United Nations' 1947
Partition Plan as a Western colonial plot to dispossess the
Palestinian people. It was 'a European-American majority' that
outvoted the 'Afro-Asian minority' at the UN, so the booklet
claimed, to establish 'a colonial Zionist state in the Afro-Asian
bridge, the Arab land of Palestine'. (The booklet discreetly
omitted the Soviet Union's support for partition.) Israel's 'vital

19

and continuing association with European Imperialism, and its introduction into Palestine of the practices of Western Colonialism' are grounds for its condemnation, the PLO booklet argued, while 'its chosen pattern of racial exclusiveness and self-segregation renders it an alien society in the Middle East'. Another PLO booklet three years later went further, comparing Zionism to Nazism: 'The concept of a "chosen race", in Zionism, differs from the concept of a "chosen race", in Nazism, only in the identity of that race – the Zionists speaking of a "Jewish race", and the Nazis of an "Aryan race"'. Algeria, too, in the years following its independence from French rule in 1962, promoted this anti-colonial view of Zionism. A booklet on Palestine published by the Algerian National Liberation Front (FLN) described Israel and Zionism in terms that began with the idea that Israel was created by an imperialist plot, and then moved into an explicitly antisemitic conspiracy theory. Zionism, the booklet claimed, is 'a colonialism based on a theocratic, racist, and expansionist system'; Israel was artificially created as 'the result of an imperialist will' and has a 'racist and fascist nature'; its creation was facilitated by 'the monopoly, by the magnate Jews, of the economic, financial and information centres of influence'; and 'armed popular struggle is the essential means' to fight Israel and Zionism.[9]

Meanwhile, the antisemitic treatment of Zionism that had developed in Soviet propaganda during the last years of Stalin's life survived Khrushchev's thaw and intensified after 1967, both

for domestic consumption and as part of Soviet outreach to
the European left and to Third World countries. Articles accusing Israel of racism and colonialism, comparing Zionism to
Nazism and using traditional antisemitic tropes were published with increasing regularity in the Soviet media, and then
translated into English and distributed in pamphlet form in the
West. One 1970 example, a booklet called *Zionism: Instrument
of Imperialist Reaction*, described Zionism as 'an ideology, a
ramified system of organisations, the policy and practice of the
Jewish big bourgeoisie that have become closely knit with
the monopoly circles of the United States and other imperialist
powers'. Israeli military operations, it claimed, were reminis-
cent of 'the barbarity of the Hitlerites', part of 'the imperialist,
neo-colonialist plot directed against the peoples and progressive regimes of the Middle East', serving the interests of
'oil monopolies and international Zionist organisations'. The
image of a global Zionist conspiracy with Israel as its tool, powered by Jewish wealth and responsible for war and oppression,
is strikingly similar to pre-war antisemitic conspiracy theories about Jews. This Soviet antisemitism percolated through
anti-colonial politics to influence the anti-Zionist discourse
to which Western New Leftists were increasingly exposed.
By the 1980s, according to Antony Lerman, in circles where
Western leftists and politicians from Third World states met,
'The formula of linking Zionism with imperialism, racism,
neo-colonialism ... serves the purpose of establishing the

speaker's credentials as part of a broad Third Worldist ideological tendency.' This tendency included those on the New Left in Europe and North America who idealised Third World liberation movements, and for whom this rhetoric of anti-colonial anti-Zionism became familiar.[10]

The New Left's break from Moscow was never a complete doctrinal split, but rather an insistence on the independence to think, and act, free from the political requirements of Soviet policy. But still, there is a certain irony in New Left activists in Europe adopting the anti-Zionism of the Arab nations and their Afro-Asian allies on the basis of Third World solidarity, when that anti-Zionism was driven in part by the very Cold War power politics that the New Left sought to escape. The rhetorical connection of Zionism to colonialism, in a broader framework that sees Zionism as a powerful international network, was a lasting invention of these political campaigns whose imprint can still be seen on today's left. Malia Bouattia, elected as president of the National Union of Students in 2016, gave a speech two years earlier in which she spoke about Palestinian 'resistance' to Israel in language that channelled Frantz Fanon through a contemporary filter of Muslim identity, with a dash of Zionist conspiracy theory added in:

> The notion of resistance has been perhaps washed out of our understanding of how colonised people will obtain their physical emancipation ... With mainstream, Zionist-led media

outlets ... resistance is presented as an act of terrorism. But instead of us remembering that this has always been the case throughout struggles against white supremacy, it's become an accepted discourse among too many ... Internalised Islamophobia has also enabled our obsession with convincing non-Muslims of our non-violent and peaceful nature, so we're taking things a step further and dangerously condemning the resistance, branding groups and individuals as terrorists to disassociate from them, but at the same time supporting their liberation which is a very strange contradiction.[11]

This all meant that by the time of the Six Day War in 1967 – that is, before the occupation of the West Bank and Gaza began – the idea that Israel is an alien presence in the Middle East, left behind by European colonialism as an agent of Western imperialism and an obstacle to the legitimate national aspirations of the native Arab population, was already easily accessible for anybody interested in anti-colonial politics. Shortly before the Six Day War, *New Left Review* published an article by Che Guevara in which he counterposed Israel, 'backed by the imperialists', with its enemies, 'the progressive countries' of the Middle East. In its next edition, following the war, *New Left Review* carried an interview with the Marxist writer Isaac Deutscher, in which Deutscher scathingly described the war as part of 'a tremendous political, ideological, economic, and military offensive over a vast area of Asia and Africa' by

'American imperialism, and the forces associated with it and supported by it'. Israel, he argued, had become a 'Western outpost in the Middle East'. This anti-Zionism existed on the British New Left before it fully recognised Palestinian nationalism: the term 'Palestinian' was not even used in the pages of *New Left Review* before the Six Day War. Tony Cliff, founder of the Socialist Workers Party and one of Britain's foremost Trostkyists, wrote a pamphlet immediately after the war that described Israel as 'a *colon*, a settler's citadel, a launching-pad of imperialism'. Furthermore, echoing Fanon, Cliff argued that Israeli workers were, like white South Africans and Algerian settlers, part of the ruling imperialism and could not be revolutionary. An article in the journal *Race & Class* in 1968 made a direct comparison between Israel and South Africa, arguing that 'Africa today lies encircled between two confident, aggressive white powers – South Africa and its satellites to the south, Israel to the north.' Attitudes on the Old Left, too, were beginning to change. Whereas the Labour Party newspaper *Tribune* had been staunchly supportive of Israel during the Suez Crisis of 1956, by 1967 its editorial line was more even-handed, and its letters pages published contributions from readers who were fiercely critical of Israel. Even in the mainstream British media, according to one survey, there were several examples of Israel being cast as a symbol of white supremacy and imperialism in the Afro-Asian world, and comparisons made between Israel's behaviour and that of Nazi Germany. All of these

ideas – that Israel is a colonial state made up of European settlers; that it belongs in the same category as apartheid South
Africa; that its very existence is part of a Western plot to deny
Arab and Muslim peoples their national rights; and that there
are no 'normal' or progressive Israelis, only colonisers, settlers and racists – comprise today's left-wing charge sheet
against Israel.[12]

After 1967, the intellectual groundwork for an anti-Zionist
political movement started to appear in more substantial form.
This did not stop at a critique of Israel's actions during and
after the Six Day War, but went back to the circumstances of
Israel's creation to directly challenge its existence and legitimacy as a state. French Marxist and Middle East expert
Maxime Rodinson did much to popularise the idea that Israel
is a settler state, mainly through an essay in Jean-Paul Sartre's
Les Temps Modernes, published at the time of the 1967 war
(and translated into English in book form as *Israel: A Colonial-
Settler State?* in 1973). Rodinson set out detailed examples
of the early Zionist movement's use of colonial practices to
build its putative state, while acknowledging that there had
been nothing controversial about colonialism at the time of
Zionism's early development: 'Except for a section (only a
section) of the European socialist parties and a few rare revolutionary and liberal elements, colonization at the time was
essentially taken to mean the spreading of progress, civilization and well-being.' Yet, by the 1960s, Rodinson went on,

it was common for 'left-wing intellectuals' to portray colonisers as 'monsters with human faces whose behavior defies
rational explanation'. In 1969, *New Left Review* published an
article by Fawwaz Trabulsi that one contemporary observer
described as the first New Left analysis of Israel, Palestine and
the Middle East in an English-language journal. Trabulsi wrote
that the Palestinian struggle 'can only be understood within
the wider framework of the revolution in the Middle East as a
whole, an area which is closely linked to the world imperialist
system'. US imperialism, Zionism, the Arab regimes and the
USSR are all to blame, he argued, for holding back national liberation and socialist revolution in the region. In 1971, *New Left
Review* published an important essay called *The Class Nature
of Israeli Society* by three Israeli anti-Zionists from the Israeli
organisation Matzpen, which was turned into a booklet and
sold by various British Trotskyist organisations and newspapers. Across the New Left, in Britain and abroad, organisations
and journals turned their attention to Israel and Palestine.
A 1973 survey of American Communist, Marxist–Leninist and
Trotskyist organisations found that all viewed the Middle East
conflict 'in terms of the imperialist penetration of the region
for economic and strategic purposes'; almost all saw 'Zionism
as a product of the forces of capitalism and imperialism'; and
the Six Day War had been the 'catalyst' that had 'eroded the
total pro-Zionist commitment of the intellectuals, left-liberals
and social democrats'. Some articles in this post-1967 period

recycled older antisemitic ideas in an attempt to provide a left-wing analysis of Zionism. A 1972 article in the *Journal of Palestine Studies* argued that Zionist ideology was a vehicle for the enrichment of 'the specifically Jewish upper bourgeoisie, led by the Rothschilds', and a way for 'big Jewish finance capital' to serve imperialism while making a profit.[13]

Left-wing campaigning for Palestine and against Israel also began to take shape after the Six Day War, having been virtually non-existent beforehand. At a Palestine Day Conference held in London in 1966 by the General Union of Arab Students (a UK-based organisation for Arab students formed in 1953), the writer Erskine Childers had berated the British left for a lack of interest in Palestinians: 'this one indigenous people in the whole of Afro-Asia who are ignored by British Socialists'. In May 1968, a *Jewish Chronicle* article about what the newspaper called 'The Pro-Arab Lobby' highlighted, through almost complete omission, the paucity of left-wing support for Palestine at that time. The article noted the activities of the General Union of Arab Students, the Arab League office in London and various Arab embassies, before concluding that the most articulate and active supporters of the Arab cause were 'native British pro-Arabs in politics, Parliament, literature, in the press, in academic life' as well as retired diplomats and army officers. The anti-colonial left commanded just one sentence in the article. This soon began to change. June 1968 saw the first edition of *Free Palestine*, a monthly newspaper based in London launched by a group of supporters of Fatah, the main Palestinian resistance movement and largest constituent body in the PLO. The following year, a group of MPs formed the Council for the Advancement of Arab–British Understanding (CAABU), which became a home for the establishment Arabists identified by the *Jewish Chronicle*'s article on Arab lobbying. One of CAABU's founders, the Labour MP Christopher Mayhew, established the Labour Middle East Council in 1969 in an attempt to change Labour's traditional pro-Israel stance. Outside Parliament, New Leftist groups dedicated to the Israel/Palestine issue also began to emerge: the Palestine Solidarity Campaign was launched in 1969, Palestine Action was formed in 1972 and the British Anti-Zionist Organisation (BAZO) was established in 1975.[14]

While the left reacted to the Six Day War with a radical critique of Israel's creation and existence and by forming various pro-Palestinian and anti-Zionist campaigning groups, Jews around the world experienced the war as a story of the imminent destruction of Israel – to many, a potential second Holocaust in the making – followed by what they saw as its miraculous salvation. Rather than being an example of Israeli aggression and territorial expansion, they felt this was an example of a small, threatened nation executing a breathtaking military victory against overwhelming odds. In Britain, as in other countries, the war triggered a surge of Jewish support for Israel even amongst those who had previously not been committed Zionists. This impact was so profound that it helped Zionism become the vehicle for a new secular form of British Jewish identity. In the United States, Norman Podhoretz observed that during and after the Six Day War, 'most American Jews experienced a passion of solidarity with the Jews of Israel that was new and shocking and powerful'. In the Soviet Union, the war triggered a revival of Jewish and Zionist consciousness; Soviet Jewish demands to leave the USSR were described in 1972 by then Israeli Prime Minister Golda Meir as 'one of the wonderful by-products of the 1967 war'. For Jews around the world, according to the late historian Robert Wistrich, Israel became 'a catalyst of Jewish identification and an undeniable core of Jewish identity, cohesion and continuity in the post-war world'. All this happened at the same moment that the New Left was settling on a hostile view of Israel as a colonial hangover that ought not to have been created and which should not endure. This alone shows how much Jewish politics had already diverged from that of the New Left on this issue. Having been part of each other's story for over a century, Jews and the left had been drifting apart for some years. After 1967, these different paths would lead to open conflict between them.[15]

CHAPTER TWO

FROM ANTI-APARTHEID TO ANTI-ZIONISM

E very year, sometime between February and April depending on whether they are in Europe, North America, South Africa, Latin America, Asia or in Arab countries, students arrive at university to be confronted by temporary walls, checkpoints and fake Israeli soldiers, sometimes carrying pretend guns. These students are forced to wait in line while the fake Israeli soldiers – who are actually pro-Palestinian activists from amongst their fellow students – denounce Israel and what they claim are its apartheid policies and practices. Once the street theatre is over and they are allowed to enter their seats of learning, the students are invited to attend meetings where speakers will explain in great depth why they believe Israel to be the world's sole successor to apartheid South Africa. The students may be encouraged to vote for a Students' Union motion supporting the growing international movement to boycott Israel. This is Israel Apartheid Week, and in 2016 it claimed to have activities in 150 universities and cities around the world.

The idea that Israel is an apartheid state based on racial segregation between Arabs and Jews is a core principle of left-wing anti-Zionism. Examples of pro-Palestinian campaigners, politicians, diplomats and journalists making this comparison are legion. Archbishop Desmond Tutu, a veteran of South Africa's own anti-apartheid struggle, has compared Israel's occupation to his own country's racist history. Former American President Jimmy Carter used it in the title of his book, *Palestine: Peace not Apartheid*. John Dugard, the former UN Special Rapporteur on human rights in the occupied territories, suggested that aspects of Israel's occupation would contravene the 1973 International Convention on the Suppression and Punishment of the Crime of Apartheid. Labour MP and former minister Clare Short claimed that Israel was responsible for 'the deliberate creation of an apartheid system' in the West Bank. In 2006, *The Guardian* published a lengthy, two-part essay on the subject by Chris McGreal, who had served as a correspondent in both Jerusalem and Johannesburg, in which he described a complex pattern of similarities between Israel and apartheid South Africa – and also noted some important differences.[1]

Most of these comparisons focus on the situation in the West Bank rather than in Israel itself. There are important differences in the history and legal status of the two territories.

The West Bank was occupied by Jordan in 1948 during its war against the new State of Israel and then annexed by Jordan after that war, remaining under its sovereignty until 1967. The border between the West Bank and Israel during that period ran along the armistice line between Israel and Jordan at the end of Israel's war of independence in 1949. In 1967, Israel conquered the West Bank, East Jerusalem, Gaza Strip, Golan Heights and Sinai Peninsula during the Six Day War. Of these, Israel returned the Sinai Peninsula to Egypt under the 1979 peace treaty between the two countries; annexed East Jerusalem in 1967 and the Golan Heights in 1981; withdrew unilaterally from the Gaza Strip in 2005; and remains in military administration, but not sovereign authority, of the West Bank, the governance of which is shared with the Palestinian Authority. In other words, Israel and the West Bank are, legally and in terms of sovereignty, different places subject to different legal and political systems. The border between them, known as the 'green line' and running along the 1949 armistice line, is not an international border of the State of Israel. The anomaly that anti-Israel campaigners cite to justify their apartheid comparison is that Jewish settlers who live in the West Bank are, in certain circumstances, subject to Israeli civil law from the other side of the green line and vote in elections for the Israeli government, while the Palestinians who share the same territorial space as them live under Israeli military law and elect the Palestinian Authority.

The construction of a barrier between Israel and the West Bank, dubbed the 'Apartheid Wall' by Israel's opponents, has emphasised the impression of physical separation between Israelis and Palestinians. While successive Israeli governments have justified this barrier as a security measure to prevent Palestinian terrorists from reaching Israeli cities, their critics have a different opinion of its purpose. In the view of Jeremy Corbyn, 'Any normal thinking person would see it as an absurd piece of 21st-century civil engineering built upon the principle of apartheid against the Palestinian people.' The apartheid charge is not limited to the West Bank: it includes, for example, claims that land ownership laws and planning regulations inside Israel comprise a legal system of racial discrimination against its Arab citizens. The primary basis for the allegation, though, is the different legal status and physically parallel lives of the two communities in the West Bank. This is 'simply another' apartheid system, according to Corbyn.[2]

The power and attraction of the apartheid charge is obvious. Apartheid is a gross offence against the most basic political morality – what Håkan Thörn called 'the global norm of racial equality' – and opposition to it enjoys universal support. It has been declared a crime against humanity by the United Nations General Assembly, whose International Convention on Suppression and Punishment of the Crime of Apartheid makes it possible to prosecute people or organisations that are involved in apartheid practices (although to date, none have been). South Africa was excluded from global sporting bodies from the 1960s and its membership of the UN was effectively suspended from 1974 until the end of apartheid twenty years later. It was subject to economic sanctions and a UN-mandated arms embargo. This structure of global exclusion was matched by a consumer boycott of South African goods that was the hallmark of grassroots anti-apartheid campaigns. The Anti-Apartheid Movement that was formed in Britain in 1960 was originally called the 'Boycott Committee', precisely because it aimed for the isolation of South Africa via a consumer boycott and economic and other sanctions by governments. For anti-Israel activists trying to promote a similar campaign against Israel – known as the Boycott, Divestment and Sanctions campaign, or BDS – the possibility of convincing people that it, too, practises apartheid, is a tremendous lure. South African apartheid could not withstand this global pressure; persuade enough people, corporations and governments that Israel is also guilty of apartheid and, so the logic goes, it will also eventually crumble.[3]

There is another reason why campaigners try to make the apartheid equation stick: because the Anti-Apartheid Movement was a model campaign group that every political campaigner would want to emulate. It was one of the most popular, and arguably the most successful, of the social movements that emerged from the new radical politics of the 1960s. It came from the fringes to shape mainstream opinion. It successfully sold anti-apartheid as both a human rights issue and a moral cause that everybody could join in with, simply by their choice of which oranges to buy at their local supermarket. It has a mythological status on the left that instantly grants moral authority to anyone who was involved with it. The pro-Palestinian movement has never enjoyed similar support, influence or moral weight, but defining itself as a new anti-apartheid movement could be a route to such status. 'Help us to build a new mass anti-apartheid movement for Palestine,' asks the website of the Palestine Solidarity Campaign. For individual anti-Israel activists, imagining themselves to be heroically tearing down a new Israeli apartheid allows them to bask in the reflected glory of their illustrious forebears.[4]

Meanwhile, Israel's supporters point to the situation inside Israel itself, on the other side of the green line from the West Bank, to defend Israel against the apartheid charge. There, Arabs and Jews enjoy the same political rights to vote, to stand for Parliament and, in theory at least, to hold the highest offices of state. There is none of the physical separation that charac-terised apartheid South Africa: no separate buses, beaches or benches, no laws prohibiting sexual liaisons between Arabs and Jews and no segregation in the workplace. Israeli Jews and Arabs study alongside each other at university and work along-side each other in offices, factories and hospitals. Israeli Arabs are not conscripted into the Israeli Army (although Israeli Druze are), but some do volunteer and serve alongside Jewish soldiers; in 2016, the highest-ranking Arab–Israeli soldier, Major Alaa Waheeb, visited the UK specifically to argue Israel's case during Israel Apartheid Week.

It is not the aim of this book to delve in any great depth into these arguments and determine which carries the greater weight. It is possible, given their primary focus on different sides of the green line, that there are varying degrees of validity in both sides' arguments. Instead, this book's contribution to this particular subject is to show that while today's pro-Palestinian activists habitually connect Israel to apartheid in their campaigning, this is not a new tactic or a response to recent developments in Israel and Palestine. It is a comparison that was hardwired into left-wing anti-Israel politics in Britain during its formative years in the 1960s and 1970s. It happened because left-wing anti-Zionism grew from the very same networks and activist groups that were campaigning against apartheid at that time. And although the apartheid charge draws most of its power from the current status of the occupation, it predates Israel's conquest of the West Bank and Gaza by some years. The PLO was formed in 1964 – three years before the current occupation began – and it used the apartheid charge almost immediately. Its 1965 booklet, *Zionist Colonialism in Palestine*, made a direct comparison between Israel and apartheid South Africa – except it claimed that Israel was the worse offender of the two. 'Nowhere in Asia or Africa – not even in South Africa or Rhodesia – has European race-supremacism expressed itself in so passionate a zeal for thoroughgoing racial exclusiveness ... as it has in Palestine,' the booklet's author Fayez Sayegh claimed. The 'Zionist practitioners of *apartheid* in Palestine', he went on, had surpassed even the Afrikaners, leaving Palestinian Arabs languishing 'under a regime of racist discrimination and oppression as harsh as any race-supremacist regime in Asia or Africa'. The Arab League used the apartheid charge even earlier: in 1963, its London-based magazine *Arab Outlook* included a lengthy article explaining that the Arab economic boycott of Israel was a response to 'Israeli apartheid'. Similar to the apartheid charge, and more common, was the grouping of Israel with South Africa and Rhodesia as white settler states, left behind as the tide of colonialism receded from Africa and Asia. One organisation that embodied this idea, promoted it earlier than most, and was directly responsible for transmitting it to the British left, was a Cold War curiosity called the Afro-Asian People's Solidarity Organization (AAPSO).[5]

Based in Cairo under the radical Arab nationalist regime of Gamal Abdel Nasser, AAPSO provided a forum in which Western New Leftists met representatives of radical Third World liberation movements and encountered their views of various conflicts around the world – including the Israeli–Palestinian conflict. Nasser's Egypt was a client state of the Soviet Union by the 1960s and AAPSO's rhetoric about Zionism reflected Soviet and Egyptian propaganda. Throughout the

1960s, AAPSO's main publication, *Afro-Asian Bulletin*, consistently portrayed Israel as a creation and tool of imperialism, artificially implanted in Palestine to divide African, Arab and Asian peoples, subvert their quest for independence and penetrate their economies for Western capitalism. In this narrative, Israeli aggression against its Arab neighbours was of a piece with American aggression in Vietnam and Southeast Asia; it followed that there could be no peace in the Middle East so long as Israel existed there. In December 1961, AAPSO held a meeting of its Executive Committee in Gaza (then under Egyptian control). Nasser himself sent a message of support, in which he claimed that 'colonialism' supported its 'lackey Israel' in order 'to establish a bridge-head for imperialism from which to threaten the Arab Nations and African and Asian peoples' security and life'. The Palestinian delegation to the meeting argued that Palestine, South Africa and other African states were all places that 'colonialism endeavours to dominate'. This all predated Israel's occupation of the West Bank and Gaza. It meant that, right from the start, British left-wing anti-Zionists who attended AAPSO's conferences as part of their anti-colonialism saw Israel and South Africa as siblings in the racial oppression of Third World peoples. However, it wasn't British Stalinists or Trotskyists who took this Soviet-designed message and put it to work on the British left. It was – believe it or not – the Young Liberals.[6]

In January 1969, AAPSO held back-to-back conferences in Khartoum and Cairo, the first for 'The Peoples of Portuguese

Colonies and Southern Africa' and the second 'In Support of the Arab Peoples'. Portugal had several colonies in Africa, of which Mozambique and Angola both produced prominent anti-colonial liberation movements. Speakers at both conferences repeatedly accused Israel of being an artificial, colonial state, planted in the Middle East to obstruct the freedom of Arab and African peoples. In this telling, Palestine, Vietnam and South Africa were all part of the same struggle that all true anti-colonialists should support. Amongst the delegates at both conferences was the international vice-chairman of the Young Liberals (the youth wing of the Liberal Party, that comprised the National League of Young Liberals and the Union of Liberal Students), called Peter Hellyer. His presence would have long-lasting effects on the Young Liberals and, indirectly, on the wider left.

The Young Liberals were going through a strange period in their history in the late 1960s. They were part of a mainstream parliamentary party, but had been swept along in the radical youth politics of the 1960s. They began the decade by helping to win a parliamentary by-election in Orpington in 1962, turned left in 1966 with an attempt to ambush the Liberal Party into opposing NATO at its annual Assembly, and by 1968 had plunged fully into the revolutionary New Left, with their political vice-chairman Bernard Greaves dismissing Parliament as a hindrance to 'the revolutionary transformation of society.' Phil Kelly, chairman of the Union of Liberal Students in 1968 (and a future Labour Mayor of Islington), brought the rebellious message even closer to home: 'There is obviously a leadership in name, but the Liberal Party is now as irrelevant to us as all the rest of the political structures.'[7]

These statements were typical of what Hellyer called 'the hothouse atmosphere of the radical extra-parliamentary left in London' in the 1960s. They didn't sit well with the wider Liberal Party leadership. The Young Liberals' hostility to NATO and their involvement in anti-Vietnam War campaigns had attracted invitations to visit the Soviet Union and other Eastern bloc nations, which some members took up. They weren't pro-Soviet, but their rejection of NATO was typical of New Left thinking at that time, which shunned the binary thinking of the Cold War and viewed both superpowers with (admittedly unequal) suspicion. For the party leadership, this apparent flirtation with communism was an embarrassment. It didn't help when a Young Liberals Executive member called Louis Eaks was fined for obstructing a police officer at an anti-Vietnam War demonstration outside the American embassy in March 1968. He was the Liberal Party's prospective parliamentary candidate for Hackney Central at the time. Eaks became chairman of the Young Liberals shortly afterwards and was the most enthusiastic and determined anti-Zionist in the organisation. Although he is hardly a household name, Louis Eaks arguably did more than anyone else to make Palestine a mainstream issue for the British left.[8]

The Young Liberals saw themselves as part of the New Left. They went on the same demonstrations, joined the same campaigns, used similar rhetoric and shared some of the same political goals as the Marxist and Trotskyist groups more commonly associated with that label. That they did so while also being part of a parliamentary party was an oddity during a particularly odd political time. Many other New Leftists viewed them as eccentric and lacking seriousness precisely because they claimed to be radical, even revolutionary, while being part of a mainstream parliamentary party. Liberalism, after all, is a bourgeois conceit and hardly revolutionary. Several Young Liberals were attracted to socialism but the truth is that, despite flirting with the language and ideas of the revolutionary left, most did not want to break their connection to the Liberal Party and, through it, to parliamentary democracy. Those who were committed to socialism, like Peter Hain and Phil Kelly, joined the Labour Party. In fact, some Young Liberals even viewed the relative superficiality of their ideology with a degree of pride compared to the stultifying rigidity of Marxist–Leninism. Hellyer thought the Labour Party Young Socialists, the International Marxist Group and the International Socialists were just 'boring'. For the Young Liberals, being on the New Left was about exciting campaigns that shocked the establishment – including their own party leadership – while pursuing what they considered to be moral political causes. There was no more moral cause than apartheid, and it was Young Liberals who led one of the most successful New Left campaigns against it: the Stop the Seventy Tour Committee.[9]

The Stop the Seventy Tour Committee, or STST as it was known, was a campaign to stop the South African cricket team from touring England in 1970. It was completely successful: the cricket tour was cancelled and South Africa did not tour England again until after the end of apartheid. Its founder and spokesman was Peter Hain, then a member of the Young Liberals. Hain arrived in Britain in 1966 as a South African émigré whose parents had been active in the South African Liberal Party before being exiled for their anti-apartheid activities. He joined the Young Liberals in 1967, attracted by their spirit and attitude:

> One of the reasons I joined the Young Liberals in that period was because they seemed to be the most radical – visibly radical – groups around. And whatever the issue was, there was just a feeling and an energy that was very attractive to lots of people who were actually more socialist then they were traditionally liberal, like me.[10]

As Hain suggests, in the late 1960s, the Young Liberals provided a home for a wide range of people on the left who didn't quite fit anywhere else. 'Sometimes', former chair George Kiloh wrote, 'they gave the impression of having wandered into the Liberal Party by mistake, rather as one might wander into a pub, find it congenial and decide to stay a while.' The Labour Party's student and youth bodies were crippled by chronic infighting throughout the 1960s and the Young Liberals tried to offer a more attractive option for young people seeking a radical, militant approach to politics.[11]

STST was typical of this radicalism and the peak of the Young Liberals' popularity. The background to the campaign was the cancellation of England's 1968 cricket tour to South Africa, after the South African authorities refused to accept Basil D'Oliveira, a South African classified as 'coloured' under apartheid, who was then playing for England, as one of the touring party. With the South Africans due to tour England in 1970, in January 1969 the Young Liberals adopted a motion drafted by Hain that pledged 'to take direct action to prevent scheduled matches from taking place unless the 1970 tour is cancelled'. Activists had demonstrated outside South African sporting events in Britain before, but Hain was the first to suggest direct action to disrupt the actual events themselves. In an example of the circulation of ideas and activism in the New Left, he was inspired by the participation of some Young Liberals in a student sit-in at the Hornsey College of Art in May 1968, as well as the 'Committee of 100' that had used similar tactics in campaigns against nuclear weapons. The Young Liberals had already held a sit-in at the offices of *The Guardian* in December 1968, in protest at the paper's publication of adverts promoting South Africa.[12]

As a prelude to the South African tour, in July 1969 Hain and others organised for a group of Young Liberal activists to disrupt matches involving a visiting all-white South African club cricket team playing under the name of the Wilf Isaacs XI. That same month, Hain and two other Young Liberals interrupted a Davis Cup tennis match in Bristol between South Africa and Britain that was being broadcast on live television. By September, Hain, Eaks and others had pulled together a network to oppose the tour that included the Young Liberals, the Anti-Apartheid Movement, the National Union of Students, the International Socialists and the International Marxist Group. This broad umbrella of enthusiastic young leftists took the name 'Stop the Seventy Tour Committee'. While the Young Liberals only contributed a minority of its activists, the leadership, direction and energy that Hain and others gave it meant that they were intimately associated with the campaign in the public's mind.

STST took direct action tactics out of student unions and introduced them into a campaign of global significance. 'From being a tactic thrown up more in frustration', Hain wrote, 'match disruption began to develop almost a life of its own.' STST's first actions targeted a tour by the Springboks, the South African rugby union side, in the autumn of 1969. Around 1,000 demonstrators turned up to their opening match against Oxford University; twice that number were at Twickenham to disrupt a match against London Counties in November, which was held

up for ten minutes when hundreds of demonstrators ran onto
the pitch. Official condemnation and media attention predict-
ably followed, in South Africa as much as in Britain, in a way
that traditional methods of protest could not have achieved.
The Home Secretary hosted a meeting of Chief Constables and
Deputy Chief Constables from fifteen police forces to discuss
policing tactics and costs. Direct action methods were controversial even within anti-apartheid circles. The Anti-Apartheid
Movement, keen to protect its law-abiding image, never sanc-
tioned direct action, although it gave STST significant informal
support and its activists took part in the disruptions. The Liberal
Party had called for the cricket tour to be cancelled but did not
support the direct action of its youth wing.[13]

The party itself had a long record of support for the Anti-
Apartheid Movement. Jeremy Thorpe MP, who succeeded
Jo Grimond as party leader in 1967, was an Anti-Apartheid
Movement sponsor from the early 1960s and its vice-president
from 1966 to 1980, including during his time as party leader.
Thorpe's successor as party leader, David Steel, was president
of the Anti-Apartheid Movement from 1966–69 and a sponsor until 1980, also while he was party leader. While they could
not match the much larger Labour Party in the scale of support
and influence it offered, the Liberal Party's relationship with
the Anti-Apartheid Movement was just as close. However, the
Young Liberals' prominent role in the direct action of STST
caused increasing discomfort for the party leadership. This

reached breaking point one night in January 1970, when fourteen of the seventeen county cricket grounds where the South
African team was due to play were daubed with slogans and the
pitches at two of them were vandalised. The scale and organisation of the raids shocked the cricket authorities. STST
deliberately did not admit responsibility, but Eaks, who was
Young Liberals chairman at the time, told the media that they
were involved. Eaks had not actually taken part in the vandalism but his statement led the Liberal Party Executive to pass
a resolution calling on the Young Liberals to remove him as
chair. Hain remembers it causing 'an enormous fuss in the
party ... huge anger and division and conflict'. An attempt by
Hain later that month to persuade the Liberal Party Council to
formally endorse the use of 'non-violent direct action' failed,
his motion being amended to support 'all lawful means of protest' before being passed.[14]

Hain later claimed, quite justifiably, that STST was 'one
of the very few British protest groups to have completely
achieved its objectives'. It also brought the Young Liberals
enormous public profile and new credibility on the extra-
parliamentary left. Opposition to apartheid became central
to the Young Liberals' self-identity as a radical movement
in the 1960s. This, then, was the movement and the mindset
that Peter Hellyer represented at the AAPSO conferences in
Khartoum and Cairo in January 1969 – the same month that
the Young Liberals voted to adopt direct action tactics against

apartheid. Hellyer personified the link between the two as he was on the Executive of the Anti-Apartheid Movement and represented both it and the Young Liberals at the Khartoum conference. He was enthralled by the presence of leaders from all the Southern African liberation movements. The South African ANC, SWAPO from Namibia, the Angolan MPLA, FRELIMO from Mozambique and the Zimbabwean organisation ZAPU were all present, as were the Vietnamese NLF and 'all sorts of other oddities' from Equatorial Guinea and elsewhere. So, crucially, was Fatah. 'For a 21-year-old radical YL', he later wrote, 'it was QUITE an experience!'[15]

AAPSO was the epicentre of the drive to connect Zionism to colonialism and apartheid. Khartoum was the first place that Hellyer had ever met any representatives of Fatah or the PLO. All the Southern African liberation movements at the Khartoum conference talked of a global anti-imperialist struggle that included Palestine. The ANC delegate named Israel amongst the 'imperialist countries' that 'render active support directly and indirectly to the oppressive white minority regimes of Southern Africa'. America's war in Vietnam was repeatedly referenced in the conference documents, enhancing the Soviet Union's status as the favoured superpower in these circles. Sam Nujoma, president of the Namibian liberation movement SWAPO, saluted 'the glorious struggle of the people of Vietnam against the number one deadly enemy of all the oppressed and exploited masses of the world:

the US imperialism'. He went on to link this directly to the Palestinian cause:

> We, furthermore, support the Palestinian Arab People's struggle to regain their country back from the imperialists instigated [*sic*] reactionary Zionists. We support the peoples of the United Arab Republic, Syria and other Arab countries in their struggle to liquidate the traces of the Israeli aggression and to regain their territories now occupied by the imperialist-backed Zionist aggressors.

Some of the conference statements described Israel in conspiratorial terms – not as the authentic expression of Jewish national rights, but as part of a Western plot to subvert the freedom of Third World peoples. One of the conference resolutions claimed that Israel was used as a channel for 'imperialist investments' to find their way to African states, 'thus constituting a tool for neo-colonialism'. The main conference declaration described the African liberation movements as part of 'the world-wide anti-imperialist struggle' that included Arab resistance to 'imperialist-backed Zionist aggression'. The conference also sent a message of encouragement to the Second International Conference in Support of the Arab Peoples that Hellyer was due to attend in Cairo the following week. This particular statement directly linked the purpose of the two conferences:

The Khartoum and Cairo Conference [*sic*] are closely
connected with each other. The Israeli–imperialist aggression
against the Arab peoples is an integral part of the imperialist
strategy in the world.

The struggle of the peoples of Southern Africa and the
Portuguese colonies is inextricably linked with the struggle
of the Arab peoples against imperialism, aggression, Zionism
and racial discrimination and exploitation.[16]

In Cairo, Hellyer had the opportunity to talk more directly
to Palestinians and delegates from other Arab countries,
in order to overcome what he called the 'distorted picture' presented by 'the press and television bias towards the
Israeli side' in the British media. Nasser addressed the conference in Cairo, whose 400 participants included British
left-wing historian Arnold Toynbee. According to one
report, Nabil Shaath, representing Fatah, used his speech
to reject United Nations Security Council Resolution 242,
passed in November 1967, because it demanded acceptance
of Israel's permanency. Fatah's published version of their delegation's address claimed Zionism was an ideology of racial
superiority by linking it to the religious concept of a 'chosen
people' (a misrepresentation of that concept that is commonly
found in antisemitic rhetoric). Their statement compared
Zionism to Nazism and committed Fatah to using violence
to defeat it:

Zionism is one of the most oppressive and aggressive forms
of imperialism … The roots of the aggression lie in the Zionist ideology itself, with its belief in the need to bring a select,
chosen people without a land, to a land that is to be evacu-
ated by its inferior people … We will not accept any substitute
to a war of national liberation and will tenaciously hold to it
regardless of sacrifices and costs. Could anybody have asked
you to accept anything less than total freedom from Nazism,
fascism or colonialism?[17]

From Cairo, Hellyer travelled to Lebanon and Jordan on a trip
organised by the Arab League. In Beirut, he discussed with the
Palestine Research Center – an organisation that was part of
the PLO – the difficulties in 'trying to counter the Zionist propaganda' in order to put across the Palestinian case in Britain.
In Jordan, Hellyer was shocked by the conditions in Camp
Baqa'a, the largest Palestinian refugee camp in the country, and
by the destruction in Karameh, scene of a battle between the
Israeli Army and the PLO in March 1968. He felt that Israel's
behaviour 'prompted a reassessment of the nature of the state
and comparisons with the settler-states in Southern Africa'.
He later wrote that he returned 'convinced that the Palestinians
did, indeed, have a case, and that the almost unthinking support for Israel in Britain, including within the Liberal Party,
needed some re-examination'. It was 'the gradually emerging
evidence of close ties between Israel and the white regimes

in Southern Africa' that helped him to convince other Young Liberals that the issue was worthy of attention. AAPSO seemed to place some importance on Hellyer's trip, claiming that he was inspired by the Khartoum conference to organise various anti-apartheid activities on his return to London.[18]

Although Hellyer was not pro-Soviet, at Khartoum and Cairo he was in a political environment where he was exposed to a view of Zionism that was heavily influenced by the language of Soviet and Egyptian anti-Zionist propaganda. This is an example of how Soviet positions on Zionism and Israel played an important role in an anti-Zionist discourse that could filter down, albeit diluted, into the British New Left's understanding of Zionism, even amongst groups that were not Marxist–Leninist. Soviet anti-Zionism was often a thin cloak for antisemitism. The early 1950s had seen a series of antisemitic show trials in the Soviet bloc. In 1952, a group of predominantly Jewish communist leaders in Czechoslovakia were tried, and most executed, for treason – an episode known as the 'Slánský trial' – and then the following year a group of doctors, again mostly Jewish, was accused of plotting to kill Stalin. In both trials, prosecutors repeatedly emphasised the fact that the majority of the defendants were Jewish, while linking this to 'cosmopolitanism' and the notion of an international Zionist conspiracy. Although Stalin died in 1953, Soviet antisemitism did not die with him. The idea that Zionism was a form of racism, or even fascism, was increasingly common in Soviet propaganda in the 1960s and

1970s, often accompanied by overtly antisemitic conspiracy theories and demonic portrayals of Jews and Zionists that echoed traditional European antisemitism. One book published by the Ukrainian Academy of Sciences in 1963, Trofim Kichko's *Judaism Without Embellishment*, was so antisemitic that communist parties around the world protested about it. These portrayals of Zionism found their way into AAPSO and other anti-colonial political circles where the Soviets had influence. By the 1980s, they had spawned a conspiratorial notion of Zionism in Third World political discourse, whereby 'Zionist' became a pejorative term applied to one's enemies, even if those enemies were not Jewish and had no actual connection to Zionism or Israel. It has had a similar long-term, indirect influence on the Western radical left, whether pro-Soviet or not.

It was not long after Hellyer's return to the United Kingdom that his experiences began to have a visible impact in the Young Liberals. In April 1969, the Liberal magazine *New Outlook* published an article by Michael Jefferson that called Israel 'a Western intrusion' on Arab land and appealed to Liberals to support the Palestinians' 'irrefutable' case. It was not Israel's 'expansionism and treatment of her Arab minority' that demanded Liberal action, according to the author, but rather the historical circumstances of its founding, 'which damn Zionism and the present State in principle and practice'. In other words, it was Israel's creation and ongoing existence, not its recent occupation of the West Bank and Gaza Strip, that was the problem. The following month a new campaign group called Liberals for Palestine was formed as an 'anti-Zionist group' that 'calls for a bi-racial, secular state of Palestine in which Jews, Muslims and Christians will enjoy complete equality'. This formulation matched Fatah's proposed solution of a single secular democratic state in Palestine that came to be the preferred option for many on the anti-Israel left.[19]

However, while the Young Liberals were moving towards this New Left view of Israel as an illegitimate, colonial state, Liberal Party policy remained firmly pro-Israel. Liberal Party leader Jeremy Thorpe was a particularly strong supporter. In April 1968, he told a Jewish audience in London that the Six Day War the previous summer was comparable to the Italian–Abyssinian war of 1935 – with the Arab nations in the role of Mussolini's fascists. He went on to explain that a peace agreement was necessary but out of reach while the 'Arab world' was deluded by 'the intrigues of Nazis and Communists'. This sympathy for Israel did not prevent him from warning with some prescience that Israel would struggle to control the population of the West Bank, 'a society seething with nationalist sentiment', and he seemed to have already sensed that Israel's staggering military victory and new-found dominance could trigger a shift in public sympathy in Britain:

> Britain suffers little from the disgrace of anti-Semitism. But the amiable weakness for the underdog, which is part of our

national character, can all too easily allow us to become sen-
timental about political problems, while the perverse British
characteristic of preferring our foes to our friends often cor-
rupts our judgement.[20]

Louis Eaks was determined to turn the Young Liberals into
an anti-Zionist organisation. If it was Peter Hellyer who introduced the Palestinian cause to the Young Liberals, Eaks was
the person who made it a major campaigning issue, first
inside the Liberal Party and then beyond. Importantly, he saw
Palestine as a natural corollary for his anti-apartheid activities. In December 1969, Eaks represented the Young Liberals
at the first International Congress of Solidarity with the People
of Palestine, held in Algiers. The conference declaration
denounced Zionism as 'a racialist, expansionist and colonialist system which is an integral part and instrument of world
imperialism, headed by the United States'. It also endorsed the
PLO's preferred single-state solution for Palestine. Fatah chairman Yasser Arafat gave a speech at the Congress that wove
together Zionism, capitalism and imperialism in conspiratorial terms that showed how easily the traditional antisemitic
notion of Jewish capitalists oppressing the masses could be
reworked to appeal to a modern, left-wing audience. Fatah
does not oppose Jews, he claimed, but only 'World Zionist
racialism which exploits Jewish religious sentiment in the interests of Zionist Capitalism linked with imperialism'. Jews, he

went on, 'are being sacrificed at the altar of the monopoly interests of the Zionists, imperialists and colonialists.'[21]

Eaks was a divisive figure who irritated some of his peers
with the priority he gave the Palestinian issue. Some Young
Liberals were suspicious of his easy access to money from the
Arab embassies of London to fund his activities. He was very
open about this fact, whether it was Arab League funding for
visits to the Middle East or Arab embassies giving him con-
tracts for his public relations and publishing business. He was
a particularly single-minded activist whom Kiloh felt 'liked the
grand gesture and chafed at the administrative routine needed
to run a campaign'. Hain felt he had a 'flair for publicity and
making an impact'. He was also a natural risk-taker. All this
was apparent in a speech he made to a meeting at the Egyptian
embassy in London in January 1970, and in his decision to issue
an official Young Liberals press release with extracts that compared Israel to apartheid South Africa and (in an even more
incendiary step) Nazi Germany:

> World opinion must be mobilised to isolate the militant
> Zionists responsible for the present situation in the Middle
> East. Racial persecution and expansionism are terms
> instantly associated with Nazi Germany – yet today Israel is
> seen pursuing the same course. In 1939 we mobilised to stop
> Hitler. In 1970 we must stop Israel's blatant attempts to escalate
> the war.

There is no place for a State based on racial or religious discrimination. Zionist apartheid is no more acceptable to Liberals than South African apartheid.

[...]

Palestine is for the Palestinians – regardless of their race or creed. Palestinian liberation movements and El Fat'h [sic] must continue to assert their rights. In Isreal [sic] all people must work to remove Zionists from power, and work with all the peoples of the Middle East to create a non-secular [sic] state of Palestine.[22]

This statement came just a few days after Eaks had publicly linked the Young Liberals to STST's overnight vandalism of fourteen cricket grounds. The timing adds significance to Eaks's comparison of 'Zionist apartheid' with 'South African apartheid'. It reflected Eaks's thinking and was an attempt to harness the momentum generated by STST's activities for his anti-Zionist campaigning. However, Eaks's statement caused outrage in the party. The allegation of 'Zionist apartheid', comparison to Nazi Germany and the implication that Israel should be replaced by a single Palestinian state went against Young Liberals policy, never mind that of the Liberal Party itself. Lord Byers, Liberal Party leader in the House of Lords, described Eaks as a 'liability', while Leonard Smith, Liberal vice-president, wrote to Byers and Thorpe demanding that they publicly repudiate Eaks's views. Eaks would not be deterred. He defied the party leadership with a second press release in March, containing extracts from a speech he had made at another pro-Palestinian meeting. After rejecting the criticism of his earlier actions, Eaks stated his opposition to Israel's existence in even clearer terms:

> The major issue is the Palestinians' rights which are being denied by the existence of a Zionist state of Israel in the Middle East today.
>
> [...]
>
> There can be no peace in the Middle East so long as a Zionist state exists in defiance of basic human rights for all people. Israel, as a Zionist state based on the supremacy of one race over all others, rejects the essential aims of the Palestinian struggle for a unitary, democratic, non-sectarian state, in which all individuals and groups will have equal rights and obligations, irrespective of race, colour or creed.

Israel, Eaks added, had built alliances with South Africa, South Vietnam and South Sudan, none of which are 'on the side of progress' or 'human rights.'[23]

Despite his escalating rhetoric, Eaks soon found that there was a limit to how far he could carry his fellow Young Liberals with him on this particular campaign. The Young Liberals annual conference in Skegness in March 1970 (which had the theme 'Liberals and the New Left') had to choose between opposing motions on Israel/Palestine: one supporting a two-state solution, the other explicitly endorsing Fatah and a single Palestinian state. The latter motion also called for 'the expulsion of the Israeli Liberal Party and Young Liberals from Liberal International and the World Federation of Liberal and Radical Youth respectively'. This call for the expulsion of Israeli organisations echoed anti-apartheid campaigns that had done the same to South African bodies. There was controversy even before the conference began, when the chairman of Skegness Council objected to the planned attendance of a representative of Fatah called Abu Omar. Eaks offered a compromise whereby Abu Omar would not address the conference from the platform but would still be able to take part in debates. This was accepted and the conference went ahead with Abu Omar (who admitted having undergone military training with Fatah) under the watchful eye of Special Branch officers. Abu Omar was opposed in the Middle East debate by Shalom Mandelbaum, a student from the Israeli left-wing party Young Mapam, and Lawry (now Sir Lawrence) Freedman, who was elected chair of the Union of Liberal Students at the conference. After a series of amendments, a rather confused motion was passed: it called for 'The creation of a secular Palestinian State' in line with the Fatah policy, but removed explicit support for Fatah from the text and called on 'the belligerent nations' to hold direct negotiations. The muddled nature of the motion reflected the Young

Liberals' divisions on the whole issue. Significantly, it concluded as follows:

> Conference calls on the National Executive to campaign for the acceptance of the above policy by the Liberal International and the World Federation of Liberal and Radical Youth, and calls on W.L.F.R.Y. [sic] to consider the expulsion of the Israeli Young Liberals and the Independent Young Liberals unless they accept the principles of a secular Palestinian state.[24]

Although the language of this clause was moderated from the original proposal (and altered to reflect the existence of two Israeli Liberal parties), it was still a seminal moment: a mainstream political organisation in Britain calling for the expulsion of their Israeli counterparts from international bodies unless they effectively renounced Zionism. This set a precedent that would influence wider anti-Zionist attitudes in the 1970s via the involvement of Eaks and other Young Liberals in pro-Palestinian campaigning. It found an echo in student efforts to apply the 'No Platform' policy to Zionism that will be described later in this book. This adoption of an anti-Zionist policy by the Young Liberals is an important moment in the development of New Left anti-Zionism in Britain. Nobody else on the left in mainstream politics at that time was thinking in these terms, or would have the impact that the Young Liberals' anti-Zionism had. The Labour Party was still firmly pro-Israel and would remain so until the early 1980s. The Marxist and Trotskyist left had little mainstream influence. In contrast, the Young Liberals' position in a parliamentary party, combined with their involvement in anti-colonial political networks and anti-apartheid campaigning, meant they were better placed than the Marxist left to reach mainstream opinion with the radical ideas that they had taken on.

Eaks was replaced by Tony Greaves (now Liberal Democrat peer Lord Greaves) as Young Liberals chair at the Skegness conference, but the anti-Zionist policy remained in place. Divisions between the Young Liberals and the Liberal Party over Israel/Palestine, now formally codified in their opposing policies, continued to cause serious problems. This was a period when the Liberal Party was at one of the lowest points in its history, winning just six seats in the June 1970 general election, while the Young Liberals were the most vibrant section of the party. In April 1970, Eaks and other Young Liberals had a public row with Thorpe in Whitehall after a disastrous meeting between them and Moshe Kol, the Israeli Minister for Tourism and head of the Independent Liberal Party in Israel. Thorpe had arranged the meeting in the hope of finding some common ground; it resulted only in Kol banging the table with his fist in anger at his awkward Young Liberal interlocutors, who responded by storming out of the meeting. In May, Thorpe used a speech marking the anniversary of the 1943 Warsaw Ghetto Uprising to offer a public apology 'that the foolish

and offensive words of a few inexperienced and unrepresent-
ative people, who apparently claim to possess Liberal beliefs,
should have wounded the feelings of the Jewish Community'.
Affirming Israel's right to exist while also reserving the right to
criticise its actions, Thorpe lamented those who 'have associated with the enemies of Israel' and thereby damaged 'the good
name of British Liberalism'. In November, there were renewed
calls for Eaks's expulsion after he was reported to have told a
Young Liberals meeting in St Albans that 'Jews see themselves
as the master race' and that 'Israel is guilty of some brutal atrocities against humanity'. His comments provoked a statement of
regret from the Executive of the Union of Liberal Students.[25]

Although Eaks's excesses sometimes proved too much for
most Young Liberals to accept, he, Hellyer and others had succeeded in embedding a pro-Palestinian position within the
organisation's international outlook. Despite the unease of
the party leadership, support for a single Palestinian state in
place of Israel and rejection of Zionism became the Young
Liberals' settled policy. In 1973, the Young Liberals annual
conference in Great Malvern added to this, again echoing the
campaign against South Africa, by calling for the expulsion
of Israel from the United Nations and for a boycott of Israeli
goods. Once David Steel replaced Jeremy Thorpe as party
leader in 1976, the Liberal Party did begin to reflect a more general sympathy for the Palestinians. Although it never adopted
a single-state policy similar to that of the Young Liberals, the

Liberal Party moved away from a wholly pro-Israel position several years before the Labour Party would do the same. For Eaks and other Young Liberals, this validated their approach of balancing New Left radicalism with mainstream influence. Their activities during this period, and their eventual influence on the Liberal Party's position, are a significant milestone in the development of sympathy for the Palestinian cause in mainstream liberal and left-wing opinion.

Yet, despite this shift, there was a limit to how far most Young Liberal activists would go in their support for the Palestinians. Anti-Zionism never commanded the same consensus support within the organisation as anti-colonialism and anti-apartheid did. Even amongst those Young Liberals who considered it an important issue, few went along with Eaks's more extreme positions. For example, Eaks supported the PLO's use of violence, seeing it as the same as the ANC's guerrilla warfare, whereas the Young Liberals repeatedly passed policies condemning Palestinian *fedayeen* operations but supported the ANC's armed struggle against apartheid. Most Young Liberals saw the Palestinian cause as one of a denial of their human rights but were not convinced that Israel ought to disappear as a result. According to Phil Kelly, 'Once the issue begins to be raised, that if you're against Zionism, are you against the existence of the State of Israel, then I think the answer for people who were basically sympathetic to the Palestinians on humanitarian grounds is one great big "Err…"'.[26]

The question of whether antisemitism or Israel's Jewishness affected the Young Liberals' campaigning produces some interesting responses. Liberal opinion in wider society at that time was largely ignorant of antisemitism and the Holocaust, but it is possible that the involvement of Young Liberals in anti-racist work made them more sensitive to antisemitism, particularly given the prevalence of Jewish anti-apartheid activists. Peter Hain, who had Jewish friends in the anti-apartheid movement in South Africa, wrote in 1973 that the legacy of antisemitism did not justify Israel's existence, nor should it prevent campaigners from opposing Zionism:

> The world cannot allow its shame over its historic persecution of Jews to rationalise the present persecution of the Palestinians ... The case for the replacement of Israel by a democratic, secular state of Palestine must be put uncompromisingly ... There is a need for an aggressive public campaign to attack the roots of Zionism.

He now says that his attitude towards Israel was influenced by feeling 'a great deal of sympathy for Israelis and the history which led to the establishment of the State of Israel ... which is why I've never put it literally in the same bracket as the anti-apartheid cause'. According to George Kiloh, it was 'the common Western guilt at the fate of the Jews under Nazism' that put a brake on the Young Liberals' pro-Palestinian campaigning. Hellyer remembers the question of whether individual Young Liberal activists were Jewish or not being irrelevant to their positions on Israel/Palestine, and claims to have been unaware of which of his peers were Jewish. Other Young Liberals agree. In contrast with his non-Jewish peers, though, Lawrence Freedman felt that his Jewishness became a political issue for the first time in his life during the debate at the Skegness conference of 1970. The second time, he says, was when he was appointed to the Chilcot Inquiry into the Iraq War, and some observers objected to the presence of two Jews on the Inquiry panel (the other was the late historian Martin Gilbert).[27]

The Young Liberals' radical phase was always driven by a relatively small number of activists at the top of the organisation, whom the membership was willing to follow as long as their radicalism produced enough conflict with the main party to be exciting, but not so much as to materially jeopardise either the Young Liberals' or the party's fortunes. As with many of the more radical explorations of policy, the Palestinian issue belonged, according to Freedman, to 'a core of politicos' who never carried the whole of the organisation with them. The exception to this was STST, which drew support from Young Liberals all over the country. This was largely because opposition to apartheid enjoyed widespread support and legitimacy beyond the party. Opposition to apartheid was seen as a moral cause representing core liberal values. The characterisation of apartheid as a racist system that contravened fundamental international norms was unchallenged across most of the political spectrum. There were still right-wing people willing to defend South Africa, but they rarely did so by trying to justify apartheid itself. Instead, supporters of South Africa would object to the pace, nature and process of changing the apartheid system, rather than defending the system on its own merits. This anti-apartheid consensus had such a strong moral character that it was difficult to argue in favour of apartheid and remain within the boundaries of acceptable democratic opinion. So while the New Left mobilised around anti-apartheid as part of its opposition to establishment norms, in doing so it aligned itself to mainstream opinion well beyond its own radical politics. The most successful radical left-wing campaigns have always been the ones that resonate with broader public opinion: the campaign against the 2003 war in Iraq is the most obvious recent example. Although the direct action tactics used by STST were controversial even within the Young Liberals, in general their anti-apartheid activism enjoyed the support of what Håkan Thörn called 'an imagined community of solidarity activists' that stretched around the world.[28]

In contrast, anti-Zionism and support for Fatah's proposed single state of Palestine in place of Israel benefited from no comparable community of support or widespread public sympathy at that time, at least in Western nations. Beyond the New Left, the Liberal Party itself was fundamentally opposed to the

Fatah position and the Labour Party was even more pro-Israel. Both parties had strong connections with their Israeli counterparts. Sympathy for Labour Zionism, contrasted with the conservatism of many Arab states and the reactionary nature of their rulers, remained widespread on the left. At that time, it was generally accepted on the left that there were two national movements in Israel/Palestine in direct conflict with each other, each at different times claiming anti-colonial credentials, making it difficult to construct any kind of consensus regarding which to support. Labour MP Fenner Brockway, who was one of the left's leading anti-colonial campaigners, admitted to having been more puzzled by the Israeli–Palestinian conflict than by any other issue. Brockway even wrote a letter to the *Jewish Chronicle* paying tribute to Golda Meir on her death in 1978 – he called her 'a real Socialist, with identity with the people' – that drew a caustic response from *Free Palestine* newspaper. The New Left argument that only Palestinian nationalism is authentic and legitimate, that Jews do not have any national rights in Israel/Palestine, and that Zionism is a form of Western colonialism or even apartheid, offers an alternative understanding of the conflict that overcomes this complexity. The successive policies passed by the Young Liberals, with calls for exclusions of Israeli Liberal parties and the expulsion of Israel from the UN, clearly mimicked its position on South Africa. At that stage, though, the supportive environment, sense of priority and simplicity of analysis that was necessary for their policies to be translated into widespread activism was lacking.[29]

A supportive environment for anti-Zionism is more easily found today. Palestine is a central cause of the global left and the idea that Israel practises a form of apartheid is much more widely accepted than in the 1970s. The Young Liberals can claim to have played a significant part in getting this particular bandwagon rolling. Their actions connected anti-Zionism to anti-apartheid from their first involvement in the issue, and it was a connection rooted in activism as much as analysis. Their use of a liberal internationalist language of human rights, colonialism and anti-racism as a way of understanding Zionism and critiquing Israeli policy is the same as that found across the left today. Furthermore, those Young Liberal activists who were most committed to the Palestinian cause were instrumental in setting up and running the first single-issue campaign groups to promote the Palestine issue in the early 1970s. Eaks became editor of *Free Palestine*, a UK-based newspaper founded in 1968 that supported Fatah, and in 1972 launched Palestine Action, which he explicitly tried to model on the Anti-Apartheid Movement. In 1974, Palestine Action published a booklet called *Israel & South Africa: Development of Relations 1967–1974* that was a reprint of a report Peter Hellyer had prepared for the United Nations. Peter Hain played a prominent role in some of Palestine Action's most successful activities. *Free Palestine* and Palestine Action between them did more than any other

British organisations to bridge the divide between radical and mainstream arenas in promoting the Palestinian cause. Using lessons learned in the Young Liberals' anti-apartheid campaigns, their methods and language were more effective on this issue than the Marxist or Trotskyist left. By the late 1970s, the Young Liberals had faded as a political force and their anti-Israel campaigning had been superseded by others. They have been mostly ignored in the history of left-wing anti-Zionism, and erased from the history of the New Left itself. This does them a disservice. In just a few short years, the Young Liberals established an enduring template for left-wing anti-Zionism in Britain.

CHAPTER THREE

CREATING PALESTINE OR DESTROYING ISRAEL?

W hen Britain's left-wingers began campaigning for Palestinian rights in the late 1960s and early 1970s, they had some decisions to make. Were they campaigning for the creation of a Palestinian state alongside Israel, or for a new, single state in Israel's place? Was their priority to seek the fulfilment of Palestinian national rights as promised in the 1947 United Nations Partition Plan; or was it to oppose the political ideology of Zionism, and worry later about what would follow? Should they seek help and support from Arab governments, or were those governments actually part of the problem? Was Palestine a problem of competing nationalisms fighting over the same piece of land, or a case of colonisers and colonised? These same dilemmas have dogged the pro-Palestinian activist movement ever since and continue to do so today. The main pro-Palestinian organisation in Britain, the Palestine Solidarity Campaign, is ambiguous about whether it supports a one-state or two-state solution to the Israeli–Palestinian conflict, saying on its website that it 'campaigns for an end to the Israeli occupation of Palestine and for peace and justice for everyone living in the region'. It doesn't specify whether it sees Palestine as only the West Bank and Gaza Strip or whether it includes all of Israel, but it does add that it supports the right of return of Palestinians to Israel – which Israel and its supporters argue implicitly negates Israel's long-term existence as a Jewish state. In addition, one of PSC's logos depicts a map of the whole of Israel, the West Bank and the Gaza Strip – implying that it views all of this territory as part of Palestine. The Stop the War Coalition says that it takes no position on whether the conflict should be settled by a one-state or two-state solution, but in May 2015 it published an article (now deleted) arguing that Israel shouldn't exist. Jeremy Corbyn is ambiguous on the subject of Israel's future existence. In August 2015, he wrote a statement on the Stop the War Coalition website (while he was its chair) calling for 'a safe and viable Palestinian State alongside a safe and viable Israel', implying support for two states. However, on the very same day, an interview with Corbyn was published on the Electronic Intifada website in which, when asked whether a one-state solution was inevitable, he suggested that it was a more likely option than a two-state solution: 'I think it's up to the people of the region to decide what kind of long-term solution there would be. At the moment, all that's on offer is the possibility of a two-state solution [but] it's difficult to see how it would operate with the degree of settlements that are there.' George Galloway is so opposed to Israel's existence that when Parliament voted to recognise the state of Palestine in October 2014 he abstained, as the resolution being voted on included recognition of Israel. Ken Livingstone, on the other hand, says that Israel should not have been created but now says it should be allowed to exist alongside a Palestinian state. And so on.[1]

By the end of the 1960s, all these different approaches, and more, could be found on the British New Left. There were Arab nationalists who wanted to create a Palestinian state; Trotskyists who wanted to liberate the Palestinians via a socialist revolution across the Middle East; Israeli Marxists who wanted to 'de-Zionise' Israel; and liberals who wanted to campaign for the human rights they felt the Palestinians had been denied. To get a sense of which approach was the most successful, you only have to look around today's left: there is much talk of human rights and Palestinian statehood, and not so much about regional socialist revolutions. While the far left usually gets the credit (or blame) for turning the broader left against Israel, in the early years of this movement they struggled to make much of an impression. Strangely, the first activism to make an impression in this New Left world was organised by someone who didn't even consider himself much of a leftist.

Ghayth Armanazi was a Syrian student in London who has

a reasonable claim to be the progenitor of British New Left anti-Zionist activism. In October 1968, he went along to a large anti-Vietnam War demonstration in London armed with leaflets for an organisation called Friends of Palestine, a name Armanazi and some of his friends had invented for the occasion. Around 100,000 people, including many young people and students, were marching against the war in Vietnam and Armanazi 'tried to ride on the back of the anti-Vietnam war movement' to encourage support for Palestine. The leaflets spoke of 'the parallels that can be drawn between the struggle against Zionism in Palestine and against the imperialistic US aggression in Vietnam'. Four months later, in February 1969, Armanazi, who supported the largest Palestinian faction Fatah, was one of the main organisers of a demonstration under the name of the 'Ad Hoc Committee for Solidarity with the People of Palestine'. This was the very first New Left demonstration for Palestine to be held in London. A few thousand demonstrators chanted the impeccably New Left slogan 'Vietnam, Palestine – one struggle, one fight!' The International Marxist Group's Fred Halliday spoke at the demonstration on behalf of *New Left Review* and *Black Dwarf* newspaper, which that month had published extracts from the proposed platform of the Popular Front for the Liberation of Palestine. Yet Armanazi's background was not in left-wing politics at all. In Syria, he was a member of the Syrian Social Nationalist Party, a fiercely secular, nationalist party that was heavily influenced by European fascism but had begun to adopt the language of left-wing radicalism. Although small, it had influenced many Arab political movements and several Palestinians came through its ranks before joining Fatah and other resistance groups. Armanazi was disillusioned by the Arab failure in 1967 and frustrated that the Syrian Social Nationalist Party was suppressed in his home country. He joined Fatah in the hope that a Palestinian revolution would usher in a better future for all Arabs, not least in his native Syria.[2]

This was a good time for Fatah and the other Palestinian resistance movements. Israel's overwhelming military victory over Egypt, Syria and Jordan in the Six Day War of June 1967 discredited Nasser's ideology of radical Arab nationalism and left a vacuum in Arab politics, which was filled by the revolutionary call of the *fedayeen*. Fatah, the dominant Palestinian organisation to this day, had already been founded in Kuwait in 1959, while the Palestine Liberation Organization was formed in 1964 and carried out its first military operation the following year. After the Six Day War, Fatah was joined by several new Palestinian resistance groups who captured the imagination with their defiant rhetoric and guerrilla warfare. They transformed the image of Palestinians from refugees to fighters, affecting Arab public opinion and Western New Leftists alike. Whereas United Nations Security Council Resolution 242, passed in November 1967 to provide a framework for resolving the conflict, didn't even mention the Palestinians (assuming it was a conflict solely between Israel and the Arab states), by the end of the decade nobody could ignore the Palestinian national movement. The resistance groups took over the Palestinian National Council and Fatah's leader, Yasser Arafat, was elected PLO president. Most of these new Palestinian resistance groups were inspired by the guerrilla movements of Algeria, Vietnam and Latin America. Some of them even named their fighting units and operations after Che Guevara and Ho Chi Minh. Many of Fatah's leaders had spent time in Algeria in the 1960s and they drew on Algeria's example and advice in presenting the Palestinian struggle as part of a wider anti-imperialist politics. In doing so, they rhetorically aligned themselves with Third World anti-colonial movements that were attracting the support of New Left groups throughout Europe and North America. In return, within those Western New Left circles emerged movements in solidarity with the Palestinian cause.

Armanazi played a leading role in two contrasting organisations that illustrate the different left-wing approaches to the Palestinian issue. In 1969, he established the first Palestine Solidarity Campaign (a different organisation from the Palestine Solidarity Campaign that currently exists), and for most of 1970 he edited the *Free Palestine* newspaper. These two organisations took quite different approaches to their campaigning for Palestine and against Israel. While both argued that Israel was created by colonialism and was allied to Western imperialism, they had fundamentally different ideas about what form their campaigns should take and how the problem of Israel and Palestine should be settled. The differences between them show just how varied left-wing anti-Zionism and Palestine solidarity work can be.

Free Palestine was set up by a group of Fatah supporters in 1968. It tried to hide this narrow affiliation, claiming that it supported all Palestinian movements 'struggling for the liberation of Palestine', but as far as Armanazi is concerned he was editing a Fatah newspaper. Armanazi was *Free Palestine*'s second editor; its first, Abdul-Wahab Kayyali, later joined the PLO Executive Committee before being assassinated in his Beirut office in 1981. Claud Morris, a publisher who printed *Free Palestine* from July 1969 until his printing press mysteriously burned down in July 1970, felt that while he dealt with a team of writers in London, the '"Mr Big" behind the paper in distant Beirut was Yasser Arafat'. The newspaper described the Israeli–Palestinian conflict in terms that are easily recognisable for anybody who is familiar with today's left-wing anti-Israel rhetoric. Israel was portrayed in its pages as the product of colonial dispossession, in which Palestinian land was handed to alien Jews who were not indigenous to the Middle East. It argued that Zionism was distinct from Judaism and exploited Jews for its own ends. Peace could not come before the land was liberated by the Palestinian resistance movements, whose use of force was entirely justified and legitimate. Israel's treatment of the Palestinians was comparable to the Nazi persecution of European Jews, at least prior to the Final Solution, while in the diplomatic sphere Israel was a natural ally of apartheid South Africa. Israel's actions should not only be of concern to Palestinians; they were part of a wider imperialist alliance confronting liberation movements in Asia and (especially) southern Africa. Israel is specifically a legacy of British colonialism, it argued, and 'the tragic fate of the Arabs of Palestine ought to be a source of singular sympathetic consideration and concern to the British public' as a result.[3]

Throughout its existence, *Free Palestine* acted as a house journal for the Palestine solidarity movement in Britain, regularly publicising the activities, statements and publications of that movement's various parts. Overt antisemitism in its pages was unusual (beyond comparisons of Israel to Nazi Germany) but not completely absent. A cartoon showing senior Anglo-Jewish figures on a cruise holiday to South Africa was headed 'Sail to South Africa: Kosher Holiday', with a caption reading 'Fully licensed strictly Kosher Europeans only'. The occasional article described pro-Israel lobbying in Washington DC in conspiratorial terms. One front-cover image showed a bow and arrow pointed at the dove of peace; the bow was marked with a dollar sign, the arrow with a Star of David. More common was the justification of Palestinian armed operations, even when the victims were civilians. This upset some of *Free Palestine*'s readers. One example came when *Free Palestine* supported an attack at

Lod Airport in May 1972 by Japanese Red Army gunmen acting for the Popular Front for the Liberation of Palestine. The attackers killed twenty-six people, mostly Puerto Rican Christian pilgrims. *Free Palestine* expressed generic regret for the lost civilian lives before claiming that simply by visiting Israel, these pilgrims had given support to the occupation of Palestine and thereby placed themselves 'in the front line in a bitter war'. That they became casualties of that war was 'inevitable'. Another example was *Free Palestine*'s coverage of a hostage-taking by the Democratic Front for the Liberation of Palestine at a school in Ma'alot, northern Israel, in May 1974, that resulted in the deaths of twenty-two children. This earned a rebuke from the Labour MP Stan Newens, who declared himself to be a regular *Free Palestine* reader 'with interest and considerable sympathy for its basic objectives'. Newens wrote a letter for publication to 'speak out very strongly indeed against the line taken on these recent events'. The newspaper responded with an editorial that warned, 'now is not the time to moralise to the Palestinian people about the ethics of violence'. Any Palestinian violence, they argued, is an expected response to the 'initial aggression' of the creation of 'an essentially European settler state' on their land and at their expense. Ma'alot and other attacks like it 'will never be looked upon with pride by the Palestinian people when their history is written', but they can achieve a valuable political goal. It is the Israelis' fault for being there, in other words, and the ends justify the means.[4]

The fact that *Free Palestine* had readers in Parliament in 1972 is a result of its efforts to reach beyond the radical New Left and influence mainstream political thinking. They had help from a Labour Party activist (and future councillor) in Westminster called Manuela Sykes. They also developed a fruitful relationship with the Young Liberals, initially via Peter Hellyer and then through Louis Eaks, who edited the paper after Armanazi. Abu Omar, the Fatah spokesman who had helped Louis Eaks to pass an anti-Zionist policy at the Young Liberals' 1970 conference in Skegness, was in the UK at the time on a visit organised by Armanazi. Anti-colonial organisations, including the Movement for Colonial Freedom and the Anti-Apartheid Movement, were also targeted for support.

While *Free Palestine* sought mainstream influence and placed the Palestinian cause in a wider context of national liberation and decolonisation, the make-up of the Palestine Solidarity Campaign gave its pro-Palestinian campaigning a much more radical complexion. The Palestine Solidarity Campaign was launched in April 1969 as a permanent successor to the Ad Hoc Committee for Solidarity with the People of Palestine that had organised the demonstration in February of that year. Its name was a deliberate effort to mimic the Vietnam Solidarity Campaign that organised the campaigns against the Vietnam War. It was made up of a coalition of Trotskyists and Maoists, including the International Marxist Group (which was the leading organisation in the Vietnam

Solidarity Campaign), the International Socialists (which later became the Socialist Workers Party), *Black Dwarf, New Left Review* and the Revolutionary Socialist Students' Federation, but it was set up and run by UK-based Arab nationalists such as the Fatah-supporting Armanazi. It was based in the office of the General Union of Arab Students – which was itself housed in the Egyptian embassy. Other signatories to the Palestine Solidarity Campaign's founding manifesto included Indian, Iranian and Pakistani leftist organisations in Britain, as well as Vietnamese and Chinese friendship groups. The establishment Arabists of CAABU were absent while the Young Liberals were briefly involved. It was this initial enthusiasm for Palestine from groups normally associated with campaigns against the Vietnam War that led *The Observer* to note in August 1969, 'Some young left-wingers now seem to have embraced the issue of Palestine as fiercely as that of Vietnam.'[5]

The Palestine Solidarity Campaign's manifesto was couched in the radical anti-imperialist language of the day. It saw Zionism as a consequence of European antisemitism, the roots of which it located in 'the capitalist structure of European society'. It argued for a 'de-Zionised, democratic Palestine where Jews and Arabs enjoy equal rights' and endorsed armed struggle to bring this about. It argued that Palestinian violence against Israel was part of a broader 'Arab Revolution' against colonial rule and 'neo-imperialist exploitation'. The manifesto committed the Palestine Solidarity Campaign to opposing 'Zionism and anti-Jewish racism as vigorously as it will fight against anti-Arab racism', and called on 'all progressive anti-Zionist Jews in Britain' to help liberate Jews 'from that aberration that has transformed many of them into unabashed racists, subservient to imperialism'. It concluded with a similar slogan to that heard on the February 1969 march: 'From Palestine to Vietnam – One Enemy, One Fight!' The involvement of the Marxist and Trotskyist left in the Palestine Solidarity Campaign gave its propaganda a more radical emphasis than *Free Palestine*: its magazine was named *Fedayeen* in explicit honour of Palestinian armed resistance.[6]

The International Socialists and the International Marxist Group preferred Nayef Hawatmeh's Democratic Popular Front for the Liberation of Palestine (DPFLP, later DFLP), a relatively small Palestinian faction that sought a regional socialist revolution encompassing Israel and its Arab neighbours, to the more mainstream (and, in their view, bourgeois) Fatah. This choice says something about the difference between a revolutionary socialist approach to pro-Palestinian campaigning and one based on the pursuit of Palestinian national rights. The International Socialists preferred the DPFLP to Fatah as it had concerns about what it called Fatah's 'conservative political outlook'. For the International Marxist Group, support for the DPFLP fitted with their strategy of 'from the periphery to the centre' – the idea that revolutionary politics was most likely to originate in Third World liberation movements, including those that were not socialist, before moving to the capitalist West. An article in *Black Dwarf* dismissed nationalism as a solution for Palestine and argued instead for a Marxist–Leninist approach:

> The Palestine problem is a national problem; yet it has no nationalist solution. It can only be waged successfully under the guidance of the revolutionary ideology of the proletariat – Marxism–Leninism. The social basis of this struggle is already in action: the refugees of peasant stock. And those who believe that those displaced peasants are going to liberate the land in order to hand it back to the very effendi families who sold it to the Zionists have another surprise coming.[7]

This highly ideological talk of solving the conflict via Marxist–Leninist peasants' revolutions baffled those supporters of the Palestinians who saw it as a straightforward case of a people, the Palestinians, deserving and needing a state. Peter Hellyer of the Young Liberals thought it was bizarre, later recalling:

> The Trotskyists and Maoists, for example, had their own somewhat peculiar approach of calling for unity between the Israeli and Palestinian working class, this being defined by a Marxist ideology that bore little relationship to the actual political facts on the ground. The YLs, on the other hand, came towards a policy of supporting the Palestinians out of a general policy of supporting 'national liberation movements' – as in Southern

Africa. 'Worker–Peasant alliances' didn't seem relevant to us (to put it politely).[8]

These differences emerged in startling circumstances in the summer of 1969 on a solidarity visit to Fatah, organised by Armanazi, when European Trotskyists and Maoists came to blows over their different approaches. Forty-eight young British activists, mostly students, joined others from Europe, Asia and Latin America on a work camp in Jordan, where they lived alongside Palestinian refugees, saw Fatah guerrillas training and were visited by Yasser Arafat. According to *Free Palestine's* report of the trip:

> While the Marxist–Leninists taking part in the camp adopted a resolution declaring 'unconditional and uncritical support for Al Fatah,' other groups, particularly those with Trotsky-ist leanings, expressed criticism of some of Al Fatah's political positions. These criticisms were welcomed by the cadres of Al Fatah who were eager to expound on the ideology of the movement and to answer the criticisms; in their turn the crit-ics emphasised over and over again that whatever criticisms they held they do so as comrades and as unconditional sup-porters of Al Fatah and the Palestinian revolution.[9]

Despite this positive spin, Trotskyist criticisms of Fatah did not go down well with other visitors whose support for Fatah was genuinely uncritical as a matter of principle. Insisting on being taken to meet representatives of the DPFLP also did not endear them to their Fatah hosts. On the last night of the work camp, a British group including Chris Harman of the International Socialists caused more problems when they smuggled alcohol into one of their tents and held a drunken sing-song. Armanazi tried to persuade them to stop because 'the young *fedayeen* are getting trigger-happy', but it was the Maoist visitors who dealt out summary justice, leaving Harman with a badly bruised nose.[10]

Back in London, the Palestine Solidarity Campaign fell apart under the strain of this Trotskyist search for ideological purity. Within months of joining, both the International Socialists and the International Marxist Group declared it a failure. They objected to Maoists and Liberals being in the coalition, but most of all they were disturbed by the fact that the Palestine Solidarity Campaign's office was in the Egyptian embassy. Given their revolutionary dream of overthrowing all the Arab governments in the Middle East, this was rather awkward. The Palestine Solidarity Campaign should not accept 'help from Arab governments via propaganda channels, finance and the use of embassies', they wrote. By the end of 1969, the campaign had lost what momentum it had gathered at the time of its launch. A march in November attracted half the number of supporters as its demonstration nine months earlier. A further march in May 1970 had half the number again. The Palestine

Solidarity Campaign remained active until the late 1970s, but its message of a regional socialist revolution for the Middle East became increasingly irrelevant and never reached beyond its initial core support. Armanazi left Britain for the Middle East at the end of 1970, disillusioned and with his hopes for revolution dashed. He came back four years later as a diplomat for the United Arab Emirates, but reminders of his radical youth were waiting for him on his return. A pro-Israel MP asked the Home Secretary to revoke his diplomatic credentials 'in view of his activities on behalf of a terrorist organisation when last in Great Britain', while Armanazi later discovered he was on a Jordanian blacklist when he tried to travel there for a diplomatic conference.[11]

This flowering of radical left-wing support for Palestine in the late 1960s disappeared so quickly that in 1973, Peter Hain, then chairman of the Young Liberals, complained that 'despite the justice of the Palestinian case, the left in Britain has responded to their side in an incredibly feeble manner. Radicals and revolutionaries have never campaigned on Palestine with the strength of, for example, the Vietnam protests.' But while the Trotskyist dream of a peasants' revolutionary war in the Middle East may have been over, the Young Liberals' version of left-wing campaigning for Palestine was about to make a profound and lasting impression. When Armanazi left Britain, he was replaced as editor of *Free Palestine* by Louis Eaks, a symbolically important change. Where Armanazi saw the Vietnam

War protests as his template for Palestinian activism, Eaks, being a Young Liberal and veteran anti-apartheid activist, used the Anti-Apartheid Movement as his model and found much more success in reaching mainstream audiences as a result. His editorship of *Free Palestine* was complemented by his role in establishing a new campaign group, Palestine Action. Between them, these two organisations transformed pro-Palestinian campaigning in Britain.[12]

Palestine Action was launched in 1972 on the fifth anniversary of the Six Day War. In classic left-wing fashion, it was formed at a meeting of a small group of activists in a pub in Camden Town, north London. The sole Palestinian present, a young female doctor called Ghada Karmi, was elected its chair, and has been a prominent campaigner for Palestine ever since. Eaks described Palestine Action in a letter to Andrew Faulds, a Labour Member of Parliament with a record of sympathy for the Palestinian cause, as 'an Anti-Apartheid type of organisation to support the Palestinian people' and identified the Labour, Communist and Liberal parties as its target audience. Palestine Action's proposed solution to the conflict was, according to one leaflet, 'The creation of a secular and democratic Palestine in which all irrespective of race or creed have equal rights, and equal protection from discrimination.' The launch was noted in a short diary piece in *The Times* that identified the Anti-Apartheid Movement as Eaks's 'model' and named three Labour MPs – Faulds, William Wilson and Fred

Evans – as its supporters. Palestine Action also had the support of the Young Liberals, who had agreed to sponsor it at the suggestion of Peter Hain.[13]

In her memoirs, Karmi describes Palestine Action as 'the first political group solely concerned with the Palestine issue'. She had not even heard of the Palestine Solidarity Campaign, another sign of its lack of impact beyond radical circles. Its goal was to promote awareness of the Palestinian cause by acting as an information and lobbying organisation, and its resemblance to the Anti-Apartheid Movement was more one of strategy and narrative than in the details of its activities. For example, Palestine Action used the language of human rights to attach its anti-Zionism to existing moral opposition to colonialism. Like the Young Liberals, it straddled New Left activism and mainstream politics: it was a grassroots campaign using methods influenced by New Left campaigning, but it sought direct engagement with parliamentarians, diplomats and governments. Karmi was strongly influenced by Fanon's writings on anti-colonialism, which she considered 'seminal'. She had no political background and was frustrated to find the Palestinian cause existing on the political margins alongside gay rights and women's issues: 'good causes but espoused by peculiar people, people on the left who nobody really wanted to talk to'. Initially, Palestine Action attracted people whom Karmi felt were quite odd and looking for a political home. She had little time for leftist 'internecine struggles', but felt the Palestinian cause was so 'impoverished' for supporters at that time that she could not turn away anybody who was willing to help. She was determined to make Palestine a mainstream issue and found Eaks's experience of political lobbying invaluable. Karmi was not short of confidence herself. She raised money by going round the Arab embassies of London, cap in hand. She remembers the Saudis being particularly generous, not knowing what to make of this 'attractive young woman who turned up burning with zeal'. The Trotskyist opposition to support from Arab governments that had undermined the Palestine Solidarity Campaign was completely alien to Karmi and Eaks. Funds provided by Arab governments, both individually and via the Arab League in London, sustained both Palestine Action and *Free Palestine* for much of their existence. Karmi managed to raise enough money from Arab embassies to employ a Yemeni research student from Bath University called Galal Maktari as a full-time organiser.[14]

Rather than the Marxist left, it was the Young Liberals who provided key activists for *Free Palestine* and Palestine Action, and it is through those vehicles that their anti-Zionism had a formative influence on left-wing and mainstream opinion in the 1970s, even though the Young Liberals itself faded as an organisation. Karmi thought, like Hellyer, that the Marxist approach to the conflict was completely wrong:

> They talked about the revolt of the working class and the
> Arab working class across the world – the Arab world and

the Palestinians would team up with the working class in this country and then so on – that sort of idea. I found it deeply irrelevant because it ignored the fact that our problems were liberation. That's what we were about, it was way before talking about what sort of society would you create. Now, that I remember was a dividing issue … but you see, some of these people were also keen on this idea of the Jewish working class and Arab working class which I found also, actually didn't understand what the conflict was about, it really didn't understand it.[15]

By the end of 1972, Palestine Action had held a demonstration outside the Israeli embassy, organised a conference to plan its activities and claimed to have attracted a growing number of sponsors from Parliament, academia and the media. The following year it held fringe meetings at the Liberal and Labour Party conferences and elected Faulds to the honorary position of president. Students were a particular target for Palestine Action, as they felt 'this section of the population is not only more open than others to fresh ideas, but also holds the key in ideas and potential to the future'. They sent speakers to student meetings around the country in 1973 and attended the NUS annual conference in April 1974. *Free Palestine* had a literature stall at the NUS conference the previous November. Karmi remembers this as 'an uphill grinding battle' because of the level of support for Israel that she encountered whenever she spoke (she still speaks on campuses and finds them transformed in their support for Palestine). Much of what Palestine Action did felt pioneering to Karmi at the time. With Eaks's flair for PR and Karmi's passion for the cause, they combined public meetings and information reports with attention-grabbing stunts. Karmi vividly remembers leading a procession of Palestinian women dressed in black with hearses to lay a wreath for the Palestinians at the Cenotaph, before handing in a letter to the Queen at Buckingham Palace. As well as developing a grassroots campaign in Britain, Palestine Action coordinated its efforts with the PLO. New full-time organiser Galal Maktari worked closely with Sa'id Hammami, the PLO's first official representative in London, while Karmi travelled regularly to Beirut to inform Yasser Arafat and the Fatah leadership of their activities.[16]

Getting the Palestinian message into the mainstream media was an important part of Palestine Action's strategy. In May 1973, they placed a full-page advert in *The Times*, headlined 'Israel: The Untold Story'. It featured four articles: 'Israel: The Settler State'; 'Human Rights Crisis'; 'A Nation in Exile'; and '385 Arab Villages Destroyed'. Taken together, the articles presented the Palestinian question as a human rights problem caused by the colonial displacement of the native people by European settlers. At the bottom of the page was a statement signed by thirty-five 'Jews Against Zionism', condemning 'Zionist racialism' and rejecting the Israeli Law of Return, that allows Jews from anywhere in the world to take Israeli citizenship. The following month, Jews Against Zionism again featured in a full-page *Times* advert, but this time, incongruously, it was part of a feature promoting the Libyan government's economic development plan. The explanation for this may lie in Eaks's close ties to Libya, which was a valuable source of funds for Palestine Action, and for Eaks's public relations and publishing business. This connection to Libya was political as well as financial. In 1973, as editor of *Free Palestine*, Eaks took a large British delegation to an International Conference of European and Arab Youth in Tripoli on a trip paid for by the Libyan government. Three delegates from the National Union of Students (NUS) were present, as were a clutch of Young Liberals. The NUS delegates held discussions with representatives of the General Union of Palestinian Students (GUPS), a constituent body of the PLO, who were at the conference, and on their return recommended that the NUS should develop an ongoing relationship with the GUPS. Eaks's Libyan connection had planted the first seeds of a Palestine policy in the NUS, though they would take a few years to bear fruit.[17]

The scale of Eaks's ambition became clear in 1976, when *Free Palestine* placed two multi-page advertisements in *The Guardian* on consecutive days, totalling twelve full pages of articles. These adverts were a significant moment in bringing the Palestinian issue to a mainstream, liberal-minded audience. Titled *The Palestine Report*, the adverts were edited by

Eaks and produced by *Free Palestine* and Eurabia Ltd., a media company run by a Palestinian exile called Leila Mantoura. The content included articles by Eaks, Karmi, Hain, Hammami and Faulds, as well as Labour MP David Watkins and Liberal MP Emlyn Hooson. Anti-Zionist Jews Alfred Lilienthal, Uri Davis and Marion Woolfson all contributed. The adverts included profiles of the main Palestinian resistance movements and of the PLO's political platform. Articles on Palestinian cooking, poetry and architecture sat alongside those titled 'Zionism and Racism' and 'Britain's vital role in Palestine'. In an article titled 'The power of Israel's "American Constituency"', Lilienthal wrote:

> None of the many powerful political lobbies in Washington is better entrenched than the brokers of the 'Jewish vote.' The Zionist-Jewish nationalists have managed to frighten the politicians with the mythical unity attributed to the Jewish people. The professional politician is too busy or too cowardly to call the bluff of the 'professional Jew,' and the individual Jew will not take the Zionist to task for usurping his voice and peddling his vote.

Zionist propaganda, Lilienthal continued, has created a 'shameful American attitude towards the Palestinian people'. Peter Hain, at that time president of the Young Liberals, cited his own anti-apartheid experience to write that 'The parallel between Israelis and Afrikaners is ironical yet far from fanciful.' The simple demand of the PLO, he explained, was a secular democratic state covering all the territory of 1948 mandate Palestine. Whether this comes about through peaceful negotiation or through force is up to the Israelis: 'They can recognise now that the tide of history is against their brand of greedy oppression, or they can dig in and invite a bloodbath.' The *Jewish Chronicle* described Hain's contribution as 'an article of mind-boggling naivety'.[18]

The Palestine Report was launched on 13 May 1976 with a press conference, addressed by Eaks and Hain, and a reception for diplomats and journalists. Eaks used the press conference to announce the results of an opinion poll, also published in *The Palestine Report*, which claimed to be 'The first ever survey of British attitudes on Palestine.' The poll showed that while many more respondents supported Israel than 'The Arabs', a majority preferred to allow Palestinian refugees to return to Israel and for Jews and Arabs to be given equal rights in the same state, rather than dividing the land into two states. *Free Palestine* claimed this to be evidence of overwhelming support for 'the PLO peace plan for a secular, democratic Palestine state'. According to Eaks, the publication of *The Palestine Report* was the beginning of a campaign to persuade the British government to support this position.[19]

This goal of changing British foreign policy to support a one-state solution to the conflict was almost certainly out of reach, but the adverts still had an impact. *The Guardian* itself considered them worthy of special comment, while Israel's supporters were stirred to respond. The second day of publication was marked by a *Guardian* leader column about *The Palestine Report,* which described it as 'one more piece of evidence of the Palestinians' growing self-confidence'. *The Guardian*'s own history of its changing relationship with Zionism describes the adverts as 'The first sign that a new wind was blowing' in its coverage of the Israeli–Palestinian conflict. According to Eaks, the content of the advertisements was subject to editorial vetting by *The Guardian* before it accepted them for publication. The *Jewish Chronicle* credited 'our PLO friends' with a new sophistication, while speculating whether *Free Palestine* paid the full advertising rates – estimated at over £45,000 – and how they could raise such an amount. The Institute of Jewish Affairs compiled a special research report to assess the validity of the opinion poll results, which it deemed 'perhaps the most important item' in *The Palestine Report*. After surveying 'no less than thirty public opinion polls' conducted in Britain since 1967 on the subject of the Israeli–Arab conflict (thereby disproving Eaks's claim that his was the first), the institute concluded that *Free Palestine*'s declaration of widespread support for the PLO plan of a secular democratic state was unfounded; there had been some weakening of public support for Israel since 1967, it argued, but this had not transformed into support for the Arab side.[20]

Eaks's strategy to get the Palestinian cause a mainstream hearing extended beyond print media. In February 1973, Palestine Action applied to the BBC's Open Door series, which gave broadcasting time to minority groups to put their case on television. Their application was shelved because Open Door was, at first, only available for domestic stories, but when this policy changed three years later the programme, titled *The Right to Return* and produced jointly by Palestine Action and *Free Palestine*, became the first edition of Open Door to cover an international issue. Hellyer drafted the script and a committee of Eaks, Karmi, Hain, Phil Kelly and Mantoura all helped to make the programme. Broadcast in November 1976, it opened with a statement by Yasser Arafat and featured contributions from Mantoura and Karmi, both of whom told of leaving Jerusalem in 1948 when they were children. Eaks explained:

> *Free Palestine* doesn't see the Palestine issue as a territorial problem, one of secure borders, in fact it's a problem of human rights, the right of the Palestinians to return to their homeland and once this has been resolved the problem will be removed and borders, the issue of borders, will become irrelevant.[21]

Peter Hain, in his contribution to the programme, accused Israel of being 'a racist state' that keeps Palestinians 'in far more oppressive conditions in fact than many black South Africans live'. As well as raising awareness of the Palestinian cause, the programme also raised the profile of Palestine Action and *Free Palestine*, which received hundreds of letters of support. It even drew a glowing tribute from Farouk Kaddoumi of the PLO, who was in London when it was broadcast and phoned Karmi to tell her it was 'the best film he had ever seen on the Palestine issue'. The *Jewish Chronicle* noted that the BBC had been 'bombarded' by calls of complaint before describing *The Right of Return* as 'a perversion of historical truth masquerading as fact' that the BBC should not have broadcast. The BBC pacified its critics by giving an Open Door slot to the Anglo-Israel Friendship League, who worked with the Board of Deputies of British Jews (generally regarded as British Jewry's main representative body) and others to produce a pro-Israel programme the following year.[22]

This turned out to be the high point of Palestine Action's achievements. By 1978, some of its core activists had drifted away without being replaced and a chronic lack of money had damaged its ability to operate. There was also a sense that the organisation had achieved its goal of putting the Palestinian issue on the mainstream agenda. On a personal level, the campaign had consumed Karmi's energies for six years and had started to affect her personal and professional life. She had also become disillusioned by what she felt was a lack of appreciation of her efforts from the PLO leadership. When it was suggested that Karmi would be an ideal replacement for London PLO representative Sa'id Hammami after his assassination in 1978, the idea was dismissed out of hand in Beirut – because she was a woman, Karmi thought.

While the Palestine Solidarity Campaign was paralysed by factional arguments typical of the far left, *Free Palestine* and Palestine Action got mainstream politicians and media talking about Palestine in a way they had not done previously. Their legacy is in the language and ideas of today's pro-Palestine movement in Britain. The Palestinian cause today is overwhelmingly presented just as Palestine Action and *Free Palestine* described it: as a problem of human rights; dispossession of the Palestinians' homeland by racist colonialism; and an apartheid Israeli state standing in the way of justice. This liberal anti-Zionism has been much more popular and durable than the Trotskyist call for a regional socialist revolution, and is much more commonly heard, even though so many of today's anti-Zionist activists have a background in Marxist politics. Nowadays it is common for supporters of Israel to blame Trotskyists and other Marxists for the spread of anti-Zionism on the left; in reality, this movement was kick-started by Young Liberal and Arab nationalist activists, funded by Arab governments and used the liberal language of anti-colonialism and human rights. They provided the grassroots foundations for the parliamentary efforts of Andrew Faulds, Christopher Mayhew and others, who had founded CAABU and the Labour Middle East Council at the end of the 1960s, and they pioneered the understanding of the Israeli–Palestinian conflict that is now common across the left.

If the Palestine Solidarity Campaign was the vehicle for a revolutionary anti-Zionism designed to remake the world, and Palestine Action articulated an anti-colonial, anti-apartheid version of pro-Palestinian activism, a third organisation called the British Anti-Zionist Organisation (BAZO) showed how a highly ideological anti-Zionism can, whether by accident or design, incubate antisemitic campaigns. Launched in 1975, BAZO focused its efforts on universities, where it went beyond simply promoting the Palestinian cause and tried to remove Zionism entirely from British campuses. BAZO's secretary, a Scottish Maoist called George Mitchell, called in 1976 for 'national campaigns that will ensure the demise of the Zionist ideology in our "places of learning"' as part of wider efforts 'to ensure the complete elimination of an effective Zionist base in Britain'. BAZO was widely blamed for campaigns to ban Jewish student societies in the 1970s, although it always denied responsibility. It argued that Zionists collaborated with Nazis during the Second World War and that they encouraged antisemitism to the benefit of Israel. In 1980, BAZO distributed an antisemitic hoax leaflet, probably produced by the Iraqi embassy in London, claiming that David Aaronovitch had been offered funding by the Israeli embassy while running for NUS president. At the time, Aaronovitch strongly suspected that BAZO was funded by Iraq's Ba'athist government. Richard Burden, now Labour MP for Birmingham Northfield and a BAZO Executive member in the 1970s, agrees: George

Mitchell had 'internalised the politics' of Iraqi Ba'athism, he says. BAZO was close to the National Union of Iraqi Students, a Ba'athist organisation excluded from NUS in 1979 due to its involvement in the violent intimidation and harassment of Iraqi dissident students in the UK.[23]

By the early 1980s, BAZO had been banned from NUS conferences for distributing material considered to be antisemitic. BAZO's involvement in overtly antisemitic activity and its connection to the Iraqi government caused irreparable damage to its reputation amongst left-wing students, in a way that its anti-Israel campaigns had not previously done. Despite this, several influential anti-Israel activists passed through its ranks. As well as Burden, George Galloway first visited the Middle East on a BAZO trip in 1977 that he credits with beginning his lifelong interest in the Palestinian cause, and Tony Greenstein, a founder of the modern Palestine Solidarity Campaign and an important anti-Zionist activist in the Labour Party in the 1980s, was also in BAZO during this period. Some of its members, though, were disturbed by the group's extreme anti-Zionism: Burden tried to have its name changed from 'British Anti-Zionist Organisation' to 'Palestine Solidarity', feeling that a name that emphasised anti-Zionism gave the wrong impression. He was partially successful – it resulted in the clumsy compromise of 'British Anti-Zionist Organisation – Palestine Solidarity' – but his efforts reflect the centrality of this unresolved question: is the aim to build Palestine, or to dismantle Zionism?

One group for whom the priority was most definitely to dismantle Zionism were Israeli Marxists from the Israeli Socialist Organization, better known as Matzpen, who were ubiquitous on Britain's anti-Zionist left in the late 1960s and early 1970s and remain influential today. Matzpen was formed in 1962 by a handful of Israeli Communist Party members who, like their New Left counterparts in Britain, sought a different approach to Marxist politics. Several of its activists left Israel in the 1960s and found a receptive audience for their views in London. Matzpen was influenced by Trotskyism but its members were not all Trotskyists. Akiva Orr, a leading figure in Matzpen, later explained that it only had two non-negotiable principles: anti-capitalism and anti-Zionism. Within those 'boundaries', members could follow whatever politics they chose. Orr and his comrades are credited as important influences by many pro-Palestinian activists of the time. *Free Palestine*, *Black Dwarf* and the International Marxist Group publications *Red Mole* and *Red Weekly* all published material from Matzpen. Activists from Matzpen often spoke at pro-Palestine meetings and demonstrations. *New Left Review* published 'The Class Nature of Israeli Society', by Orr, Moshé Machover and Haim Hanegbi, which was then republished as a booklet by the International Socialists' publishing arm Pluto Press and sold in *Socialist Worker*, *Red Weekly* and *Free Palestine*. Orr's home 'became a centre for radical political discussion and a meeting point for dissenters'. Karmi describes herself as one of Orr's 'acolytes' and says that she cherished the political education she received from him in 'ways of thinking ... an analytical method' in interpreting events. Tariq Ali, then editor of *Black Dwarf*, regarded Matzpen as his 'educators' on the subject of Israel and 'automatically published' anything they gave him.[24]

Initially Matzpen's political programme focused on Israeli society, but under the influence of an Arab–Israeli Trotskyist called Jabra Nicola they developed a New Left critique that viewed the Israeli–Palestinian conflict as colonial in nature, sought its solution through a regional 'Arab revolution', and called for Israel to be 'de-Zionized'. Shortly before the Six Day War, Matzpen published their new analysis in a statement that said Israel's creation was 'the outcome of the colonization of Palestine by the Zionist movement, at the expense of the Arab people and under the auspices of imperialism'. The 'de-Zionization' of Israel would entail an end to the Law of Return (that allows Jews from around the world to claim Israeli citizenship), full right of return for Palestinian refugees and a fundamental change in Israeli foreign policy. Matzpen's analysis of Zionism and its proposed solution of a regional Arab-Jewish socialist federation were well received by the International Marxist Group in particular. However, Matzpen's views also highlighted the fundamental division within the pro-Palestinian movement about whether there is room for a Jewish national home in the Middle East. Matzpen argued that while Israel was created by colonialism, there is a 'unique complication' in this case: because the Zionist settlers had sought to replace the indigenous population rather than to rule it, they had formed 'a Hebrew nation with its own national characteristics', complete with its own 'capitalist class structure'. Consequently, according to Matzpen, 'a true solution of the Palestine problem necessitates the recognition of the right of the Hebrew nation to self-determination', as a unit of a proposed Middle Eastern socialist federation that would serve the interests 'of both Arab and Israeli masses'. Machover has even argued that it is only in Israel that secular Jewish identity has any reason to exist. This call for Jewish national autonomy within a broader regional structure was not welcomed by Palestinians. Karmi was one who objected to it. A conference for anti-Zionists in London in 1974 saw her argue with one of the Israelis present, Nira Yuval-Davis, over exactly this point.[25] Karmi later recalled:

> I remember I said, 'Listen, do you not understand if there was a way of turning the clock back to 1917 [before the Balfour Declaration], there is not one Palestinian who wouldn't turn the clock back.' So, and you know she went, 'Ah ...', and I said, 'Do you really think we want all these people in our homeland? We don't want them. What we're talking about is what can we do? They're there so we're trying to find a way.' And what it illustrated for me was the completely different standpoints from which we start. These people start, with however understanding, however passionate about justice, they stand

from an initial point which says 'we have rights here'. Well, actually, no, you don't have rights here. You're here, that's not the same as having had rights here. You're here or you've acquired rights because you're here, and it's not to be compared with the original native population of this country.[26]

This gets to the heart of the different narratives over the Israeli–Palestinian conflict: is it a conflict between two competing national movements, both with a legitimate claim to the same piece of land; or is it a case of coloniser and colonised, with all the right on one side and all the wrong on the other?

The celebrated Jewish writer Isaac Deutscher, speaking to *New Left Review* shortly after the Six Day War, likened the relationship between Israeli Jews and Palestinians to that of a man who jumps from a burning building, only to land on another man standing below. 'The jumping man had no choice; yet to the man with the broken limbs he was the cause of his misfortune. If both behaved rationally, they would not become enemies.' Deutscher was no apologist for Israel. In the same interview he described Israel as 'the Prussians of the Middle East', marked by 'chauvinistic arrogance, and contempt for other peoples'. Yet he could recognise the humanity of both sides and the tragedy of two competing national movements in the same small piece of land. Ghada Karmi hates Deutscher's analogy. 'It's a complete misunderstanding of what happened,' she says.

> It wasn't an accident that these people fleeing from something horrendous happened to fall on some poor man walking along the street ... There was a plan to ensure that they went to Palestine and not to other European countries which didn't want them and that is the brutal truth. So, it wasn't an accident, it was the design.

This is where anti-colonial anti-Zionism leads: if Israel's creation was the result of a Western colonial plan, then Holocaust survivors were imperialist pawns rather than refugees and their migration to Palestine is neither a tragic accident of history nor an authentic Jewish yearning for national self-determination, but simply part of the West's ongoing colonial instinct to dominate the world.[27]

The 1974 conference at which Karmi argued with Yuval-Davis highlighted other differences between Israeli anti-Zionists and their Palestinian comrades at that time. Israeli left-wingers were shocked by the DFLP's hostage-taking at a school in Ma'alot (the same operation about which Stan Newens MP had written to *Free Palestine*). The Palestinians felt that Israelis had no right to demand condemnation of such acts, while the Israelis present were angered by this view. Karmi found this debate exasperating. She resented Israeli demands that Palestinian resistance 'had to consider Jewish sensibilities, that you could resist, but in a nice way'. She also felt that the Israeli anti-Zionist insistence on the recognition of a Hebrew nation revealed a reluctance to relinquish completely 'the idea of a Jews-only state'. 'They are in the end Jewish,' she explains, and it was naive to imagine that 'if somebody Jewish worked with you and felt like you, that they felt with you all the way and that they were like you. They are not like you. In the end they have a sticking point.' This idea, that Jewish anti-Zionists retain a residual Jewish identity that prevents them from fully supporting the Palestinians, is today voiced in its most extreme form by Gilad Atzmon, an Israeli saxophonist whose writings have included Holocaust denial, Jewish conspiracies and other antisemitic tropes. Atzmon is shunned by most pro-Palestinian activists, but Karmi thinks he has a point:

> I think the reason why Gilad Atzmon, they hate him so much, is because he's pointed out something absolutely true that they don't want to face, that with all the cosmopolitan internationalism in the world, in the end, there's a narrow little tribal feeling which a true internationalist wouldn't have.[28]

It is important not to overstate the impact of these differences. Israeli and Palestinian anti-Zionists have always worked together and will continue to do so. Karmi never lost her admiration or affection for Orr. These were parts of the same movement, not rivals or opponents, and the borders between them were, and are, blurry and porous. All the UK-based activists and groups described in this chapter worked with Jewish and Israeli anti-Zionists in the 1970s. Some were impressed by what they perceived as a courageous position taken against the majority Jewish and Israeli view; some felt that any and all support for the cause was welcome; and some appreciated the opportunity to demonstrate that theirs was not an antisemitic movement. But as Karmi discovered, Matzpen's anti-Zionism belonged to a Jewish tradition of anti-Zionist politics rather than being a response to Palestinian nationalism. Support for Palestinians was a consequence of their anti-Zionism, not the other way round.

Jewish Marxist anti-Zionism even has its own key texts and theoretical writings. Perhaps the most important is Abram Leon's *The Jewish Question: A Marxist Interpretation*. This wartime work made an appearance in the Labour Party in 2016, when Gerry Downing, an aging Trotskyist and Labour Party member, was expelled, readmitted to and then re-expelled from the party for antisemitism. One of Downing's offences was an article on his Socialist Fight website called 'Why Marxists must address the Jewish Question concretely today'. The 'Jewish Question' Downing was referring to was Leon's Jewish Question, which was itself a response to Karl Marx's 1843 essay *Zur Judenfrage* (*On The Jewish Question*). To understand why these aging, obscure Marxist texts are relevant to today's Labour Party, and how dramatically different the various approaches to anti-Israel campaigning can be, it is necessary to explain a little of Leon's theory.

Leon was a Jewish Trotskyist who wrote *The Jewish Question* while in hiding during the Nazi occupation of Belgium. He was later caught and deported to Auschwitz, where he died. His book was published in Mexico City in 1950, republished in French with an introduction by the influential Middle Eastern expert Maxime Rodinson in 1968 and finally published in English by the Trotskyist Pathfinder Press in New York in 1970. Leon's contribution to Marxist theories about Jews was the concept of the 'people-class': a distinct ethnic, religious or racial group, whose characteristics become effectively synonymous with their economic function. Using this theory, Leon argued that Jews had survived in medieval Europe because they were economically useful. More controversial was his claim that Jews in the Middle Ages had become money lenders willingly, contradicting the conventional view that they were forced to do so by being excluded from other professions. He also dismissed as naive the idea that medieval Christianity had systematically tried to convert Jews: so long as Jews provided a necessary economic function, he argued, Christianity needed them to remain Jewish. Hatred of Jews during this period was a result of genuine 'social antagonism' caused by Jews' economic role, rather than being due to religious prejudice. However, Leon argued, Jews have no specific economic role under capitalism (they became a 'declassed element') and therefore should disappear. Antisemitism prevents this from happening, but socialism would facilitate 'The end of Judaism' – something that Leon welcomed.[29]

Leon's work is certainly influential. In the introduction to the 1970 edition of Leon's book, Belgian Trotskyist Nathan Weinstock described it as 'among the masterpieces of Marxist historiography'. It was sold by the International Marxist Group via *Red Mole* as well as *Red Weekly*. In 1972, it was described in the *Journal of Palestine Studies* as providing 'the theoretical basis for the New Left critique of Zionism'. John Rose, writing for the Socialist Workers Party (the successor to the International Socialists) in the 1980s, claimed that 'Leon's book is today recognised as *the* authority on the Jewish question by both Jewish and non-Jewish opponents of Zionism.' It is striking, then, that *The Jewish Question* is an economic history of European Jewry that was written before the creation of Israel, only discusses Zionism in its final twenty pages and has nothing of substance to say about Palestinians, who appear as props in a Jewish story. It is a highly theorised anti-Zionism that is all about Jews and not really about Palestine at all. This is a world away from the anti-colonial, anti-apartheid, Palestinian nationalist discourse that motivated the Young Liberals to pass their anti-Zionist policy in 1970, or that dominated the pages of *Free Palestine*, or that Palestine Action used to promote the Palestinian cause on the BBC and in *The Guardian*. The fact that Leon's theories are so important for Marxist anti-Zionists shows just how far removed they are from mainstream left-wing sensibilities. Looking at the language and ideas used by Britain's anti-Zionist left today, it is clear which approach has proven more successful in winning over mass support to the Palestinian cause.[30]

CHAPTER FOUR

WHEN ANTI-RACISTS BAN JEWS

It is an article of faith for Israel's left-wing opponents that Zionism is a racist ideology and that Israel has racial discrimination woven into its fundamental structures and daily life. Some element of this accusation of racism appears in every left-wing critique of Israel and Zionism; the apartheid analogy is just a more developed version of this basic idea. This association of Zionism with racism received the official approval of the United Nations in November 1975, when the General Assembly passed a resolution declaring Zionism to be a 'form of racism and racial discrimination' (the resolution was rescinded in 1991). It is difficult to overstate the importance of this resolution, or the gravity of the charge of racism that it made. In the collective opinion of the international community, Zionism – the political movement that created Israel, a movement that most Jews around the world

see as a perfectly legitimate expression of their collective identity – was in contravention of the post-Holocaust, post-colonial
world's most heinous moral crime: racism. It gave anti-Zionist
activists a huge boost of confidence and a platform on which to
build their political campaigns – after all, what could be a stronger
endorsement than the word of the United Nations? – and so, in
the decade following that United Nations resolution, left-wing
students in Britain began to use it to campaign against Israel and
Zionism. Some went further than simply trying to persuade people that Zionism was racist, and actually tried to apply this idea
in a practical way within British Students' Unions. They mostly
did this for honourable anti-racist reasons, but in doing so they
discovered something disturbing: when you use the 'Zionism
is racism' idea as the basis for practical politics, you can end up
with an antisemitic campaign.

The United Nations' anti-Zionist vote is possibly the most
important moment in the history of post-war left-wing anti-
Zionism, and like so much of the anti-Zionism in this story
it had Soviet origins. It was the culmination of two years'
effort by a coalition of Communist and Arab states to have
Zionism formally bracketed with racism and colonialism at the
United Nations. This had begun in December 1973, when the
General Assembly passed a resolution on apartheid that condemned 'the unholy alliance between Portuguese colonialism,
South African racism, Zionism and Israeli imperialism'. This
was the first time that the United Nations had formally

associated Zionism with colonialism, apartheid and racism, although the Soviet delegation had attempted to link Zionism with racism, colonialism and even Nazism a decade earlier. In the summer of 1975, the idea of having Israel's United Nations membership suspended (as had happened to South Africa in 1974) started to circulate at Arab and Third World intergovernmental conferences, while a United Nations conference in Mexico City marking International Women's Year called for the 'elimination' of Zionism alongside apartheid, colonialism and racial discrimination. Strong resistance from the United States and West European countries forced a change of tack. Rather than call for Israel's suspension, its opponents sought to have Zionism bracketed with recognised forms of racial discrimination as part of ongoing preparations for a United Nations Decade of Action to Combat Racism and Racial Discrimination. A resolution was proposed by Somalia, a Soviet ally, and co-sponsored by several Arab states, that declared Zionism to be a 'form of racism and racial discrimination'. Despite vigorous opposition from the United States and more considered disapproval from Western Europe, it was a foregone conclusion that the General Assembly, with its in-built majority of Communist, Soviet-aligned, Arab and post-colonial states, would pass it.[1]

While Israel and its supporters around the world were shocked and outraged by the vote, Palestinians and their supporters were triumphant. 'Palestinians Score Triple Victory' was the headline on the front page of *Free Palestine* newspaper, which saw the vote as evidence that 'the world community is committed to a campaign for the restoration of Palestinian rights and for the eradication of Zionism'. The US ambassador to the United Nations, Daniel Patrick Moynihan, was certain that the resolution was antisemitic. To equate Zionism with racism 'reeked of the concentration camp and the gas chamber', he later argued. Israel's United Nations ambassador Chaim Herzog agreed. It was 'symbolic', he said in his speech to the General Assembly immediately following the adoption of the resolution, that the vote had taken place on 10 November, the anniversary of the Nazi pogrom of Kristallnacht; and ironic that the United Nations, he said, 'which began its life as an anti-Nazi Alliance, should, thirty years later, find itself on its way to becoming the world centre of antisemitism'. Whether or not the resolution was antisemitic in itself, it gave left-wing anti-Zionism a Soviet-inspired slogan and ideological basis that connected anti-Zionism directly to Soviet antisemitism. This antisemitism was an increasingly frequent Soviet contribution to United Nations debates. In 1971, Soviet ambassador Yakov Malik made a speech in which he connected Zionism to Nazism via the Jewish theological notion of the 'chosen people'. The following month, in another debate, Malik used crude antisemitic language when scolding the Israeli delegation for raising the issue of Soviet antisemitism: 'Do not poke your long noses in our Soviet garden ... Anyone who pokes his long nose in our garden will find himself without a nose. You had better carve this on your own noses, Zionists.'[2]

Moynihan recognised that the resolution was not just an attack on Israel; it was part of a broader assault on the United States and its Western allies. He was one of the first Western politicians to grasp that anti-colonialism had emerged as a third ideology in world politics, distinct from Soviet communism and Western capitalism but associated with the emergence of a bloc of newly independent, post-colonial states that leaned away from the West. He linked anti-colonialism to the British left in particular. It was heavily influenced by 'British socialism', he thought, especially Fabianism, which he described as 'the least Marxist, by far the most liberal, and the most brainy' of all socialist movements. The United Nations resolution effectively associated Israel with South Africa and Rhodesia as the only remaining states in Africa and Asia 'still dominated by European whites'. As Moynihan explained, in the anti-colonial United Nations, 'Only regimes based on racism and racial discrimination were held to be unacceptable.'[3]

Racism and racial discrimination were also unacceptable in British Students' Unions. In April 1974, the year before the United Nations equated Zionism with racism, the National Union of Students passed what has come to be known as the 'No Platform' policy. It was an amendment to a lengthy policy on anti-racism that included condemnation of the treatment of overseas students by immigration officials, sought to repeal the 'extremely racist' 1971 Immigration Act while calling for the Race Relations Act to be strengthened, highlighted racial discrimination in wider British society and opposed links with South Africa and Rhodesia. The No Platform amendment read:

> Conference recognises the need to refuse any assistance (financial or otherwise) to openly racist or fascist organisations or society [*sic*] (e.g. Monday Club, NF, Action Party/Union movement, National democratic party) and to deny them a platform. However, conference believes that in order to counter these groups, it is also necessary to prevent any member of these organisations, or individuals known to express similar views from speaking in colleges by **whatever means are necessary** (including disrupting of the meeting).[4]

The policy had only one aim, NUS secretary (and Communist student) Steve Parry told the conference: 'to destroy and smash fascism no matter how it reared its ugly head, nor what form it took'. It was not enough to disrupt one or two meetings, Parry explained. Mass action of the sort that stopped Mosley's Blackshirts, or could have stopped Hitler, was necessary. 'Britain introduced the concentration camp in South Africa,' the conference minutes record Parry saying, and 'He did not want to see those concentration camps back and he was prepared to support any action which was necessary to stop fascism rearing its ugly head and gaining power in Britain or any country.'

After a close vote on the No Platform section, the policy as a whole passed comfortably.[5]

Unsurprisingly, the decision of NUS to arrogate to itself the right to use force to prevent others from speaking drew strong criticism both within and without academia. The Association of University Teachers condemned the policy and the National Council of Civil Liberties pledged to actively campaign for its reversal. Shirley Williams was one of three Labour ministers who publicly refused to speak on any NUS platform as long as the policy stood. A principled supporter of free speech, she told the conference of the Association of Headmistresses: 'The greatest single threat to education is not the theories of one political side or another, but a strange recrudescence of a crude faith-fanaticism which says it does not wish to listen to beliefs it does not want to hear.' Secretary of State for Education Reg Prentice pledged not just to boycott NUS platforms, but in addition to refuse speaking engagements at any individual Students' Union that had not disassociated itself from the No Platform policy. There was also enough opposition to the policy from within NUS to force a rerun of the debate at an Extraordinary Conference in June 1974. This second debate took place in a feverish atmosphere, with TV crews and journalists present. In what the minutes note as a 'dramatic interruption', an anti-fascist demonstrator, who had been at a nearby demonstration against the National Front, burst into the conference clutching a bloodied handkerchief to his face

and berated those who endorsed non-violence. The No Platform policy was confirmed, albeit with the implicit threat of
violence in the original policy toned down. External criticism
continued but NUS president John Randall later recalled this
being a very simple point of principle: 'There are some boundaries that a civilised society adopts, and there are some
behaviours that clearly lie outside those boundaries.'[6]

As Jewish students would discover, the flaw in the policy is
that those boundaries are movable. The No Platform policy was
supposed to be a tool to stop violent fascists from operating
on campus but in reality it was used much more broadly. In
the late 1960s, students regularly disrupted meetings addressed
by Conservative MPs, officials connected with immigration or
defence, government scientists and anyone else deemed too
right-wing. Lectures by Enoch Powell were a particular target
for disruptions all over the country. Charles Clarke was NUS
treasurer in 1974 and became president the following year. As he
remembers, while NUS conference could 'instruct' Students'
Unions as much as it liked, in practice the national union had no
influence over any individual unions that took a different view.
Clarke estimates there were ten or fifteen Students' Unions
where ultra-left activists, normally from the International
Socialists or the International Marxist Group, were determined
to apply the No Platform policy in a much looser way than NUS
had envisaged. Randall remembers his discomfort at having to
explain to the media why some students at Kent University had

branded the morality campaigner Mary Whitehouse a fascist and prevented her from speaking.[7]

Within eighteen months of the United Nations passing its 'Zionism is racism' resolution, British Students' Unions began discussing motions to ban Zionism from campus. These policies had the impact of restricting the activities and funding of Jewish Societies, or even banning them entirely, on the basis that their promotion of Zionism was racist and therefore contravened the No Platform policy. In 1977, this gathered enough momentum, and caused enough controversy, to provoke a debate in the House of Commons and commentary in the national press, but few people saw it coming. British students had shown little interest in Palestine for much of the first half of the 1970s, concentrating instead on South Africa, Vietnam and Chile as their favoured international causes. 'The issue of Palestine has been avoided in NUS,' complained Kate Hoey, then vice-president of NUS and now a Labour MP, in *Free Palestine* in 1971. 'Unquestionably the mass media has given no prominence to the Palestinian case which is understandable because of the Zionist influence among the people who control it,' she wrote, but 'the left has also been guilty of failing to make any real effort to push the Palestinian revolution through its own vehicle of information.' There were some hints that this was beginning to change by the middle of the decade. Representatives of NUS had already made contact with GUPS on their 1973 trip to Libya that was organised by

Free Palestine and paid for by the Libyan government. In 1974, the NUS Technical Colleges Conference featured a motion on the Middle East that instructed Students' Unions 'to campaign against any Zionist societies or propaganda on campus'. In January 1975, the Board of Deputies of British Jews received reports that Leeds University Students' Union had passed a motion 'expressing opposition to the activities of pro-Zionist organisations'. A motion 'to expel Zionist student bodies affiliated to the NUS' was on the agenda of NUS national conference in April 1975, but does not appear to have been debated. Jewish students were alert to the danger. The 1974 national conference of the Inter-University Jewish Federation – the predecessor to the Union of Jewish Students – discussed the possibility of 'sanctions against "Zionist" activity on campus' that would 'threaten entire Jewish students movement in this country [*sic*]'. Presciently, in May 1974, an article in the *Jewish Telegraph*, a local newspaper in Manchester, drew attention to the newly adopted No Platform policy of NUS and asked: 'Will Jewish, and especially Zionist speakers, be banned from Manchester University campus?'[8]

These straws in the wind turned into a national campaign to ban Jewish and Zionist speakers from campus, and it was in Manchester where it first came to national attention. Salford University Students' Union, where BAZO's NUS organiser Peter Wragg was on the Student Council, had already adopted an anti-Zionist policy in October 1976 and began to restrict

Jewish society activities shortly after. In March 1977, following a 'Palestine Week' at the university that featured Louis Eaks of *Free Palestine* and Akiva Orr of Matzpen as speakers, the Jewish Society was denied permission to organise a similar 'Israel Week', for which a rabbi had been invited to speak about Zionism. The Students' Union said that the rabbi could talk about the differences between Judaism and Zionism, but not the links. The Jewish Society was also prevented from setting up a bookstall to distribute leaflets about Israel. The small Jewish Society sought a legal injunction against Salford University Students' Union and the Palestine Solidarity Society to overturn the decision to ban its Israel Week meetings, but was unsuccessful. A Students' Union meeting subsequently reaffirmed Salford's 'Zionism equals racism' policy, despite the presence of Charles Clarke, who warned that NUS opposed any restrictions being placed on Jewish societies. Jewish students at the nearby University of Manchester Institute of Science and Technology (UMIST) were more successful in their use of a legal writ to prevent a Students' Union debate on a motion about Zionism and racism. Although the UMIST motion did not explicitly call for Jewish Society activities to be restricted, the Jewish Society chairman, Stuart Benson, told the *Daily Telegraph* that if it passed 'our activities would be restricted to purely religious matters'. While the Jewish Societies at Salford and UMIST sought legal protection, the larger Jewish society at Manchester University successfully won a Student Union vote to defeat an anti-Zionist motion proposed by Wragg.[9]

The events in Manchester were not isolated and anti-Israel motions, some explicitly banning Zionist activity, began appearing at Students' Unions elsewhere. By late March, according to the Union of Jewish Students, motions equating Zionism with racism had been debated by at least seventeen Students' Unions, and York, Salford, Warwick and Lancaster University Students' Unions had all passed motions 'expelling Jewish societies on the grounds that they are Zionist and therefore racist'. All four denied the claim. 'I think they are suffering from a persecution complex,' said the president of Salford University Students' Union. At the heart of this dispute was a disagreement about what restricting Zionist activity actually meant. Those far-left activists pushing the anti-Zionist motions thought they were having just another political argument. For the majority of Jewish students, though, it was an attack on a fundamental aspect of their Jewishness. Many on the far left – if they were not anti-Zionist Jews themselves – suffered from a profound cultural ignorance about the place of Israel in mainstream Jewish identity. Motions at York, Salford and Lancaster Universities proposed that Jewish Societies could exist with cultural and religious rights, but not political ones: a position that most Jewish students thought was patronising and discriminatory. Many were not satisfied with a purely cultural or religious Jewish identity and wanted to express their Jewishness in a political way through Zionism and support for Israel.[10]

The leaders of the Union of Jewish Students quickly understood that campaigns based on the 'Zionism is racism' idea would brand their members as racists who belonged outside the boundaries of acceptable democratic life, as defined by their Students' Unions. They explained in a letter to *The Times* that, while the campaigns themselves may not have been motivated by antisemitism, their impact was just as bad:

> ...to describe this trend as anti-Semitic would perhaps lay us open to a charge of sensationalism ... the attacks we are facing, though perhaps not inspired out of racial hatred, have implications equally as serious. Resolutions equating Zionism with racism not only result in the appellation 'racist' being laid at the door of every supporter of Israel, but have also led to a denial of the democratic rights of some Jewish students.[11]

This was a consequence of a simplistic political logic that combined NUS's No Platform policy with the United Nations' 'Zionism is racism' motion, not realising (or caring) that, because the only organisations on campus promoting Israel and Zionism were Jewish societies, efforts to restrict or ban Zionism would only affect Jewish students. In the view of Sue Slipman, Clarke's successor as NUS president, campus anti-Zionists ended up banning Jewish societies 'more by accident than design' without stopping to realise that 'banning Jewish societies is in itself a racist act'.[12]

Although the Union of Jewish Students did not claim that its political opponents were antisemites, there were isolated cases of Jewish students complaining that their opponents had made antisemitic comments or distributed antisemitic literature. While most participants limited their discussions to issues of Jewish nationalism, Palestinian dispossession and United Nations resolutions, antisemitic notions of Jewish wealth, power and influence did sometimes make an appearance in the campus debates. For example, an International Marxist Group pamphlet argued that campus bans on Zionism were futile because of the power of Zionism in Britain: 'Not only do the Zionists have a significant proportion of the bourgeois publishing world more or less at their disposal, but also the puny resources of individual student unions are incomparable to the sort of resources that the Zionist movement is capable of mobilizing in Britain.'[13]

However, few (if any) anti-Zionist activists on campus during this period were consciously antisemitic; several were Jewish and all considered themselves to be anti-racist. Instead, it was the impact on Jewish students of the anti-Zionist campaigns and policies, rather than the language used to promote them, that was the reason why they were antisemitic. This was a foreseeable consequence of addressing Zionism and anti-Zionism through the No Platform policy, given the insistence of most Jewish student activists that their Jewish identity, and therefore their Jewish Society activities, should involve support for Zionism and Israel.

The campaigns snowballed as they gained publicity in the student movement and the national media. Anti-Zionist motions appeared at universities and polytechnics in all parts of the United Kingdom, some of which included explicit calls to ban Zionist activities. The School of Oriental and African Studies (SOAS) Students' Union, where there was no Jewish Society, adopted a policy to 'refuse money and facilities to societies whose aim is to propagate Zionism and organise support for the state of Israel'. Whereas at first anti-Zionist motions were passed at several campuses, as the year progressed and the Union of Jewish Students became more organised, the anti-Zionist campaign ran into increasingly strong opposition. At Sheffield University, the small Jewish Society defeated an anti-Zionist motion and put a pro-Israel policy in its place by allying with the much larger Christian students' society. The largest general meeting of the year at Manchester University passed a pro-Israel policy, while Cambridge University Students' Union passed a motion condemning those Students' Unions that had restricted Jewish Society activities. At Salford, a new policy was passed that reaffirmed the association of Zionism with racism but removed the ban on Zionist speakers.[14]

At campuses where there were few Jewish students, the pressure of the debate sometimes proved too much for the small

Jewish Society to continue its activities. At North London Polytechnic, an anti-Zionist motion was proposed by the local branch of the Socialist Workers Student Organisation, the student wing of the Socialist Workers Party. (Confusingly, the International Socialists changed its name to the Socialist Workers Party in 1977, and its student wing changed its name from the National Organisation of International Socialist Students to the Socialist Workers Student Organisation. For simplicity's sake, they will be referred to here as 'Socialist Workers Party students'.) The motion ordered that there should be 'no material aid for Zionist propaganda', although it acknowledged that 'Jewish students have to [sic] right to organise in Societies'. Despite this caveat, the small Jewish Society found the whole experience debilitating, as its last chair, Jonathan Fisher, explained:

> We were threatened that if we tried to maintain our activities, such as running a Zionist book stall and getting in speakers, we would be cut off from the union. That would have deprived us of funds, accommodation and other resources. We were a small body against a large left-wing group of International Socialists and other extreme political factions ... The tacit agreement was that if we didn't engage in any so-called provocative activity they would leave us alone and we would not be harassed ... I don't know whether it was the right thing to do, or whether we should have tried to take a hard line. But the

union would have made it impossible for us to operate or exist.
And so our society was abandoned at the end of last year.[15]

At North East London Polytechnic, a motion proposed by the local Socialist Workers Party students branch was passed denying Students' Union funds or facilities to any organisation supporting Israel, and preventing any Zionist speakers from being invited onto campus. The debate was marred by abuse and threats to the Jewish students who spoke against the motion. Union of Jewish Students chairman Moshe Foreman told the *Daily Telegraph*:

> This was one of the most vicious anti-Zionist debates I have ever attended. Pro-Israel speakers were subjected to a barrage of abuse from hecklers. It was not a debate, it was a ritual. I have never seen such venom and hatred as I saw on this day and it was not coming from Arab students but from supporters of the Socialist Workers Party.[16]

Foreman was right that students from the Socialist Workers Party were prominently involved in the anti-Zionist campaigns, although at first this was a case of activists acting on their own initiative rather than following a directive from the party. Some students from the International Marxist Group were also involved, but the organisation itself – a strong supporter of No Platform for fascists – came out in opposition to campus bans on Zionism mid-way through 1977. The Socialist Workers Party, on the other hand, was initially confused and then came up with a position supporting some restrictions but not others. In May, Andy Durgan of the Socialist Workers Student Organisation National Council explained to activists that although a blanket application of the No Platform policy to Zionism was not appropriate, 'in some cases we should be against Zionists being allowed to speak. A meeting or event which actively promotes Zionist ideas should be banned from the college ... We do not stand for the banning of organisations such as Jewish Student societies, most of which are at least objectively Zionist.' However, the following month an activist from the York University student branch of the Socialist Workers Party was quoted in the *Socialist Worker* newspaper appearing to endorse bans on Jewish Societies if they supported Israel:

> We support unconditionally the right of the Jewish Society
> to exist as a cultural and religious body within the students
> union. We support unconditionally the right of all people of
> all races to live in and participate freely in a secular state in
> Palestine. It is because we oppose all racism that we oppose
> an openly Zionist and racist Jewish society.[17]

This confusion remained visible throughout the year. In October, Andy Strouthous, a Socialist Workers Party student on the NUS Executive, told *Socialist Worker*, 'We think pro-Israel government meetings should be treated like the one in Salford last term' (in other words, they should be banned). He was contradicted two weeks later by Alex Callinicos, a more senior member of the Socialist Workers Party, who stated that their policy of denying Students' Union money and facilities to Zionists did not extend to 'physically preventing Zionists from meeting'. This became their official position and was confirmed in a Socialist Workers Party students' pamphlet on Palestine:

> What we do argue is that student unions should refuse money and facilities to societies whose aim is to propagate Zionism and support for the state of Israel. This does not mean banning Jewish societies what it means is not paying money for Zionist propaganda or paying speakers fees for Zionists.[18]

The Socialist Workers Party and its student arm were effectively trying to separate the two parts of the No Platform policy that NUS had adopted in 1974. This involved denying union funds or facilities for Zionist speakers or meetings, but not preventing their meetings from taking place. This approach ignored the consequences of such restrictions, as the withdrawal of Students' Union funding often meant that Jewish Societies could no longer operate. Some anti-Zionist students from that period assumed that Jewish Societies had independent financial resources not available to other student societies

– an assumption that was uncomfortably close to yet another antisemitic stereotype. In practice, the Socialist Workers Party's attempt at nuance passed many people by; even other anti-Zionists thought they were responsible for motions banning Jewish Societies. Richard Burden, who succeeded Wragg as BAZO's NUS organiser, wrote in *Free Palestine* in 1978 that Socialist Workers Party members had a 'policy of refusing union recognition of Zionist organisations within NUS'. While Burden criticised the Socialist Workers Party for this, BAZO was also believed by many to be behind the campus bans on Zionism. *Free Palestine* hailed BAZO's 'campaign in British universities to bar explicitly Zionist groups under the National Union of Students ruling that no platform should be provided by university facilities to racists'. BAZO, like the Socialist Workers Party, denied supporting the bans, but few believed them. For the Union of Jewish Students, a policy equating Zionism with racism naturally raised the question of a ban on Zionism, whether it was mentioned explicitly in the policy text or not.[19]

It is a sign of how Zionism and Israel divided the left that, while the Trotskyists of the Socialist Workers Party were the main activists trying to ban Zionism on campus, the Union of Jewish Students' most important allies were the Communist and other left-wing students in the NUS leadership. Sue Slipman was on the Executive of the Communist Party of Great Britain and most of the top posts in NUS were taken by students from the Broad Left, an alliance of Communist, Labour and unaffiliated socialist students. Jewish student activists spent a lot of time trying to build a relationship with the NUS leadership, helped by the fact that their offices were conveniently located on the same central London street. The Union of Jewish Students' political officer (and later the eminent historian) David Cesarani remembered Slipman being genuinely sympathetic to their concerns and she spoke in their support in the debate at SOAS in October 1977. Slipman found Union of Jewish Students activists to be politically naive at first, but felt a vague affinity with them.

It helped that there was a meaningful difference between the Communist Party's position on Israel and that of the Trotskyist groups. Communist students like Slipman followed Eurocommunism, a popular idea in the late 1970s that tried to combine Communist Party membership with a more critical attitude towards the Soviet Union. This included a more moderate stance towards Israel. The Communist Party itself was hostile to Israel and Zionism but it tended to shun the more egregious anti-Zionist and antisemitic rhetoric that emanated from Moscow. It also maintained formal support for Israel's existence, based on United Nations Security Council Resolution 242 of November 1967, in line with Soviet policy. When war broke out between Israel, Egypt and Syria in October 1973, for example, the Communist *Morning Star* newspaper blamed Israel for the crisis, but emphasised that any peace settlement would have to recognise 'the sovereignty and right of existence of all the states in the area, including Israel'. This was quite different from the reaction in the International Socialists' journal *International Socialism*, which argued at the time: 'There is only one way to real peace in the Middle East and that is through the destruction of the Zionist state, with its preferential citizenship rights along racial lines, and its replacement by a Palestinian state, in which Jews and Arabs have equal rights.' The International Marxist Group had greeted the war with the typically New Left slogans: 'No to the Ceasefire! Against Security Council Resolution 242! For a Revolutionary Offensive against Zionism and Imperialism!'[20]

Whether or not the position of the NUS leadership was influenced by attitudes to Israel or by sympathy for Jewish students, it meant that the campus bans on Zionism became another fault line in their ongoing struggle with the Trotskyist factions within NUS. Jewish student activists played on these tensions, calculating, rightly, that the Broad Left would welcome any opportunity to 'smash the Trots', as Cesarani put it. Anti-Zionism divided the left on campus, as it continues to divide the left today, and on this occasion it resulted in Communist students paradoxically helping the Union of Jewish Students to undo the consequences of the Soviet-sponsored United Nations resolution equating Zionism with racism. There was also support from the parliamentary left. A meeting between the Union of Jewish Students and a group

of MPs (including three Labour Cabinet ministers) was followed in late November by an adjournment debate on the
subject in the House of Commons, led by Eric Moonman,
Labour MP for Basildon and a member of the Select Committee
on Race Relations. Shirley Williams, by then Secretary of State
for Education and Science and a consistent opponent of the
No Platform policy, endorsed the NUS Executive's position
against campus bans on Zionism.[21]

NUS decided to deal with the problem by sending a student delegation to the Middle East in August 1977 that would
recommend a policy for the NUS conference in December.
Their visit provides a compelling portrait of young, politically
motivated student activists trying to make sense of a complex
and divisive issue. GUPS and the Union of Jewish Students
each arranged a week's itinerary in Lebanon and Israel
respectively. The delegation was unusually high-level, com-
prising two senior NUS officers from the Broad Left (NUS
vice-president David Aaronovitch and NUS national secretary Trevor Phillips), an NUS Executive member from the
International Marxist Group (Colin Talbot), one Conservative
Student (Eddie Longworth) and NUS international manager
Roger Trask. In Lebanon the group visited refugee camps and
Palestinian institutions. They met Abu Jihad from the Fatah
Central Committee, plus representatives of other Palestinian
factions. In Israel, they met former Prime Minister Golda Meir
and a future Prime Minister, Yitzhak Shamir; the Mayor of

Ramallah Karim Khalaf; and Israeli anti-Zionists Israel Shahak and Leah Tsemel from Matzpen. Looking back, all the participants remember the trip being an emotional and humbling experience. The damage to Palestinian refugee camps from the Lebanese civil war shocked everybody. Every wall seemed to have bullet holes or shell damage. In Israel they visited the national Holocaust memorial at Yad Vashem. Being students, there were inevitably moments of light relief. Talbot remembers the momentary panic when one of their Palestinian guides at Lebanon's southern border with Israel offered to open fire on some Israeli tanks in the valley below, to show their British guests what a real firefight was like. Phillips managed to smuggle home a metal plate from a wrecked Israeli tank on the Golan Heights, a memento he retains to this day. On their return they produced a report for NUS that contained something for everybody. It concluded that the Palestinians are a nation with commensurate national rights and endorsed a two-state solution for Israel and the Palestinians. Only Talbot deviated from this line, arguing the International Marxist Group's standard line that the Jewish people do not constitute a nation and that Israel should be replaced by a single secular democratic state. He explicitly rejected bans on campus Zionism. Talbot has changed his views since: he left the International Marxist Group a few years after this trip, now describes his politics as social democrat and supports a two-state solution.[22]

The report was adopted by the NUS conference in December

1977, by which time NUS had brokered a deal between GUPS and the Union of Jewish Students that 'No limitations on the rights of Jewish or Palestinian students or Jewish or Palestinian societies whether they are religious, political or social groupings, should be contemplated.' GUPS had always been reluctant followers of what was a far-left campaign to ban Zionism. The motion that was passed at NUS conference was heavily critical of Israel, but met UJS's needs by stating that 'Both the Palestinians and the Jews have historic rights to the same land' and 'Both the Palestinians and the Jews have a right to national self-determination.' Jewish students welcomed this recognition of Israel's right to exist and the affirmation of their rights to hold Zionist activities. The *Morning Star* heralded NUS's recognition of Palestinian national rights. The entire No Platform policy was also revoked in a separate motion, having been discredited by its use to ban Jewish Societies, but was reinstated the following year.[23]

This policy did not put an end to campus anti-Zionism, but for a few years it meant that Jewish Societies were safe from the threat of being banned. The next time the question of banning Jewish Societies returned to national student politics was in 1985, in the midst of Labour's own internal struggles between moderate and hard lefts, with Zionism a dividing issue on and off campus. The row over Jewish Societies that rocked NUS throughout 1985 began at Sunderland Polytechnic, when its existing policy declaring Zionism to be a form of racism was renewed at a Union General Meeting in January. At the same time, a small group of Jewish students was trying to set up a Jewish Society with a clause in its constitution that included the aim 'to promote a greater understanding of the Jewish religion, culture, people, the state of Israel and Zionism'. This was deemed to contravene the anti-Zionist policy and they were told that they could not receive Students' Union funds or use its facilities if the Jewish Society constitution mentioned Israel. Posters advertising the new Jewish Society were taken down because they bore an image of the Israeli flag and the Jewish Society's application was rejected. In a clumsy and counter-productive effort to find a compromise, the Students' Union created an alternative Jewish Society with a constitution that omitted any mention of Israel or Zionism, but this was dismissed as a 'stooge society' by most Jewish students. Despite the obscurity of the location, the affair attracted national attention and an article in *The Guardian* quoted Charles Slater, the leader of Sunderland Council and a governor of the Polytechnic, recommending that the Jewish students should consider legal action.[24]

That this should happen at Sunderland Polytechnic caught out just about everybody in national student politics. It was an initiative of local students led by the Students' Union treasurer, a Stalinist called Mick Flaherty, but once NUS and all the various national student factions were involved it became inevitable that the issue would escalate. The Jewish students at Sunderland forced an Emergency General Meeting and Phil Woolas, then president of NUS (and later a Labour MP), addressed an 800-strong march and rally alongside Union of Jewish Students chairperson Simon Myerson. Jewish students arrived on coaches from all over the country, many having successfully moved motions at their own Students' Unions condemning Sunderland. At the emergency meeting, the would-be Jewish Society and the Union of Jewish Students were opposed in the debate by the GUPS national president, Nabil Kassim, and by Israeli anti-Zionist Uri Davis. The meeting rejected a motion allowing the Jewish Society to choose a constitution that included Zionism and voted instead to uphold the position of the Students' Union. A *Jewish Chronicle* editorial the following week, titled 'This is racism', called the vote 'a manifestation of anti-Semitism in the guise of anti-Zionism'. The Union of Jewish Students argued that Sunderland Polytechnic should be suspended by NUS because the decision contravened the minority rights of Jewish students:

> The second reason [to suspend Sunderland Polytechnic Students' Union from NUS] is to maintain the rights of all oppressed minorities to organise autonomously within the Student Movement. This right has been denied to Jewish Students at Sunderland Polytechnic. Every other minority group, be it Black, Gay, or Feminist has the right. Why should the Jews be different? There is no justification for Sunderland

Polytechnic's crude attempt to dictate to their Jewish Students what they can and cannot believe.[25]

This was an important step for UJS. When Jewish Societies came under threat in 1977, they made their case using the liberal language of democratic rights and free speech. By the 1980s, identity politics was the dominant political language in NUS. In adapting to this change UJS was ahead of the Jewish communal leadership, which still preferred the community to be defined as a faith than as an ethnicity at that time.

Students' Unions all over the country held debates about the events in Sunderland, with both sides bidding to control their delegations' votes at the forthcoming NUS conference, where the issue would be settled. The Union of Jewish Students was successful at several locations. A victory at the Polytechnic of Central London was marred by a letter in the Polytechnic's magazine that warned of 'the racist nature of Jews' and called the Jewish Society 'this Jewish propaganda shop'. They were assisted by Socialist Organiser, a Trotskyist group that was moving towards a position of supporting a two-state solution to the Israeli–Palestinian conflict. As well as arguing the case in Students' Union debates, a series of articles in the *Socialist Organiser* newspaper set out a left-wing case against bans on Jewish Societies. They also argued that the bans were the consequence of a specifically left-wing form of antisemitism. In a sign of how the political climate had changed in NUS since the

1970s, this time Socialist Workers Party students did not support restricting Students' Union funding or denying facilities for Zionist activities, although they still argued that Zionism was racist. Instead, they insisted that, while it may have been tactically mistaken to ban Zionists, it could not be construed as antisemitic and was certainly not worthy of condemnation or suspension by NUS.[26]

Individual Socialist Workers Party student branches, however, sometimes went a step further on their own initiative. At City of London Polytechnic, a motion was proposed by the Socialist Worker Students Society that supported Sunderland Polytechnic and called for the de-recognition of City's own Jewish Society. David Osler was a Socialist Workers Party member who spoke in the debate, alongside Mick Flaherty, who had come down from Sunderland, and Nabil Kassim of GUPS. Osler thought it was the Socialist Workers Party line, 'and the party line just had to be correct'. His student branch was being squeezed by a very left-wing Labour Club and a strong contingent from the Revolutionary Communist Party, and here was a chance for some 'brand positioning' to make the Socialist Workers Party the most radical faction. Unfortunately for them, the debate was held at the Polytechnic's Moorgate campus, which had a strong representation of Jewish Society and Conservative students. Phil Woolas and John Mann, then the chairman of the National Organisation of Labour Students (NOLS) and now a Labour MP, joined Simon

Myerson and the heads of the national Liberal, Conservative and Communist Party student groups in signing a statement that condemned the motion as 'anti-Semitic in effect, whatever the motivation', and the proposal to ban the Jewish Society was overwhelmingly defeated. Osler, who is no longer a Trotskyist, did not at the time believe the motion to be antisemitic; but he would not repeat his actions today. He remembers this being 'the most controversial issue during my entire student political career'. Just like in Sunderland, the Jewish Society drew on the examples of feminism and gay rights to claim the language of identity politics for themselves, arguing:

> Zionism is an integral part of Jewish identity ... It is the expres-
> sion of the Jewish aspiration to achieve self-determination.
> If this motion passes the Jewish Students at this Poly will be
> denied the right to define their own identity ... The proposers
> of this motion would certainly preach self-determination for
> other minority groups (such as Blacks, Asians, Women, Gays,
> and Lesbians). Why do they deny the same rights to Jews?[27]

Support for Sunderland Polytechnic was isolated and mainly came at campuses where GUPS or the Socialist Workers Party were strong. SOAS Students' Union, where there was no Jewish Society, passed a motion supporting Sunderland's position. North London Polytechnic passed a motion from its Socialist Workers Party student branch that endorsed Sunderland's 'principled stand against Zionism' and condemned the NUS Executive and Woolas 'for their woolly liberalism in confusing anti-Zionism with anti-Semitism'. But when the issue reached NUS national conference in March 1985, the Union of Jewish Students and its allies won a vote that condemned Sunderland Polytechnic and instructed it to reinstate the Jewish Society by the end of the year. By successfully arguing that Zionism was a legitimate expression of their Jewish identity, allied to effective political tactics and organisation, Jewish students had altered the terms of the debate in the student movement so that it was anti-Zionists, not Zionists, who had to defend themselves from charges of racism.[28]

The eight years between these two waves of Jewish Society bans had seen a transformation in attitudes to Israel and Zionism in the Labour Party. The election of a right-wing Likud government in Israel in 1977 meant that, for the first time, Israel was led by a government for which the British Labour Party did not feel an automatic political affinity. The new social and cultural class associated with the New Left was making its presence felt in Labour as the party increasingly attracted members from public sector professions. By the early 1980s, Israel's occupation of the West Bank and Gaza Strip had been ongoing for over a decade and, despite the peace treaty with Egypt, the anti-Israel politics that had grown from the New Left in the late 1960s was starting to have an impact. Younger Labour Party activists who had experience of single-issue campaign groups from the New Left saw support for the Palestinian cause as a natural fit with their broader anti-American sentiment and anti-racist politics. It was also a time when Anglo-Jewry increasingly voted Conservative and Labour looked to more recently arrived minorities for its political support, with socio-economic class an important factor in both trends. This was the decade when Jeremy Corbyn first became a prominent activist for the Palestinian cause in one of the new anti-Israel groups that emerged on the left at that time. He did so by embracing an organisation that promoted a fully anti-Zionist position, rejected Israel's existence and campaigned to 'eradicate Zionism' from the Labour Party.

The 1982 Lebanon War was a seismic event in the development of left-wing anti-Zionism in Britain. 'Never before did Israel's image reach such a low ebb as in this war,' one survey of Western media coverage concluded. The war led to many civilian casualties in Lebanon, of which the massacres of Palestinians in Beirut's Sabra and Shatila refugee camps by Israel's Lebanese allies came to be emblematic. Support for the Palestinian cause, normally associated with the Labour left, was found across the party after the massacres. The war sparked the creation of a new generation of pro-Palestinian and anti-Zionist campaign groups in and around the party. One of these was the Labour Committee on Palestine, which was formed in June 1982, the same month as the Israeli invasion, with a platform to campaign for Palestinian self-determination;

for recognition of the PLO and 'their fight for a democratic, secular state'; 'Opposition to the Zionist state as racist, exclusivist, expansionist and a direct agency of imperialism'; and 'Opposition to the manifestations of Zionism in the Labour movement and the Labour Party in particular'. This was a much more radical position than that proposed by the older Labour Middle East Council, which supported a two-state solution to the conflict. The chair of the Labour Committee on Palestine was Tony Greenstein, a Trotskyist and former BAZO activist from Brighton, and amongst its early supporters were Ken Livingstone (then leader of the Greater London Council) and Ted Knight, the leader of Lambeth Council in south London. Knight had a background in Trotskyism and was close to Gerry Healy, leader of the Trotskyist Workers Revolutionary Party, which was increasingly influential in the London Labour Party. According to Alex Mitchell, a senior activist in the Workers Revolutionary Party, Knight, Healy and Livingstone would hold regular 'semi-clandestine gatherings' in Healy's flat. One consequence of these meetings was the decision to launch the *Labour Herald* newspaper, edited by Knight and Livingstone, for which Knight secured financial support from the PLO and which was printed on the Workers Revolutionary Party's Libyan-funded printing press.[29]

The Labour Committee on Palestine was behind an emergency resolution at the 1982 Labour Party conference that recognised the PLO as 'the sole legitimate representative of the Palestinian people', and that called on the party to support 'the establishment of a democratic secular state of Palestine as the long-term solution to the Palestinian problem'. This formula of a 'democratic secular state' meant that Israel would be replaced entirely by a single state of Palestine. Embarrassingly for the party leadership, the resolution was passed at conference, with Knight leading the way, despite the party's National Executive Committee advising against it. This didn't have the power to change Labour party policy, but it did show how much the tide was now flowing against Israel. This challenge to the long-standing support that Israel had historically enjoyed from Labour shook the Anglo-Jewish leadership and relations became increasingly strained. Ken Livingstone's efforts to replace Reg Freeson as Labour candidate for Brent East in the 1983 general election included attacks on Freeson's support for Israel. Similar disagreements between Labour Zionists and anti-Zionists arose in Hackney. The Labour-run council in Dundee, encouraged by George Galloway, twinned Dundee with Nablus and flew the Palestinian flag from the town hall. This drew an outraged response from the Board of Deputies, who organised a petition of 5,000 names against the move and protested to the Scottish Office, to no avail.[30]

The Jewish community leadership's concerns coalesced around the figure of Livingstone, elected as leader of the Greater London Council in 1981. In June 1982, the Board of Deputies asked the Attorney General to prosecute Livingstone's *Labour*

Herald after it published a cartoon of Israeli Prime Minister Menachem Begin wearing a Nazi uniform and giving a *Sieg Heil* salute while standing astride a pile of bloody skeletons. Instead of a swastika, Begin's armband bore a Star of David. They also complained about a March 1982 review of three books alleging collaboration between Zionists and Nazis. The reviewer, a Scottish BAZO activist called Harry Mullin, wrote that 'the Zionist is a greedy and selfish upholder of capitalism, with its love for property' and that Israel

> is a state entirely built on the blood of Europe's Jews, whom
> the Zionists deserted in their hour of greatest need. These
> books will shock and horrify, for they expose the hypocrisy
> of Zionist leaders who used the sympathy stirred up for Jews
> after the Holocaust for their own devious ends.

A few weeks later, *Labour Herald* published a letter from the non-Zionist Jewish Socialist Group demanding an apology for printing Mullin's 'blatantly anti-Semitic' review and calling it 'a disgrace to a socialist newspaper'. No apology was forthcoming and the Attorney General declined to prosecute *Labour Herald* for either the review or the Begin cartoon. Harry Mullin later moved from far left to far right, joining the British National Party, where he continued to claim that Zionists collaborated with the Nazis, while also denying that six million Jews were killed in the Holocaust.[31]

This argument over *Labour Herald*'s book review and cartoon took place a year before Lenni Brenner published *Zionism
in the Age of the Dictators*, the book that Livingstone later said
'helped form my view of Zionism and its history'. Livingstone
recounted these events in his 2011 memoirs, alleging that various
people and organisations in the Jewish communal leadership
in Britain and America, and in the pre-state Zionist leadership, were either soft on fascism or sympathetic to it before and
during the Second World War. He claims to have been most
shocked by 'the role of Israel's respected Labour party leaders
... it was a catastrophic error of judgement not to throw all
the resources of Zionism into the campaign against Nazism'.
(The implication that the Zionist movement in the 1930s
and 1940s could add significant weight to the combined war
effort of the British Empire, the Soviet Union and the United
States suggests that Livingstone has an inflated estimation of
Zionism's power and influence.) When Livingstone endorsed
Brenner's work in 1983 and again in 2011, few people in the
Labour Party seemed to mind. When he repeated his views
in 2016, his party membership was suspended within hours.[32]

Under Livingstone, the Greater London Council regularly
hosted meetings for anti-Zionist groups, including a press conference for Brenner when he visited the UK on a speaker tour
in 1983. In 1984, it held an 'anti-racist year', which included a
conference on anti-Arab racism organised by a newly reformed
Palestine Solidarity Campaign and funded by the Greater

London Council. The Palestine Solidarity Campaign produced a booklet for the conference titled *Israel-South Africa:*
The Natural Alliance, which included the text of the 1975
United Nations resolution declaring Zionism to be a form of
racism. The conference was chaired by Jeremy Corbyn and
included talks on 'Apartheid in Israel' and 'Western imperialism and anti-Arab racism', as well as sessions about the status
of Arabs in Britain. Shortly afterwards, Livingstone gave an
interview to the Israeli newspaper *Davar*, in which he claimed
that 'The Board of Deputies of British Jews has in recent years
been taken over by Jews who hold extreme right-wing views'
and that since Menachem Begin had become Israeli Prime
Minister, 'the Jews' in Britain and elsewhere 'became reaction-
aries, turned right nearly to be fascists'.[33]

Meanwhile, Knight had engineered a complete takeover of
the Labour Committee on Palestine by the Workers Revolutionary Party, leaving himself as chair and Livingstone on its
committee. In typical Trotskyist fashion, this led to a split and
the creation of a rival group, the Labour Movement Campaign
for Palestine (LMCP); and it was this new group that Jeremy
Corbyn sponsored and supported throughout the 1980s. The
Labour Movement Campaign for Palestine continued the
radical approach of its predecessor, campaigning for a democratic, secular state of Palestine in place of Israel and pledging
to oppose 'manifestations of Zionism' in Labour. Its mission
statement included the pledge that 'The Labour Movement

Campaign for Palestine will fight within the Labour Movement – and the Labour Party in particular – to eradicate Zionism'. LMCP was not formally affiliated to Labour, but the party was the main focus of its activism. It was run by Tony Greenstein, who was, and remains, an avid proponent of the view that the Zionist movement benefits from, and proactively encourages, antisemitism (including, he alleges, collaborating with Nazism). Greenstein wrote his own pamphlet on the subject, called *Zionism: Anti-Semitism's Twin in Jewish Garb*, which the LMCP advertised. Corbyn became a sponsor of the organisation early in 1983, not long after it was formed, when he was Labour's candidate for the Islington North constituency in the 1983 general election. He spoke regularly at LMCP fringe meetings at party conferences and at its other events. Israel's Labour Party was a particular target for its campaigns in an attempt to undermine the link between the British and Israeli Labour parties. One LMCP conference in 1984, that Corbyn chaired, was promoted by Greenstein in an article that claimed: 'Labour Zionism was responsible for the main burden of colonisation of Palestine ... Historically Labour Zionism has been more racist than its revisionist opponents.' The LMCP even brought out a special booklet on the subject, 'to expose the monstrous myth of Labour Zionism's progressive or socialist nature'. The booklet's 'recommended reading list' included Lenni Brenner's *Zionism in the Age of the Dictators* and Greenstein's *Zionism: Anti-Semitism's Twin in Jewish Garb*.[34]

When Sunderland Polytechnic Students' Union banned its Jewish Society in 1985, the LMCP supported the Students' Union. An unsigned article in its newsletter declared that while 'it was a *tactical* mistake on the part of Sunderland Polytechnic Students' Union to ban an overtly Zionist Jewish Society ... We totally reject the assertion that Sunderland Poly's action was in any way anti-Semitic.' The article went on to insist that anti-Zionism cannot possibly be antisemitic: 'Zionism is inherently racist ... we can make no compromises with the nationalism of a colonising movement, even when dressed up in the ideology of an historic oppression.' Corbyn did not comment directly on events in Sunderland, but the same Labour Movement Campaign for Palestine newsletter that printed this article supporting Sunderland Polytechnic also carried a message from Corbyn encouraging people to join the organisation. 'The Palestine question is one of the most important issues facing the Labour movement,' Corbyn wrote, and 'The Labour Movement Campaign for Palestine is the only campaign rooted in the Labour Movement whose platform really tackles the important issues in relation to this question. Its activities ought to be supported by every Labour Party member.' As well as its pledge to 'eradicate Zionism' and its support for a democratic, secular state in place of Israel, the LMCP had a particularly cynical attitude to terrorism against Jews outside Israel. When Palestinian gunmen shot dead twenty-two worshippers at the Neve Shalom synagogue in Istanbul in 1986, its newsletter insisted that while the LMCP didn't condone the attack, 'it is Zionism that gains ... So whatever Israel may feel about the massacre of the Turkish Jews, the truth is that the Zionist State actually benefits from such attacks.' By this stage Livingstone had joined Corbyn as a LMCP sponsor, alongside around a dozen MPs and MEPs and a clutch of Constituency Labour Parties and student Labour Clubs.[35]

The divisions in the Labour Party, and the wider left, over Zionism are illustrated by the choices made by two current Labour MPs, John Mann and Richard Burden, who were on opposite sides of the student campaigns described here. Both are still active in this debate: Mann as chair of the All-Party Parliamentary Group Against Antisemitism and Burden as chair of the Britain–Palestine All-Party Parliamentary Group. Burden was a former Young Liberal and a BAZO activist in 1977 when, as president of York University Students' Union, he proposed a motion that condemned Zionism as 'a discriminatory, racist and unjust ideology'; cited the UN 'Zionism is racism' resolution; endorsed Palestinian 'armed struggle'; and resolved 'To sever all connections between NUS and Zionist groups and organisations' and 'To sever links with all explicitly Zionist student bodies and thus make clear the total rejection by the NUS of racialism wherever it is practiced [sic] and under whatever misleading terminology.' Burden wrote the motion himself and says now that he had not considered the possibility that the Jewish Society would be caught by the call to cut all links with Zionist student groups. The Jewish Society felt differently and forced the issue by changing its constitution to include 'explicit support for the Zionist ideal and the existence of the State of Israel', thereby triggering a decision by the Union Council to withdraw both funding and recognition of the society. This meant that as well as losing its funding, the society would not be listed in the Union's handbook or allowed to hold a stall at the next Freshers' Fayre. The Union Council explained in a statement that 'It should not continue to recognise or fund an organisation, one of whose explicit aims is to mobilise support for the Zionist State of Israel.' Burden went into more detail in a statement that tried to separate Jewish student activities from support for Israel:

> We feel that the existence of a Jewish Society on campus is both healthy and worthy of union support; an organisation of Jewish students has much to contribute culturally, religiously and in the fight to combat racism and fascism in this country ... I should emphasise that our policy is in no way anti-Jewish, but rather in opposition to the political creed of Zionism. It would be both irresponsible and hypocritical of the union to recognise or fund groups, whose stated aim is to support Israel, and thus contribute to the further subjugation of the Palestinian people.[36]

Burden's problem was that the Jewish Society resisted this separation between Jewish activities and Zionism. An Emergency

General Meeting of the Students' Union was arranged for the following week and the university Vice-Chancellor threatened to intervene if the Students' Union did not revoke the ban. Burden proposed a motion to the emergency meeting that was similar to the one that had provoked the original crisis. His new motion resolved 'To oppose any denial of Union rights to any members of SUs who respect the rights of other members', but also 'To refuse to support, fund or recognise any organisation whose constitutional purpose is support of Zionist Israel and to refuse to support or fund any activities supporting Zionist Israel.' The Jewish Society at York was small but, in the recollection of its head Gill Schiller, 'totally united about how to react'. A rival motion, proposed by Communist Party students at York on behalf of the Jewish Society, endorsed a two-state solution to the Israeli–Palestinian conflict; reinstated the Jewish Society; and granted the Jewish Society the right to express its support for Israel and Zionism. This motion was passed, restoring the Jewish Society and leaving the Students' Union with an official policy that recognised Israel and the legitimacy of Zionism. The cooperation with Communist students was significant and mirrored UJS's strategy at a national level. Schiller was 'exhilarated'.[37]

Burden gives the impression of having been rather more bruised by the experience. It didn't put him off pro-Palestinian campaigning: the following month he went on a BAZO-organised trip to Lebanon in a group that included a young

George Galloway, and he has continued to campaign for Palestine ever since. But Burden's experience at York did affect how he conducts that campaigning. Reflecting on the episode many years later, and from his position as a serving Member of Parliament, he concluded: 'If I had the political experience then that I have now, I would have recommended that we take no action – you don't leap into the trap that somebody is setting for you.' While this suggests that he feels the Jewish Society out-manoeuvred him, the episode also led him to reflect on his entire approach to the conflict. Burden is still a leading parliamentary advocate for Palestine but he says now that analysing the conflict through a theoretical analysis of Zionism, or trying to undermine Israel by alleging Nazi/Zionist collaboration, are blind alleys that do nothing practical for the Palestinians. Similarly, he changed his views on armed struggle and now supports a two-state solution. More profoundly, he came to understand the importance of listening to other people's fears:

> People on both sides need to recognise and validate the deeply held beliefs and collective memory of the other side … If people, especially Jews, feel threatened, then they feel threatened and you should reach out to them and have a dialogue. You should try to be careful about the use of terminology, not leave room for misinterpretation, and avoid words and actions that run the risk of being counterproductive.[38]

Eight years after Burden's troubles at York, John Mann was the chair of the National Organisation of Labour Students (NOLS) when Sunderland Polytechnic Jewish Society was banned. He had become friendly with Jewish Society activists at Manchester University in the early 1980s after speaking against an anti-Zionist motion there. He and Phil Woolas saw political potential in the Union of Jewish Students and encouraged it to get more involved in NUS politics. This advice was timely as several Jewish student activists had come to a similar conclusion at around that time. By 1985, Mann had visited Israel and his relationship with the Union of Jewish Students had become profound and lasting. His time as chair of NOLS coincided with Neil Kinnock's efforts to reduce Trotskyist influence in the party as a whole. Mann had similar battles to fight amongst Labour students. NOLS had been taken over by Trotskyist students from Militant in the early 1970s and was subsequently the subject of a factional fight between them and moderate Labour students. The moderates initially called themselves 'Operation Icepick', named after the weapon used by a Soviet agent to assassinate Leon Trotsky in 1940, but their faction came to be known as 'Clause 4'. By 1976, the Clause 4 group had won back control of NOLS, largely by matching Militant's organisational discipline and sectarian plotting, but the bitter conflict between the two continued well into the 1980s, at which point Militant was estimated to hold the loyalty of around 40 per cent of NOLS members. Mann was from the Clause 4 group and faced opposition from Trotskyists within NOLS itself. NOLS' policy was to support two states but with the aspiration that they would voluntarily merge into one 'secular democratic state' at some point in the future. This didn't translate into the more extreme anti-Zionism of the Socialist Workers Party or GUPS, but Mann remembers facing strong opposition to his candidacy for NOLS chair simply because he supported a two-state solution to the Israeli–Palestinian conflict.

When the Jewish Society was banned in Sunderland, Mann backed the Union of Jewish Students' position and set about ensuring that NOLS would do the same at the forthcoming NUS conference. This depended more on controlling the balance of the political factions in NOLS and NUS than actually winning the argument over Zionism. The debate at NUS conference was an opportunity for Mann and Woolas to deal a blow to their internal opponents while also overturning a policy they considered antisemitic. As part of this they ensured that the Union of Jewish Students rejected an offer of a compromise deal that might have left the Jewish Society with something less than the full restoration of its rights – and left their own political opponents suffering something less than total defeat. Amongst Labour students, as in Labour as a whole, policy differences on Israel/Palestine were part of a wider struggle between left and right.

The different experiences of Burden and Mann show just how divisive and contentious debates over Israel and Zionism can be on the left. Burden acted from genuine anti-racist principles and humanitarian concern for the Palestinians, but found that his own political assumptions led him to the point of banning the Jewish Society at his university. Mann saw clearly how those same anti-Zionist ideas had contributed to a political campaign with antisemitic consequences, but had to fight internal opponents in his own political faction to have that recognised. The fact that Jewish students managed to find allies on the left to help them defend Zionism in 1977 and 1985 – despite the damage done to Israel's reputation by the intervening Lebanon War – further highlights these divisions.

The primacy of identity politics in the student left was crucial. Jewish students insisted that their own democratic rights depended on being allowed to support Israel and to define antisemitism on their own terms. 'Hands off Jewish identity' was the slogan on stickers handed out to delegates at the 1985 NUS conference. The logic of identity politics meant that this simple demand was irresistible. To deny Jewish students this right would be discriminatory within the left's own political framework; but for anti-Zionists, to allow Jewish students to promote Zionism would be acquiescing in racism. This is the conundrum that Jewish students forced left-wing anti-Zionists to confront when they demonstrated the practical consequences of political campaigns based on the 'Zionism is racism' idea. This wasn't about preventing people from criticising Israel or about the details of the Israeli–Palestinian conflict.

Jewish students viewed their successes not as a propaganda triumph for Israel, but as validation for their own place as Jewish students in Britain. As the Union of Jewish Students wrote in its journal after the crucial NUS conference of December 1977: 'the national union decided that Jews have as many rights as anyone else. And that, after all, was all we ever wanted.'[39]

CHAPTER FIVE

THE NEW ALLIANCE: ISLAMISTS AND THE LEFT

April 2002. The second Palestinian Intifada that had begun nineteen months earlier was at its peak. Widespread rioting that followed Israeli Likud Party leader (and future Prime Minister) Ariel Sharon's visit to Jerusalem's Temple Mount, the holiest site in Judaism and one of the holiest in Islam, had quickly escalated to shootings and suicide bombings. March 2002 had been the deadliest month so far: 247 Palestinians and 117 Israelis killed. A suicide bombing by the Palestinian Islamist group Hamas had killed thirty people at a Passover Seder (festive meal) being held in a hotel in the Israeli beach resort of Netanya. The Israeli Army reoccupied West Bank cities that they had left under the Oslo Peace Accords during the previous decade, Palestinian fighters were holed up in Bethlehem's Church of the Nativity and false rumours circulated of a massacre of Palestinian civilians in Jenin.

In London, Jeremy Corbyn was preparing, not for the first time, to speak at a rally for Palestine in Trafalgar Square. Unlike most of his previous engagements, this one was not organised by the left-wing pro-Palestine organisations that he was used to working with, but by the British arm of the Muslim Brotherhood, the world's oldest and most influential Islamist movement. The Muslim Brotherhood was formed in Egypt in the 1920s and spawned branches in most Arab countries, with supportive groups in several other countries where there are Muslim minorities. Its goal is to achieve political power and social influence in order to reshape society according to Sharia (Islamic law). Most significant Islamist organisations in the Middle East, from the democratic Islamists in government in Turkey to the violent jihadists of al-Qaeda and Islamic State, can trace their genealogy back to the Brotherhood. Hamas, which uses both democratic means and violence to pursue its goals, is the Brotherhood's Palestinian branch. Members and supporters of the Brotherhood had arrived in Britain during the 1980s and 1990s as part of a wave of Islamist and jihadist exiles who found home in what came to be called, somewhat pejoratively, 'Londonistan'. One of these exiles was Kamal Helbawy, an Egyptian veteran of the Brotherhood who had been exiled from his native country for most of his life. In 1994, he moved from Pakistan to London, where he served as the Brotherhood's official spokesman in the West. Helbawy was keen to exploit the advantages offered by Britain's open society. In 1997, he founded the Muslim Association of Britain, with help from other Brotherhood exiles, and became its first president. It was the Muslim Association of Britain that organised this demonstration for Palestine in April 2002. Muslim and left-wing groups had held several protests against Israel since the Second Intifada began in late September 2000, but not together and not on this scale. Labour MPs Corbyn, Galloway and Tony Benn, and veteran left-wing campaigners Lindsey German of the Stop the War Coalition and Carole Regan of the Palestine Solidarity Campaign, spoke alongside the Muslim Association of Britain's Helbawy and Azzam Tamimi. Hezbollah and Muslim Brotherhood flags mixed with Socialist Workers Party and Stop the War Coalition placards in the crowd. After the speeches were finished, the event concluded with a prayer from Sheikh Rached Ghannouchi of the Tunisian Islamist Ennahda Movement.

The Muslim Association of Britain claimed that 100,000 people marched in London that day. Those present from the Palestine Solidarity Campaign and the Stop the War Coalition were impressed that it could mobilise so many British Muslims from a community that was usually absent from left-wing political protests. The Palestine Solidarity Campaign invited the Muslim Association of Britain to co-organise another rally in May that they had already scheduled. In September, the Stop the War Coalition and the Muslim Association of Britain jointly organised a much larger protest for Palestine and against the impending war in Iraq. And in February 2003, their combined efforts produced the largest political demonstration Britain has ever seen, when anywhere between one and two million people marched under two slogans: 'Freedom for Palestine' and 'Stop the war in Iraq'. This new protest movement, built on an alliance between Islamists and the far left, held the promise of a different kind of political campaigning that is more inclusive of British Muslims. This is one reason why Corbyn has called the Stop the War Coalition, which he helped to set up and chaired for four years, 'one of the most important democratic campaigns of modern times'. Encouraging political engagement amongst British Muslims (or people from any minority) is, in principle, a good thing, but this came with the prospect of putting radical leftists at the head of a movement with energy and numbers beyond their dreams. It didn't stop the invasion of Iraq and it hasn't brought freedom for Palestine, but it has changed the complexion of the left in Britain. Tony Blair's decision as a Labour Prime Minister to join the United States in the 2003 Iraq War opened a deep wound in the Labour movement that has still not healed, and the anger and shame felt by left-wing opponents of the war play a large part in explaining how Jeremy Corbyn became Labour Party leader.[1]

This new alliance has also brought new risks for the left, that might have been apparent to those veteran leftists at the April 2002 rally if they were paying attention. They would have seen some marchers dressed as suicide bombers, as if to emphasise the meaning of all the Hezbollah flags being waved. Others had brought banners and placards equating the Star of David with the swastika. One man, wearing a fake suicide bomb belt, climbed onto one of the fountains in the middle of Trafalgar Square and set fire to a huge American flag. A specially produced Muslim Association of Britain newspaper handed out at the September demonstration included a full-page article on 'Islam and Human Rights' written by Azzam Tamimi. It contained little that a conscientious leftist would agree with. Man is on earth to serve God, he wrote, while Western political thought denies this divine service. Muslims and non-Muslims should not be equal citizens in Islamic states and non-Muslims should have fewer rights there than Muslims. Freedom of belief does not extend to the freedom for a Muslim to choose to leave the faith; he or she is either an apostate or a traitor, and risks execution. This support for terrorism, antisemitism and religious bigotry common to Islamist politics was easy to spot, but it didn't put off the leftists running the Stop the War Coalition.[2]

Two years later, Ken Livingstone, by then Mayor of London, hosted perhaps the strangest meeting of all his eight years in office. At a press conference in City Hall arranged by the Muslim Association of Britain, Livingstone sat and listened while Sheikh Yusuf al-Qaradawi, the most influential Muslim Brotherhood scholar in the world, answered questions from journalists who had been drawn to the event by negative press coverage about Qaradawi's presence in the UK. He was on record as supporting Hamas suicide bombings in Israel, and was also accused of making controversial comments regarding female genital mutilation and homosexuality. Qaradawi had been to London several times before, but since the 9/11 terrorist attacks in the United States the British media had begun paying more attention to Islamist extremism. Qaradawi answered their questions and gave interviews, while Livingstone called him an 'honoured guest' and the two men embraced for the cameras. Livingstone was determined to stand by Qaradawi, who had condemned the 9/11 terrorist attacks and was, in Livingstone's view, a moderate voice, and it took the quick thinking of the Muslim Association of Britain's people in the room to keep Qaradawi from embarrassing his left-wing host. According to one bilingual observer, when journalists asked the Egyptian cleric about his previous comments endorsing Palestinian suicide bombings, Azzam Tamimi – acting as translator for the Arabic-speaking Sheikh – did not fully translate his reply. 'Their women are not like our women,' Qaradawi is reported to have said in Arabic, because military service is compulsory in Israel, and consequently there is no such thing as an Israeli civilian. This put a different spin on Qaradawi's condemnation of terrorism and the killing of innocents, but the Mayor and the assembled journalists never heard this part of Qaradawi's talk, because, it is claimed, Tamimi didn't translate it. Livingstone was therefore unaware of the irony when he said that the media's lack of religious and ethnic diversity meant they were ignorant of Qaradawi's true views.[3]

This 21st-century alliance between Islamists and leftists has profoundly changed Britain's pro-Palestine movement. Collaboration with Islamists has introduced new people and ideas to a movement that had previously relied on the same small circles of left-wing activists and groups for, in some cases, decades. It has brought this movement new energy and focus, but also given it a more extreme and controversial aspect. It has ensured, for example, that the radical left's traditional support for the violence of Third World liberation movements transferred to the Islamist suicide bombers of Hamas. At the same time, and largely for the same reasons, pro-Palestinian activism has become part of a much broader anti-war movement. The Stop the War Coalition was formed by veterans of Britain's radical left in September 2001, just ten days after 9/11, initially to oppose the coming invasion of Afghanistan. By the time it found mass public support via its opposition to the 2003 Iraq War, its partnership with the Muslim Association of Britain ensured that Palestine had equal billing with Iraq in its campaigns. Just as left-wing anti-Zionism first emerged from anti-colonial politics, it now has a home in the global anti-war movement that emerged in response to the wars in Afghanistan and Iraq.

Strangely, though, British Muslims came relatively late to the Palestinian cause. While groups from the radical left began campaigning for Palestine in the late 1960s, British Muslim interest only took shape twenty years later. In 1988, Yusuf Islam (the musician formerly known as Cat Stevens) joined a delegation of British Muslim converts who visited Palestine and returned convinced that Palestine was 'a matter of concern for Muslims all over the world'. When peace talks began between Israel and its Arab neighbours in 1991, leading to the Oslo Peace Accords between Israel and the PLO in 1993, Britain's Islamist organisations were unanimous in their rejection of any peace deal. The Oslo Accords involved recognition of Israel by the PLO and was the beginning of a long process that envisaged – in spirit, if not in their explicit wording – an eventual two-state solution to the Israeli–Palestinian conflict. This was anathema for Islamists because it involved accepting Israel's permanency on what they considered to be Muslim land. However, unlike left-wing anti-Zionists, Islamist groups used religious language rather than anti-colonialist politics to justify their opposition to Israel. 'The Jews seem neither to respect God nor His creation,' read the statement issued by the 1988 British Muslim delegation. It continued: 'Their own holy books contain the curse of God brought upon them by their prophets on account of their disobedience to Him and mischief in the earth. We have seen the disrespect displayed by those who consider themselves to be "God's chosen people".' This religious language, so alien to leftists, made it clear that for these British Islamists, Palestine was primarily a religious conflict.[4]

The emergence of this Islamist anti-Zionism in Britain coincided with a wave of jihadist enthusiasm sweeping through British Muslim politics. The war in the former Yugoslavia and mass killings of Bosnian Muslim civilians during the early 1990s heightened fears about anti-Muslim prejudice in Europe. Bosnian Muslims had been in Europe for centuries and were mostly white, secular and integrated into Yugoslav society. That their Christian neighbours turned on them with such ferocity shocked British Muslims, most of whom were relatively recent arrivals from South Asia and East Africa. The reluctance of Western governments to intervene until late in the conflict reinforced these fears. Instead, British Muslim organisations started to look to jihadists to defend Muslim lives and honour. Thousands of foreign *mujahideen* fought in Bosnia in the early 1990s, just as they do in Syria and Iraq today. Many had previously fought in Afghanistan against the Soviet Union. Blood-curdling videos of atrocities carried out by Serb and Croat soldiers circulated amongst British Muslims to encourage people to volunteer. Several different Muslim organisations held campaigns to raise money for arms to send to Bosnian Muslims, or to recruit British Muslim volunteers to go and fight. Thousands of people heard this message at meetings and conferences, including directly from Abu Abdul Aziz, the Saudi Commander of Arab jihadi fighters in Bosnia, who visited Britain to make his plea for volunteers in person. According to one report, UK intelligence estimated that up to 1,000 British

Muslims answered the call during the 1990s; several thousand more joined aid convoys or gave money. Usama Hasan, a former jihadi fighter and recruiter, estimates that tens of thousands of British Muslims at that time either visited Bosnia or knew somebody who did.

This growth in jihadism didn't occur in isolation. The 1980s had ended with the Rushdie Affair, when some British Muslims protested against the publication of Salman Rushdie's novel *The Satanic Verses* and Iran's Ayatollah Khomeini issued a fatwa calling for the author's assassination. This was a traumatic experience for many British Muslims and played a large role in the formation of a separate Islamic political identity. The 1990s was also the decade when the word, and the concept, 'Islamophobia' came into common use, to describe the perception of growing prejudice towards Muslims and Islam. Bosnia was, for many British Muslims, a sign of what might be to come. Islamist groups didn't miss this opportunity: 'Bosnia Today, Britain Tomorrow', read one leaflet by the radical Hizb ut-Tahrir organisation. Meanwhile, the collapse of the Soviet Union following its defeat in Afghanistan had been put to good use by the propagandists of the Arab *mujahideen* who fought there. Kashmiri jihadi leaders toured British mosques encouraging recruits and as the 1990s progressed, increasing numbers of British Muslims went to Kashmir to visit jihadi training camps there. British Muslims felt under attack and the call to jihad was an alternative source of pride and action. It had a profound effect on British

Muslim politics and is the precedent for today's British Muslim involvement in the Syrian jihad.

The glorification of jihadi fighters transferred easily from Bosnia and Kashmir to other foreign conflicts. Hamas was the Palestinian organisation of choice for most British Islamists, who dismissed the PLO and Arab governments as collaborators and secular sell-outs. *Trends* magazine, a popular Muslim youth publication at that time, dedicated an issue to Hamas shortly after the Oslo Accords were signed. It dismissed the Accords as 'a breath taking [*sic*] capitulation' by 'secular apologists among the Muslims'. Hamas, one article hoped, could 'draw inspiration and energy from their youth who desire to live and die for Allah's cause'. Some of *Trends* magazine's young journalists travelled to Sudan to interview a Hamas spokesman (they had already visited Kashmiri jihadist training camps in 1991). 'Our prayers are with our brothers and sisters of Hamas in Palestine,' they told their interviewee. The centrefold was a full-colour, pull-out poster with the word 'Hamas' emblazoned across a map of Palestine and a drawing of an AK-47 assault rifle. Inayat Bunglawala, who later became a senior figure in the Muslim Council of Britain (MCB), wrote a column for *Trends* on international affairs. His Islamist ambitions at that time included the overthrow of all pro-Western Arab governments as a prelude to the destruction of Israel:

> The Muslim masses must overthrow these oppressive regimes
> so that the resources of these Arab countries can be put to the

service of Islam. Only then can the Muslims effectively remove
the Zionist cancer. For the Islamic movement the road to Jerusalem goes through the capitals of all the Arab nation-states.[5]

As we have already seen, from the late 1960s, sections of the far
left had embraced the glamour of Che Guevara and the anger
of Frantz Fanon to legitimise the violence of Palestinians and
other groups fighting against the West. In the 1970s, groups
like Palestine Action, the Palestine Solidarity Campaign and
the *Free Palestine* newspaper helped to establish the notion
that Fatah and other Palestinian factions had the right to use
violence, although they sometimes differed over the precise
tactics used. Since then, attitudes ranging from sympathy for
the motivations of terrorists to outright justification of their
actions have spread beyond the radical left to become commonplace in mainstream left-wing and liberal thought. British
Islamists, though, brought support for Hamas into the heart of
pro-Palestine activism in the UK. Jihadist fervour married to
long-standing leftist support for the violence of Third World
liberation movements produced a groundswell of left-wing
sympathy, or even support, for Palestinian suicide bombers.

Although support for violent resistance groups was not a
new development for pro-Palestinian campaigners, in the post-
9/11 world, the argument that suicide bombers were heroic
freedom fighters rather than terrorists carried an extra sting.
Liberal Democrat MP (and now Baroness) Jenny Tonge was

sacked from her front-bench position for saying of Palestinian suicide bombers, 'If I had to live in that situation – and I say that advisedly – I might just consider becoming one myself.' Ted Honderich, a philosophy professor at University College London, went further, claiming that Palestinian terrorism was a form of 'terrorism for humanity'; morally right, necessary and rational. A 2001 article in *New Left Review* called suicide bombing (including by al-Qaeda) 'the ultimate weapon of the weak against the powerful of this earth'. In 2003, the youth wing of the Socialist Labour Party (a left-wing breakaway from the Labour Party, formed by Arthur Scargill in 1996) published an article in its newsletter *Spark* that hailed Rachel Corrie, Tom Hurndall and Asif Mohammed Hanif as 'heroes of the revolutionary youth', who had 'given their lives in the spirit of internationalism'. While Corrie and Hurndall were both unarmed activists who had been killed by Israeli soldiers during pro-Palestinian protests in Gaza, Hanif was a British suicide bomber who murdered three people and injured fifty at Mike's Place bar in Tel Aviv in 2003.[6]

The problem for British supporters of Hamas is that jihadism does not respect national boundaries. It is, by definition, a global ideology that seeks to spread itself all over the world, and support for Hamas suicide bombings grows from the same soil as support for suicide bombings in Western countries. Muslim support for Hamas was part of a much broader support for jihadist movements that was expressed openly in the years before 9/11. In March 2001, the Muslim Council of Britain, which is generally seen as the largest leadership body of its type in British Muslim life, objected to a new law that banned, for the first time, membership of or support for a range of foreign terrorist organisations. The list included several jihadist groups including al-Qaeda, Hamas Izz ad-Din al-Qassam Brigades, Palestinian Islamic Jihad, the Kashmiri Harakat-ul-Mujahideen and others. These are 'legitimate resistance movements' that have been 'forced to adopt armed struggle', not terrorists, the Muslim Council of Britain claimed. This law was also opposed by Corbyn and the man who would become his shadow Chancellor, John McDonnell, both of whom voted against it in Parliament. The following month, Muslim Council of Britain secretary general Yousuf Bhailok led a delegation to a conference in Tehran in support of the Second Intifada. The heads of Hamas and Hezbollah were also there: Hezbollah secretary general Hassan Nasrallah called on Muslim countries to 'finish off the entire cancerous Zionist project which has been threatening our region for fifty years'. Bhailok was applauded for explaining that the MCB refused to take part in Britain's Holocaust Memorial Day commemorations. The conference pledged to 'revive' the United Nations' 1975 resolution defining Zionism as a form of racism. In August, Muslim journalist Faisal Bodi, writing in the *Guardian* newspaper, made his support for suicide bombing explicit: 'In the Muslim world, then, we celebrate what we call the martyr-bombers. To us they are heroes defending the things we hold sacred.'[7]

The connection between British Muslim support for Hamas and the global jihadists that kill their fellow citizens in Europe is evident in links between Britain's two Tel Aviv suicide bombers, Asif Mohammed Hanif and Omar Khan Sharif, and the 7/7 London Underground bombers. In 2001, Hanif and Sharif were trying to recruit young Muslims in Manchester with Mohammad Sidique Khan, who led the 2005 terrorist attack on the London Underground that killed fifty-two people and injured more than 770. That year, all three travelled to Afghanistan to train or fight in jihad; Khan before 9/11 and Hanif and Sharif afterwards. They all imbibed the same jihadist rhetoric from Britain's Islamist extremist organisations and leaders. This was a period when extremist preachers, including the hook-handed Abu Hamza al-Masri, his close associate Omar Bakri Mohammed who ran the extremist groups Hizb ut-Tahrir and then al-Muhajiroun, and the Jordanian al-Qaeda cleric Abu Qatada, used fiery sermons to encourage young British Muslims to aspire to jihad. All three have since been convicted of terrorism offences, or removed from the UK, or both, as a result of their extreme views and activities. There is little difference between what they were preaching and the language used by the Muslim Association of Britain's Azzam Tamimi to encourage support for Hamas. 'Do not call them suicide bombers, call them *shuhada* (martyrs) ... We love death, they love life,' Tamimi told a conference in 2003. Carrying out a suicide bombing for Palestine 'is the straight way to pleasing my God and I would do it if I had the opportunity', he told the BBC in 2004. 'If fighting for your home land [*sic*] is terrorism, I take pride in being a terrorist. The Koran tells me if I die for my homeland, I'm a martyr and I long to be a martyr,' he told students at London University's SOAS in 2010. Hanif and Sharif became suicide bombers for Hamas in Israel in 2003 and Khan became one for al-Qaeda in London two years later.[8]

By the time that Tonge and Honderich expressed their support for Palestinian suicide bombers, the fact that they targeted civilians was beyond dispute. In June 2001, a suicide bomber blew himself up next to a queue of teenagers outside the Dolphinarium nightclub in Tel Aviv, killing twenty. In August 2001, a suicide bomber from Palestinian Islamic Jihad killed fifteen (including seven children and a pregnant woman) at the Sbarro pizzeria in Jerusalem. Other attacks targeted buses and street markets. Given this violent context, leftist support for Hamas does British Muslims no favours; nevertheless, some on the left have even argued that Hamas and similar jihadist groups are actually part of the same broad political movement as the left itself. In 2009, when Jeremy Corbyn invited 'friends' from Hezbollah and Hamas to speak in Parliament, he said of Hamas: 'The idea that an organisation that is dedicated towards the good of the Palestinian people, and bringing about long-term peace and social justice and political justice in the whole region should be labelled as a terrorist organisation by the British government is really a big, big historical mistake.' According to American academic Judith Butler, 'Understanding Hamas/Hezbollah as social movements that are progressive, that are on the left, that are part of a global left, is extremely important. That does not stop us from being critical of certain dimensions of both movements.' Whereas leftist support for the PLO in the 1960s and 1970s could be justified by pointing to the PLO's largely secular character and the fact that it spoke the language of the global left, the idea that Hamas is a progressive, left-wing organisation dedicated to social justice stretches credulity. In the Hamas Covenant, written in 1988, Hamas describes itself in strictly Islamic terms:[9]

> The Movement's programme is Islam. From it, it draws its ideas, ways of thinking and understanding of the universe, life and man ... By adopting Islam as its way of life, the Movement goes back to the time of the birth of the Islamic message, of the righteous ancestor, for Allah is its target, the Prophet is its example and the Koran is its constitution ... The Islamic Resistance Movement welcomes every Moslem who embraces its faith, ideology, follows its programme, keeps its secrets, and wants to belong to its ranks and carry out the duty. Allah will certainly reward such one.[10]

In contrast, the 1968 Palestinian National Charter – in effect, the charter of the PLO – doesn't mention Islam or Muslims once, preferring instead to describe itself in the secular language of national liberation. There is another contrast between the Hamas Covenant and the PLO Charter that catches the eye: the Hamas Covenant is much more antisemitic. It even cites the *Protocols of the Elders of Zion,* an antisemitic hoax created by Tsarist secret police in pre-revolutionary Russia and used by antisemites ever since, to claim that Zionists manipulate other world powers:

> With their money they were able to control imperialistic countries and instigate them to colonize many countries in order to enable them to exploit their resources and spread corruption there ... It was they who instigated the replacement of the League of Nations with the United Nations and the Security Council to enable them to rule the world through them ... Their plan is embodied in the 'Protocols of the Elders of Zion', and their present conduct is the best proof of what we are saying.[11]

This language alone should prevent Hamas from being considered a progressive or left-wing organisation. The PLO Charter is hostile enough to Zionism, depicting it as racist, fascist and destined for destruction, but it doesn't rely on old antisemitic myths usually peddled by neo-Nazis and conspiracy cranks. Instead, it uses familiar New Left language to argue that Israel is a tool of larger world powers:

> Zionism is a political movement organically associated with international imperialism and antagonistic to all action for liberation and to progressive movements in the world. It is racist and fanatic in its nature, aggressive, expansionist, and colonial in its aims, and fascist in its methods. Israel is the instrument of the Zionist movement, and geographical base for world imperialism placed strategically in the midst of the Arab homeland to combat the hopes of the Arab nation for liberation, unity, and progress.[12]

This leftist identification with violent Islamist movements extends further than Hamas. In 2006, when Israel fought a bloody war with the Lebanese Shia organisation Hezbollah, anti-Israel demonstrators marched through London carrying placards that read 'We are all Hizbullah' [*sic*]. The wording is significant. It goes beyond sympathy or support with the Lebanese people to suggest political identification with Hezbollah as part of the same movement. It consciously echoes the words of support extended from Britain to the United States after the 9/11 attack, as if to say that where the governments of the UK and US share values, goals and interests – so those demonstrators in London shared values, goals and interests with Hezbollah. George Galloway, then the MP for Bethnal Green & Bow, drew huge cheers when he told the crowd:

> Hezbollah has never been a terrorist organisation ... I am here to glorify the Lebanese resistance, I am here to glorify

the leaders of the Lebanese resistance, Hezbollah, and I am
here to glorify the leader Sayyed Hassan Nasrallah ... victory
to the Lebanese resistance.[13]

In 1994, twelve years before Galloway spoke these words,
Hezbollah – working with its patron, Iran – had carried out
the worst massacre of Jews since the Second World War,
when eighty-five people were killed by a suicide bomber at
the AMIA Jewish Community centre in Buenos Aires. In 2001,
five years before British leftists declared 'We are all Hezbollah',
the Hezbollah TV channel Al-Manar invented the antisemitic
lie that 4,000 Israelis (or Jews) did not turn up for work at
the World Trade Center on 11 September 2001, because the
9/11 attacks were supposedly a secret Jewish or Zionist plot.
In 2002, Hezbollah leader Hassan Nasrallah gave a speech in
which he said it is good that Israel gathers all the world's Jews
in one place, because it saves Hezbollah 'from having to go to
the ends of the world' to kill them. It is not necessary to be
Jewish or to support Israel to find this language chilling or to
be alarmed by the readiness with which some on the British
left could identify with such an organisation.[14]

It sometimes seems as if opposition to the United States, to
Western power more broadly, and to Zionism, have become
defining values of progressive politics for many radical leftists.
By this logic, any movement that is fighting against America
or one of its allies is treated as progressive, irrespective of its

actual character. An article in the Socialist Workers Party journal *International Socialism* argued that anyone who supports Hamas is, by definition, more progressive than anyone who supports Israel: 'From the standpoint of Marxism and international socialism an illiterate, conservative, superstitious Muslim Palestinian peasant who supports Hamas is more progressive than an educated liberal atheist Israeli who supports Zionism (even critically).' Any attempt to identify the common values and goals that bind together Islamists and leftists struggles to get far beyond this foreign policy mixture of anti-Zionism, anti-Americanism and a vague hope that Islamism can be the latest movement to challenge the dominance of Western power. Foreign policy is a much easier arena for Islamists and leftists to find common ground than domestic politics, where standard left-wing views about homosexuality, gender equality and religious freedom make for a difficult fit with an Islamist agenda.'[15]

This alliance began as a pragmatic one, to avoid duplicating efforts in campaigns for the Palestinians and against the wars in Afghanistan and Iraq. It then became a proactive one, as Islamists and leftists saw advantages and benefits in working with each other. While the Labour Party had relied on votes from Asian communities for many years, the radical left had ignored the Muslim community, and particularly political Islamists, viewing them with suspicion as not only religious but also socially reactionary. 'The Islamists are not our allies,' wrote the Socialist Workers Party's Chris Harman in 1994, and they are not 'progressives'. However, he argued, Islamism is still a movement that seeks to overthrow the existing order and transform society, and this is something that socialists can exploit. 'When we do find ourselves on the same side as the Islamists, part of our job is to argue strongly with them, to challenge them,' and, where possible, to convert them to socialism. This typical Trotskyist opportunism turned out to be hopelessly optimistic. His warning that Islamists are not progressive clearly fell on deaf ears; if anything, it is Islamists that have had the greater influence over socialists, not the other way around.[16]

Those on the left who clung to this suspicion of Islamism were in the minority once the Stop the War Coalition began working with the Islamists of the Muslim Association of Britain. The Trotskyist group Alliance for Workers' Liberty (formerly Socialist Organiser, that had opposed the banning of Jewish Societies in the 1980s) objected to working with the Muslim Association of Britain due to its links to the Muslim Brotherhood, and suggested that the left should be working with secular, progressive Muslim groups instead. The *Weekly Worker* newspaper took a similar stand, pointing out in one article that

> At the same time as our secularist and Marxist comrades are
> being murdered by groups allied to the MAB, we are lining

ourselves up as co-sponsors of demonstrations. This is like communists lining up with Nazi sympathisers on demonstrations during World War II, because we are both against British imperialism.

There were also Islamists who objected not just to working with the left, but also to the very idea of engaging with democratic politics. Muhammad al-Massari, a Saudi Islamist living in London, argued that by giving primacy to the will of the people, democracy stands in direct contradiction to the Islamic belief that Allah is the ultimate source of authority. The radical Islamist group Hizb ut-Tahrir objected to any Muslims marching under a Stop the War Coalition banner, because

> It is clear that many of the heads of the Stop the War campaign are atheists, communists, anarchists and believers in sexual freedoms. These are people who believe that Allah does not exist, that the Prophet Muhammad was an impostor, and that religions such as Islam are barbaric, oppress women, forbid sexual expression and remain as the 'opium of the masses'.[17]

Despite these objections, many more people were excited by the possibilities offered by a left-Islamist alliance than were opposed to it. This has involved some compromises on both sides. Lindsey German, when challenged on the attitude of

Islamists to homosexuality, told a Socialist Workers Party conference that 'I'm in favour of defending gay rights, but I am not prepared to have it as a shibboleth.' The Muslim Association of Britain refused to actually affiliate to the Stop the War Coalition, fearing (rightly) that it would be dominated by the leftists who ran it, but agreed to work with it as long as it would provide 'gender-segregated spaces and halal food' at meetings. Andrew Murray, the Stop the War Coalition's first chair, found the prospect of gender-segregated meetings 'uncomfortable' but agreed to it as a way of allowing Muslim women to take part. For their part, the Muslim Association of Britain said it 'could overcome misgivings' about sharing platforms with 'socialists and atheists' as long as 'Zionists and Israelis' were not involved. That would be a compromise too far.[18]

The left's support for Palestine was part of the mindset of this anti-war movement from its beginning. At the founding meeting of the Stop the War Coalition, held in London ten days after 9/11, a large banner reading 'Campaign for Palestinian Rights: Stop Israel's War Crimes' hung from a balcony. The coalition had organised a demonstration outside the Israeli embassy even before it began working with the Muslim Association of Britain. It did not take a formal position on whether the Israeli–Palestinian conflict should be settled by one state or two, but the Muslim Association of Britain's opposition to Israel's existence was clear and the chant 'Palestine must be free, from the river to the sea' – in other words, replacing Israel in its entirety

– has become common on pro-Palestinian demonstrations. The linkage of Palestine and Iraq became firmly embedded in the Stop the War Coalition's activities despite a request from the Board of Deputies of British Jews for it to drop the Palestine issue. The Board of Deputies argued that it would deter Jews from supporting the anti-war movement and might encourage a backlash against Jews in Britain. They were also aware of reports of antisemitism on anti-war demonstrations. After the first joint demonstration co-organised by the Stop the War Coalition and the Muslim Association of Britain in September 2002, a group of Jewish leftists, all opponents of the war and supporters of Palestinian statehood, wrote to *The Guardian* to complain about 'hate-filled chanting and images in which anti-Israel and anti-Jewish imagery were blurred'. The Stop the War Coalition dismissed the board's request but did try to limit such chanting on future marches. It didn't help that some prominent opponents of the war made a direct connection between Israeli policy and British Jews. The *Morning Star* published an article by Azzam Tamimi that warned 'the end of US imperialism … will be very bad news for Israel and the Jewish lobbies that support them in the US and Europe'. A column by John Pilger in the *New Statesman* blamed Israel for causing the 2004 Madrid train bombings and for being 'the guiding hand' behind American foreign policy, then smoothly drew 'middle-class Jewish homes in Britain' into the circle of 'destructive' Zionist complicity.[19]

For the Islamists in this alliance, Palestine, not Iraq, was always the priority, even to the extent that the Muslim Association of Britain and the Stop the War Coalition put their two slogans, 'Freedom for Palestine' and 'Stop the war in Iraq', in a different order on their respective leaflets for joint demonstrations. There was also a level of open antisemitism in Islamist campaigning that would make most leftists blush. The ubiquity of swastikas and comparisons of Israel to Nazi Germany on Islamist placards was a visceral example. In October 2000, shortly after the Second Intifada began, a Muslim Association of Britain newsletter called *New Dawn* reproduced a notorious antisemitic hoax, called 'The Jewish Threat on the American Society', that is supposedly based on a speech by Benjamin Franklin but was in fact written in the 1930s by an American fascist called William Dudley Pelley. Another leaflet distributed in London that month with the contact details of a UK-based Islamist organisation claimed that 'the Zionist occupiers' had used 'their financial control of the international media' to suppress information about Israeli crimes. Qaradawi himself, five years after meeting Livingstone, was reported to have said that the Holocaust was 'divine punishment' for the Jews.[20]

In this alliance, anger over Palestine is treated as both understandable and justified, whatever the consequences. During a three-week conflict between Israel and Hamas in Gaza in January 2009, a series of protests outside the Israeli embassy in London, organised by the Stop the War Coalition, Palestine Solidarity Campaign and other groups, resulted in scenes of violent disorder that left over fifty police officers injured and caused extensive damage to nearby shops. A branch of Starbucks was singled out for vandalism because some of the protestors believed that Starbucks gives money to Israel. After a lengthy evidence-gathering process by the police, over 100 people were arrested, most of whom were young Muslim men. Many were convicted of a variety of offences and around two dozen were imprisoned. The organisers of the demonstrations showed no contrition for the crimes committed at their protests: on the contrary, they declared the prosecutions to be an affront to justice and a threat to democratic protest. Public meetings were held, petitions signed and further demonstrations organised. Jeremy Corbyn was one of the leading voices in this campaign. 'People get angry,' he told a meeting in London in 2010:

> ... and the events that happened at the end of the demonstration were an expression of anger about what was happening in Gaza by a lot of very young people, many of whom were on their first ever demonstration, who wanted to express their anger. The sentences they have suffered as a result of it are absolutely appalling ... So what I'm supporting is a call for a judicial inquiry into the whole process surrounding that demonstration, surrounding the charging, surrounding the

convictions, so that we can re-open all of the cases, because
it seems to me that there's an injustice going on here that is
actually very unfair against some of the young people who've
been put into prison sentences, essentially for attending a
demonstration. The purpose behind this, I believe, is to try
to deter anyone from going on demonstrations.[21]

A support meeting for the imprisoned demonstrators in
Parliament issued a set of demands that included the release
of those imprisoned, dropping all further charges, to 'end the
criminalisation of the Muslim community' and to 'defend the
right to peacefully demonstrate'. Seumas Milne, writing in
The Guardian, claimed the sentences were motivated by a racist desire to deter Muslims from getting involved in politics.
Neither Milne nor Corbyn, nor the Stop the War Coalition
nor the Palestine Solidarity Campaign, appeared to consider
that they have a responsibility to channel young Muslims away
from illegal protests. Nor did they acknowledge, publicly at
least, the impact that the violent demonstrations may have had
on the mood of London's Jews.[22]

The relationship between leftists and Islamists brought
practical benefits beyond the numbers that could now be
mobilised for demonstrations. Muhammad Sawalha, a director of the Muslim Association of Britain, set up a new company
called Islam Expo that hosted a large festival and cultural
event at London's Alexandra Palace in 2006. Sawalha is a

former Hamas activist who came to the UK in the 1990s and, according to BBC's *Panorama*, is alleged to have distributed funds to Hamas's armed wing from exile in London. His fellow directors of Islam Expo were all connected to the Muslim Brotherhood, including the Muslim Association of Britain's Azzam Tamimi and Anas Altikriti. Islam Expo attracted thousands of people, Muslim and not, as well as national media coverage. It was paid for partly by a grant of £200,000 from the Greater London Authority, then under the mayoralty of Ken Livingstone. The rest of the funding came from Qatar. Two years later, Altikriti and Tamimi set up 'Muslims4Ken' to campaign for Livingstone in the 2008 mayoral election. Its website described his Conservative opponent, Boris Johnson, as 'an Islamophobe who has insulted and condemned Islam and Muslims'. Johnson won the election, but Altikriti claimed that their campaign had still managed to boost Livingstone's vote.[23]

At a more ideological level, the Israeli–Palestinian conflict is seen as the exemplar of the global struggle that the anti-war movement thinks it is fighting. In a world divided by left-wing typology into a wealthy, aquisitive, imperialist North and a poor, occupied and exploited South, Israel/Palestine is a frontier where these two blocs meet. According to a 2001 article in *New Left Review*, 'Israel is part of the North, backed up by the Northern superpower; while the Palestinians are the quintessential poor and dispossessed Southerners.' This frontier, it went on, is where violent jihad is at its most popular and potent amongst Muslim masses, for whom religious movements 'have come to replace many socialist movements as self-proclaimed resistors of imperialism'. The suggestion is that the Israeli–Palestinian conflict is not a relatively small national dispute over land but is in fact a symbol of Western oppression of what used to be called the Third World, and is now called the Global South. According to this theory, European colonialism has been replaced by American cultural, financial and military imperialism – with Israel seen by many on the left as a Western colony that now enjoys more American support than any other of its client states. One consequence of this reading of world affairs is that some leftists view Hamas as part of a progressive struggle that needs their support.[24]

The international arm of this alliance was forged at a series of conferences held in Egypt between 2002 and 2007. Called the Cairo Anti-war Conference, this international network brought together leftists, Islamists and Arab Nationalists in a broad anti-American and anti-Zionist front. The Stop the War Coalition was heavily involved from the beginning and John Rees (then a leading activist in both the Stop the War Coalition and the Socialist Workers Party) was appointed its European vice-president at the first Cairo Anti-war Conference, held in December 2002. There have been large British delegations of anti-war activists at all five conferences. Rees and George Galloway have attended most of them while Corbyn and

Tony Benn MP were at the second, in December 2003. Rees felt the conferences were an invaluable opportunity to meet people from groups that are considered extremists, or even terrorists, in Britain, saying, 'Where else can you sit down in a single evening and listen to senior people from Hamas, Hezbollah, the Muslim Brotherhood, people from the revolutionarly [sic] left and people from the anti-war movement around the globe?' The conferences reflected this radical, jihadist input. Successive conference declarations stated their opposition to American capitalism and democracy, endorsed the right of Palestinians and Iraqis to resist occupation by all means, including 'military struggle', and rejected 'the legitimacy of the racist Zionist entity'. The declaration of the second Cairo Anti-war Conference connected Iraq and Palestine via the conspiracy theory that the Iraq War was 'part of the Zionist plan, which targets the establishment of the greater State of Israel from the Nile to the Euphrates'. This declaration, like all the others, was adopted by the Stop the War Coalition. Conspiracy theories of this nature are easily found in the politics of this new alliance.[25]

The formative role of anti-Zionism in the anti-war movement is important because the anti-war movement played an important role in ushering Jeremy Corbyn to the leadership of the Labour Party. Corbyn was centrally involved in the Stop the War Coalition from its beginning. He spoke at its founding meeting and at many others around the country, helping to build support, and was its chair from 2011 to 2015. When the Blair government produced its case for going to war in Iraq prior to the parliamentary vote – what opponents called the 'dodgy dossier' – Corbyn was the Member of Parliament who went through it point by point for the Stop the War Coalition to help them build their rebuttal. Undoing the work of New Labour was always a strategic goal for the leaders of the Stop the War Coalition. Lindsey German of the Socialist Workers Party and Andrew Murray of the Communist Party of Britain were the two most important leaders of the Stop the War Coalition in its early years and both expressed the hope that it would transform the left as a whole. As early as 2003, German claimed in the *Socialist Worker* newspaper that 'The anti-war movement marks a new politics in Britain and has created an atmosphere in which socialists can build.' Faced with the question of whether this new socialist future could be constructed inside or outside the Labour Party, German plumped for the latter and, with her Socialist Workers Party comrade John Rees and George Galloway (who had been expelled by Labour for his comments about the war in Iraq), set up the Respect Party. This was an electoral vehicle for the left–Islamist alliance that had mobilised so many people to demonstrate against the war, but it failed to convert that support into political power. While Respect's economic and social policies were largely left-wing, it explicitly targeted Muslim voters through the priority and emphasis it gave its positions on Palestine and Iraq. Galloway described Respect as a party for 'all those people who are against imperialism, against Zionism and against globalization', and said that in the 2005 general election he would stand in a seat 'where we're strong and the Member of Parliament is a pro-war, pro-Israel activist'. His choice was Bethnal Green & Bow, then held by Labour MP Oona King, who was partly Jewish and had voted for the war in Iraq. Galloway defeated her in a bitter campaign that left King complaining of anti-semitism. He lost the seat five years later, returned to Parliament by winning a by-election in Bradford West in 2012, and was then defeated once more by Labour's Naz Shah in 2015.[26]

Andrew Murray, the other leader of the Stop the War Coalition alongside German, was prevented from joining Respect by a vote of the Communist Party Executive in 2003. This turned out to be a blessing in disguise for Murray: for while Respect has failed as a political project, the real prize of the Labour Party leadership has fallen into the left's lap. Murray is the only person other than Corbyn to have chaired the Stop the War Coalition, having held that position from 2001 to 2011. He then became Chief of Staff at the trade union Unite, which gave crucial support to Corbyn during his leadership campaign, and returned to the post of Stop the War Coalition chair when Corbyn stepped down in 2015. For Murray, Corbyn's path to victory in the Labour leadership election 'began on February 15, 2003 when he addressed the two million people who marched in London against the Iraq War'. Murray is adamant that anger about the war in Iraq is what helped to unite and mobilise the left, and that the Stop the War Coalition gave it organisational shape and focus. There is much truth in this. Corbyn's victory was not the result of a long-term plan or conspiracy, and there were many other factors that played a role in making it possible and bringing it to pass. But his election fulfilled a prediction made by Murray in October 2001, shortly after the Stop the War Coalition was created:

> In fighting for peace, and against imperialism, we are also fighting for our own future and our own freedom. By defeating New Labour and the class interests which it serves, we will also be opening up our own road to Socialism, and to a world in which the peoples of British [sic], like peoples everywhere, can flourish in peace.[27]

Murray argues that Corbyn's victory and the accompanying surge in new members of the Labour Party is rooted in new forms of radical left-wing politics, particularly the anti-war movement. This is true both in terms of political sentiment and the actual organisation of Corbyn's campaign: the Stop the War Coalition made its email lists available for Corbyn's team, as did the Palestine Solidarity Campaign and other groups from a similar part of the political spectrum. The Stop the War Coalition's Carmel Nolan became Corbyn's press officer, while the Palestine Solidarity Campaign's Ben Soffa drove his online and social media campaigning. In their history of the Stop the War Coalition (written in 2005), Murray and German claimed that although they failed to stop the war, they had success-fully transformed British politics by uniting the left and putting 'anti-imperialism ... at the heart of left-wing politics in Britain for the first time'. Not just anti-imperialism, but anti-Zionism too. Both have made their way to the heart of the Labour Party, for so long Britain's most pro-Israel political party, under a new leadership that views Zionism as a hostile, discriminatory ide-ology and Hamas as a progressive movement. It has also made antisemitism a national political issue in Britain for the first time in a generation.[28]

CHAPTER SIX

ANTISEMITISM, THE HOLOCAUST AND THE LEFT

The problem of antisemitism in left-wing politics became front-page news in Britain in April 2016, when Labour MP Naz Shah was suspended for alleged antisemitism due to a series of posts she had put on Facebook nearly two years earlier. One of her posts suggested that Israel should be 'relocated' to the United States; another called on her supporters to vote in an online poll about Israel and Gaza because 'the Jews are rallying to the poll'. As if the suspension of a Labour MP was not bad enough, Shah was soon followed by Ken Livingstone, when, in trying to defend her, he told an interviewer on BBC radio: 'Let's remember when Hitler won his election in 1932, his policy then was that Jews should be moved to Israel. He was supporting Zionism – this before he went mad and ended up killing six million Jews.' Livingstone's claim that Hitler supported Zionism turned a problem into a full-blown political crisis. Livingstone – one of the most recognised politicians in the country, Labour's former Mayor of London, a member of the party's National Executive Committee and a long-standing colleague of Jeremy Corbyn's on the Labour left – was suspended within hours.[1]

Three days later, Corbyn was due to speak at London's May Day rally, an annual left-wing event to mark International Workers' Day. The calls from inside and outside the Labour Party for him to condemn antisemitism, to show clear and decisive leadership on the issue that had gripped his party, were irresistible. Corbyn took the opportunity to do so, but the way he did it, the words he used and the political context he gave to antisemitism revealed much about why so many left-wing people struggle to comprehend modern antisemitism. Addressing the marchers before they set off from Clerkenwell Green, a traditional site for radical protests, Corbyn said:

> We also have to stand up against racism in any form whatsoever in our society. We've stood in this green and Trafalgar Square and many other places, against apartheid South Africa. Eventually apartheid South Africa was defeated. We stood in solidarity with many in the USA, fighting for civil rights during the '60s and '70s. We stand in solidarity now against the growth of the far right across Europe, that are more interested in blaming migrant workers, blaming victims of war who are refugees, than facing up to the reality that we're all

human beings living on one planet, and you solve problems by human rights, humanity and justice and respect, not by blaming minorities. And so we stand absolutely against antisemitism in any form. We stand absolutely against racism in any form. We stand united as a Labour movement, recognising our faith diversity, our ethnic diversity, and from that diversity comes our strength. That is the strength of our movement.

This is Jeremy Corbyn's understanding of antisemitism. He sees it only as a far-right phenomenon: part of a broader xenophobic politics that is against diversity and stigmatises refugees and minorities. He opposes it because he opposes fascism, and as part of his internationalist politics that opposed apartheid and racial inequality overseas. During a husting for the 2015 Labour leadership campaign at the JW3 Jewish community centre in London, Corbyn answered a question about antisemitism by mentioning that his mother was at Cable Street in the East End of London in 1936, when local Jews, Communists, dockers and others prevented a march by Oswald Mosley's fascist Blackshirts. This is commendable – but it isn't necessarily relevant. Describing antisemitism in this way suggests that those Labour members who have been suspended or expelled for alleged antisemitism were guilty of parroting political ideas and language that were alien to the left. It implies that a growing list of people suspended from the party, including the former Mayors of London, Bradford and Blackburn, and councillors from Luton, Nottingham, Burnley, Newport and Renfrewshire, held views that would have been more at home in the British National Party than in the Labour Party. If Corbyn is right, then these individual cases were anomalies from which there is little to learn about left-wing attitudes to Jews or Zionism.

Corbyn's narrow understanding of antisemitism being part of fascism is common across much of the left. It often comes with the logical, but false, assumption that because people on the left are opposed to fascism and racism, they cannot say or do antisemitic things. The *Morning Star* denied that either Shah's or Livingstone's comments were antisemitic on the basis that the left is anti-fascist. George Galloway argued that leftists, by definition, cannot be antisemitic, because antisemitism is a right-wing condition. Writing in the *American Herald Tribune* shortly after Shah's suspension, Galloway explained that 'Anti-Semitism is a right-wing "nationalist" curse which deems, for example, British Jews as not British at all but aliens'. Corbyn and his shadow Chancellor John McDonnell cannot possibly be antisemitic, he went on, because 'McDonnell is a former Trotskyite. Trotsky was a Jew. Both men are influenced by Karl Marx. Marx was a Jew. Both men are anti-racist as an article of faith. They have spent their lives fighting racism in all its forms. Given their politics, how could it possibly be otherwise?'[2]

Despite this, few of the alleged cases of antisemitism in the Labour Party in 2016 involved people who could be mistaken for fascists. There are other forms of antisemitism to which many on the left appear oblivious, one of which appeared directly before Corbyn when he made his May Day speech. The audience that stood and listened to the Labour Party leader that day included marchers carrying banners with images of Joseph Stalin. In the late 1940s, Stalin crushed Jewish political and cultural activity in the Soviet Union. In the early 1950s, he oversaw antisemitic purges of Jewish Communist Party figures in the Soviet Union and its satellite states in Eastern Europe. These purges were not just antisemitic because they targeted Jews in the local Communist parties; they also used explicitly anti-Jewish language and antisemitic conspiracy theories in their prosecution. It is likely that Stalin's death in 1953 prevented the mass round-up and deportation of Soviet Jews that was being planned. Anybody who truly stands against antisemitism 'in any form' ought to recognise that Stalin was an antisemite, but if Corbyn was aware of this contradiction when he made his May Day speech, he didn't show it.

It is precisely because people on the left think and act as anti-fascists and anti-racists that they have such a problem recognising modern antisemitism. This is a paradox that takes some explaining. Parts of the left have always struggled to understand the importance of antisemitism within fascism and Nazism. This was the case before the Holocaust, and even afterwards it was argued that the Nazi genocide was primarily an extreme manifestation of capitalism, racism or imperialism.

More recently, it has become popular on the left to see the Holocaust as part of a pattern of genocides in the history of European colonialism rather than the culmination of European antisemitism. These are 'little family quarrels' between European whites, Frantz Fanon wrote in *Black Skin, White Masks*, and not the same as racism against black people. Tony Greenstein complained that, 'For over forty years, Zionism has had a monopoly on the history of the Holocaust and its interpretation ... for socialists the Holocaust is but one example of imperialism's genocidal character.' Whether the Holocaust is seen as a consequence of capitalism or of colonialism, the antisemitism at its heart can sometimes be downplayed.[3]

This may be related to the fact that the left has its own tradition of antisemitism that dates back to socialism's formative years in the late nineteenth century. During that period, when socialist and Marxist thinkers were developing the left's core critique of capitalism and international finance, a strand of thinking emerged that drew on existing antisemitic conspiracy theories associating Jews with capitalism. According to this way of thinking, the working classes were not just oppressed by the concentration of financial power in the hands of a rich few; these rich few were predominantly Jewish, and it was a specifically Jewish network of power and wealth that needed to be broken. At the same time, a similar process was happening in reverse amongst antisemitic theorists, who developed a specifically left-wing version of those same antisemitic conspiracy theories. The term 'anti-Semitism' was invented as a political label in 1878 by Wilhelm Marr, who had a background in radical, pro-democracy politics in Germany at the time. Marr came up with the name 'anti-Semitism' because he did not want to be associated with older religious prejudice towards Jews, which he considered to be irrational and reactionary. Instead, he came to believe that social emancipation for all Germans required Germany to be freed from Jewish influence. Marr didn't have much success with this amongst his fellow leftists. Despite his belief that antisemitism and radical democratic politics suited each other, his fellow radicals in Hamburg disagreed and rejected his new, anti-Jewish outlook. Marr discovered what other antisemites from the left have encountered in the decades since: most left-wing people are not antisemitic and, overall, the left's history of opposing antisemitism outweighs its history of indulging it.

What Marr tapped into, though, is that the left has its own specific forms of antisemitism that are not fascist or xenophobic, but are a distorted reading of the left's own commitment to freedom and emancipation. This antisemitic version of left-wing politics is what led German social democrat August Bebel to warn against a 'socialism of fools'. It feeds on the fact that antisemitism differs from other forms of racism because it uses conspiracy theories to claim that Jews are a powerful, controlling influence in society. Whereas racism tends to depict non-white people as dirty, poor, diseased and even subhuman, antisemitism accords Jews massive power, wealth, political influence and media control (Nazism did both, by comparing Jews to rats and vermin while also claiming that there was a global Jewish conspiracy). Antisemitism promises to be a liberating politics that can free the world from the hidden hand of Jewish power. Socialism claims the same thing, but with global capital as its nebulous foe.

Sometimes, particularly at moments of conflict and stress in society, these two worldviews combine to produce an eruption of antisemitism within the left. In Britain at the end of the Victorian era, left-wing and liberal opposition to the Second Boer War merged opposition to imperialism with precisely this kind of socialist antisemitism through talk of 'Jew financiers' being behind a 'Jew Capitalist war'. The leading advocate of this strand of left-wing antisemitism in the last decade of Victorian England was Henry Hyndman, the founder of the Social Democratic Federation. He repeatedly used antisemitic language, sometimes crude and at other times sinister, to identify Jews as enemies of the working classes. In an 1896 essay titled 'Imperialist Judaism in Africa' that eerily anticipated Soviet and Egyptian anti-Zionist propaganda of the 1960s and 1970s, Hyndman warned that Jewish business interests were planning 'an Anglo-Hebraic empire stretching from Egypt to Cape Colony and from Breira to Sierra Leone'. When the war began in 1899, this antisemitic critique became prominent on the left. The Trades Union Congress in 1900 passed a resolution decrying the war as one 'to secure the gold fields of South Africa for cosmopolitan Jews, most of whom had no patriotism and no country'. Even Keir Hardie wrote in *Labour Leader*, the newspaper of his Independent Labour Party, that 'modern imperialism is really run by half a dozen financial houses, many of them Jewish, to whom politics is a counter in the game of buying and selling securities'.[4]

This is an example of how antisemitism can feed parasitically off left-wing politics and drag the left away from its core values. There are also some authentic left-wing ideas that can have troubling consequences for Jews. Marxist theory has never been comfortable with the idea that Jews form a nation or that Zionism is an authentic movement of national liberation. Karl Marx's 1843 essay *Zur Judenfrage* (*On the Jewish Question*) set out the Marxist view of Jews and Judaism that has changed little in its fundamentals since then. Marx argued that Jews are not a real, authentic people, but a 'chimerical' people defined by money, business and commerce. 'What is the worldly religion of the Jew? Huckstering. What is his worldly God? Money,' he wrote. Marx wrote this essay in response to a German philosopher, Bruno Bauer, who thought Jews should be forced to give up their Judaism in return for full emancipation. Marx disagreed with Bauer, but said that Jews would disappear anyway once their capitalist activities had been removed from society. His essay concluded: 'Once society has succeeded in abolishing the empirical essence of Judaism

– huckstering and its preconditions – the Jew will have become impossible … The social emancipation of the Jew is the emancipation of society from Judaism.' Marx's other writings about Jews were peppered with hostile and pejorative language. He found Judaism 'repugnant' and rarely condemned anti-semitism, even after extensive pogroms in Russia in 1881. His ideas provided a Marxist tradition for understanding Jews and Judaism that has endured through the writings of others, most recently Abram Leon's *The Jewish Question* that was described in Chapter Three. Stalin described the Jews as 'a nation whose future is denied and whose existence has still to be proved'. In Russia, Zionism and Marxism developed in parallel in the decades before the Russian Revolution of 1917 and were rivals for the support of Russian Jews. Zionism was depicted by Russian Marxists as counter-revolutionary, as it took Jews away from the class struggle. Lenin himself only ever wrote about Zionism within the Russian context, never addressing its concrete development in Palestine. It is not difficult to see how this older Marxist denial of Jewish collective identity dovetailed with the more recent New Left argument that Zionism is not an authentic national movement, and Israel is not a legitimate nation state. The Marxist idea that Jews are not a genuine people and ought to wither away as history progresses is clearly not one that most Jews would welcome.[5]

These traditions in left-wing thought about Jews provide the ground for antisemitic ideas to take root and flourish. The left's instinctive anti-racism ought to prevent this from happening – and often it does – but this protection has been weakened because Jews and antisemitism have been gradually squeezed out of popular understandings of what racism is. This might seem strange given the role of racism and racial theories in Nazi antisemitism. It happened because, from the 1950s onwards, the idea that racism is exclusively about skin colour spread as a consequence of the arrival in Britain of large numbers of non-white immigrants from Britain's colonies and former colonies in the Caribbean, South Asia and East Africa. Political and public debate came to treat non-white immigration and racial discrimination in Britain as two parts of the same policy issue, with legislation on both appearing in parallel throughout the 1960s and 1970s. One reason for this was because it was feared and expected that excess numbers and concentrations of immigrants would provoke hostile responses from the indigenous population. The broader framework that joined these two issues of immigration and racial discrimination together was the disintegration of Britain's empire overseas. Most of the new immigrants to Britain came from British colonies or former colonies and political considerations in Britain's remaining colonies directly influenced the British government's approach to immigration controls. Whereas in the United States race relations are a direct legacy of slavery and the civil rights movement, in the United Kingdom decolonisation, immigration and domestic race relations were entwined as part of the same, overarching problem. Race became one of the animating ideas of the New Left and anti-racism emerged as a political idea in its own right, but it didn't just relate to racism and anti-racism in Britain: from the very beginning it incorporated attitudes to colonialism and immigration.

The politics of anti-racism follows this path. According to this political idea, racism is defined by colour and is not simply a matter of prejudice: it is the consequence of prejudice plus power, and can be found in society's structures of power and inequality. Domestically, this might include immigration restrictions, unequal access to housing or employment, or, more recently, anti-terrorism legislation and counter-extremist policies that disproportionately affect British Muslims. Globally, it would include Britain's imperial legacy in its former colonies, the economic and financial policies of global institutions like the International Monetary Fund, or Western military interventions overseas. Anti-racism, accordingly, is not just about opposing prejudice, but about resisting the power structures that impose and encourage discrimination and inequality between racial or ethnic groups. The Institute of Race Relations, originally a liberal organisation taken over by radical leftists from amongst its own staff in the early 1970s, epitomises this view of racism. It defines racism as 'an act or system of discrimination, oppression or exploitation', which it distinguishes from prejudiced opinions and ideas. Its regular 'Calendar of racism and resistance' focuses on what it argues is state or institutional racism, such as asylum and immigration policy or discrimination in education and employment, as well as racist violence and the extreme right. Racism is the exercise of prejudice via concrete discrimination. In this view, those who have power cannot be victims of racism and those without power cannot be racist.[6]

Antisemitism in today's Britain does not fit with this understanding of racism. Official and popular histories of race relations in Britain begin with post-war Commonwealth immigration, excluding previous immigrant groups – such as Jews – from this history. While the arrival of the *Empire Windrush* in 1948 bearing immigrants from the Caribbean is now seen as a landmark in the development of modern Britain, nobody remembers the names of the ships that brought around 150,000 Jews from Russia and Eastern Europe to Britain between 1880 and 1914. At that time, Jews were widely viewed in racialised terms as non-white and culturally alien to Britain. In the 1930s, Jewish immigration to Britain from Nazi-occupied Europe was limited due to fears that large-scale immigration would trigger a rise in antisemitism in Britain: a similar attitude to that evidenced during the 1960s in relation to Commonwealth immigration. But by the time the post-war race relations debate took shape, and as the political idea of anti-racism became a defining part of left-wing politics, Jews were increasingly seen as white, integrated, relatively wealthy and not suffering social or economic exclusion. Fanon condemned antisemitism but also argued that it is not the same as racism because the Jew 'is a white man' and can hide in the European crowd. During the same period, the New Left was developing its critique of Israel as a powerful, white, Western nation, born of colonialism and oppressing a people of colour – the Palestinians. This meant that Israel, Zionism and Jews all fell on the wrong side of the new anti-racist politics. It is why historian Gil Troy described the 1975 United Nations vote to declare Zionism a form of racism as 'the blackening of the Palestinians and the whitening of Israelis'. As Jewish students found in the 1970s, it is a short but dangerous leap from this to conclude that Israel's Diaspora Jewish supporters are part of a global network of racism.[7]

The relative places that Muslims and Jews have in this anti-racist binary, and the general anti-Western orientation of Islamist political movements, mean that many on the left find it difficult to recognise antisemitism when it comes from Islamist or jihadist actors. In March 2012, after the jihadist Mohamed Merah shot dead three Jewish children and a teacher at a Jewish school in Toulouse, the Stop the War Coalition published an article by Lindsey German that blamed the shooting on racism against French Muslims and the legacy of French colonialism in Algeria. The article did not mention antisemitism. When Jeremy Corbyn described Hamas as 'friends' and as an organisation dedicated to 'long-term peace and social justice and political justice' in the Middle

East, he was speaking at a Stop the War Coalition meeting alongside Dyab Abou Jahjah, a Belgian Hezbollah supporter who had previously posted Holocaust denial cartoons on his website (for which he was eventually convicted and fined by a Dutch court). The Board of Deputies of British Jews had written to the Home Secretary to complain about Abou Jahjah's presence in the United Kingdom. Corbyn's response to these complaints was to tell the meeting that 'I refuse to be dragged into this stuff that somehow or other because we're pro-Palestinian, we're antisemitic. It's a nonsense.' As faith has come to rival colour as the primary identity of some in Britain, so the perceived power disparity between white and black has been transposed onto religions. In 2006, John Rees, then a leading figure in the Socialist Workers Party and the Respect Party, was quoted as saying:

> There are some religions that are overwhelmingly held by the poor and excluded and there are some religions that back up the establishment, the rich and the powerful. So when the rich and the powerful attack the religion of the poor and excluded, then everyone should know what side they are on.

If these are the factors by which some on the left decide which 'side they are on' between Muslims and Jews – both defined in homogeneous ways – it is no wonder that some fail to properly recognise and condemn Islamist antisemitism.[8]

In recent years the idea has taken hold that Jews have not just been removed from the anti-racist landscape but have been actively replaced by Muslims, and that antisemitism has been succeeded by Islamophobia as Europe's prejudice *du jour*. 'It's open season on Islam – Muslims are the new Jews,' columnist India Knight wrote in the *Sunday Times*. 'Today the new Jews of Europe are Muslims ... We are today's despised "other", blamed for all the ills of the world which is still largely controlled by Christians,' according to Yasmin Alibhai-Brown. Kevin Ovenden, a former aide to George Galloway, who has been a prominent activist in both the Socialist Workers Party and the Respect Party, wrote in the *Morning Star* that 'Islamophobia is the Jewish question of our day. It is not simply one reactionary idea among many ... It plays a particular corrupting role across politics and society as a whole.'[9]

Some have taken this idea a step further, combined it with the notion that Israel and its supporters are part of the West's structures of racist power and influence, and argue that Zionist organisations and funders are partly responsible for a rise in anti-Muslim prejudice in Europe. The Spinwatch organisation, a campaigning group run by a sociology professor at Bath University, claims to have identified Islamophobic networks 'funded by wealthy businessmen and financiers, and conservative and pro-Israel trusts and foundations'. By creating 'a transatlantic alliance between anti-Islam groups and those unconditionally supportive of Zionism', Spinwatch argues, 'the Islamophobia network has successfully tapped into the financial and political resources of the Israel lobby'. From Jews being the ultimate victims of European racism in the twentieth century, now Zionists stand accused of being behind what is seen by many on the left as the primary form of racism in the twenty-first.[10]

The insistence that Jews and Israelis cannot be victims of racist behaviour at the hands of left-wing pro-Palestine campaigners sometimes runs into problems with the law. In 2011, a student at St Andrews University called Paul Donnachie was convicted of a racially aggravated offence after a late-night incident involving a Jewish student called Chanan Reitblat, who had an Israeli flag on his bedroom wall. According to a report from the Scottish Council of Jewish Communities, Donnachie and a friend, Samuel Colchester, both of whom were drunk, entered Reitblat's room:

> Donnachie then launched into a tirade of expletives about Israel, and calling Chanan a 'terrorist', wiped his hand on his genitals and then onto what he called a 'terrorist flag', and then went out into the hallway in the halls of residence shouting about Israel being 'terrorists, an illegitimate state, and Nazis', disturbing other students. The court also heard that Colchester jumped on Chanan in his bed, and urinated around the room, including on his toothbrush.

Donnachie, who was a member of the Scottish Palestine Solidarity Campaign, was convicted of 'acting in a racially aggravated manner which caused distress or alarm' and expelled from the university. His offence was racially aggravated because national groups are protected under British laws against racial hatred. This was a case of illegal, racist harassment against Israel as a nationality, rather than antisemitism against Jews. Members of the Scottish Palestine Solidarity Campaign supported Donnachie in court, campaigned in his defence and raised money for an appeal (which Donnachie lost). Even the conviction of one of their own for a racist offence was not enough for them to rethink their political assumptions. 'This is a ridiculous conviction,' Donnachie said afterwards. 'I'm a member of anti-racism campaigns, and I am devastated that as someone who has fought against racism I have been tarnished in this way.'[11]

When Tony Blair's New Labour government joined the American-led invasion of Iraq in 2003, the idea that the war was devised by pro-Israeli, mainly Jewish, lobbyists and politicians in Washington DC, and that American Middle East policy had been hijacked by a Jewish or Zionist clique, became common in left-wing and liberal opinion. The combination of anti-imperialism, anti-Zionism and opposition to American power produced an antisemitic conspiracy theory that was much more widespread and potent than its predecessor during the Second Boer War. It even spilled over from the anti-war movement and left-wing publications into the mainstream media. An article in *The Guardian* described neo-conservatism, an ideological position within American Republican politics followed by many supporters of the war, as 'Trotsky's theory of permanent revolution mingled with the far-right Likud strain of Zionism', and warned that this was an alien ideology with 'no precedents in American culture or political history'. Israel, in other words, had infected American politics with its warmongering. A BBC *Panorama* documentary focused on the alleged Jewish or Israeli interests of 'the small and unelected group of right-wingers, who critics claim have hijacked the White House'. This is 'a story of people who stick together', said the narrator, echoing an old antisemitic trope, who then went on to discuss whether American Jewish neo-conservatives were guilty of 'dual loyalty'. This thinking affected left-wing attitudes to Middle East policy in general. Scottish Labour MP Tam Dalyell complained that Tony Blair was 'being unduly influenced by a cabal of Jewish advisers'. Left-wing journalist Paul Foot tried to excuse the antisemitism in Dalyell's comment by arguing that 'obviously he is wrong to complain about Jewish pressure on Blair and Bush when he means Zionist pressure'. Perry Anderson, in a 2001 editorial in *New Left Review* (still the intellectual house journal of the New Left), wrote that 'the Jewish community' in America – which he used interchangeably with 'American Zionism' – is 'entrenched in business, government and media' with 'a firm grip on the levers of public opinion and official policy towards Israel', making it a 'state within a state'.[12]

Some on the left began compiling lists of Jews to explain global political events. The Revolutionary Communist Group, who held stalls outside Marks & Spencer stores encouraging people to boycott it because of its supposed support for Israel, published an article directly linking neo-conservative support for the Iraq War to the number of Jews amongst their ranks. 'It is no surprise that so many of the NeoCons are pro-Israeli Jews,' the article claimed, and even Christian Zionists in America 'practise Jewish culture'. A letter in the *Morning Star* from a former British serviceman who served in Britain's colonial Palestine mandate included an apology to the Palestinians for his role in their dispossession, before putting it down to the fact that 'there were sixty-three known Jewish MPs in our Parliament at the time' (this is not correct: there were twenty-nine Jewish MPs elected in the 1945 general election). Often these conspiracy theories were discussed in terms of 'Zionists' or the 'Israel lobby' rather than openly talking about Jews, but the British far right thought it could hear a familiar dog whistle. One supporter of the violent neo-Nazi Combat 18 group posted a link to the *Panorama* documentary on the Combat 18 website with a message: 'Allow me to introduce you to the biggest puppet masters of them all The Neo Conservatives. There must be something in it if f**king PANORAMA went sniffing around Washington.' The late John Tyndall, one of Britain's foremost fascist post-war leaders and founder of the British National Party, wrote gleefully that 'certain things are coming out into the open which not long ago would have been tightly censored and suppressed ... We are witnessing a gigantic conspiracy being unveiled.' Tyndall understood what many on the left didn't: that the word 'Zionism' was being used in ways that had little in common with how most Jews define it – the belief that Israel should exist and that Jews should have a state – and much more in common with how he and his fellow antisemites use the word, as a euphemism for a vast, malevolent Jewish conspiracy.[13]

An edition of the *New Statesman* in January 2002 became emblematic of left-wing antisemitism during this period. Its front cover showed a shiny, golden Star of David piercing a supine Union Jack. The strapline posed a question: 'A kosher conspiracy?' and trailed articles on 'Britain's pro-Israeli lobby'. It would be hard to find a more blatant combination of antisemitic motifs than this image, with its combination of conspiracy, wealth and power dominating Britain's interests. The cover would not have been out of place in a neo-Nazi publication. Inside, Dennis Sewell wrote: 'That there is a Zionist lobby and that it is rich, potent and effective goes largely unquestioned on the left. Big Jewry, like big tobacco, is seen as one of life's givens.' Sewell did not challenge the idea that this lobby, run by 'wealthy Jewish business leaders' and the Israeli embassy, exists, but argued that it is ineffective. On the next page, John Pilger explained Tony Blair's support for Israel partly by pointing to his choice of Lord Levy, 'a wealthy Jewish businessman', as his special envoy to the Middle East. After weeks of protest, and a visit from a group of left-wing Jewish protestors, *New Statesman* editor Peter Wilby published an apology. 'We (or, more precisely, I) got it wrong,' wrote Wilby.

> The cover was not intended to be anti-Semitic; the *New States-man* is vigorously opposed to racism in all its forms. But it used images and words in such a way as to create unwittingly the impression that the *New Statesman* was following an anti-Semitic tradition that sees the Jews as a conspiracy piercing the heart of the nation.

However, Wilby insisted that the articles by Sewell and Pilger were not in any way antisemitic.[14]

Whether Wilby was right about this or not, the suggestion that 'Big Jewry' (used interchangeably with 'Zionist lobby' on this occasion) uses money and political influence to damage British interests appeals to the idea of emancipatory anti-semitism that has existed on the left since its earliest years. This can sometimes be found in the strangest of contexts. In 2011, Pilger wrote another *New Statesman* column protesting against the building of a large Westfield shopping centre in east London as part of the plans for the London Olympics. Complaining that the shopping centre replaced small independent shops and traditional manufacturing with a glossy, consumerist mall inaccessible to the local poor, Pilger felt it relevant to point out that Westfield was co-founded by Frank Lowy, 'an Australian-Israeli billionaire ... a former Israeli commando, [who] gives millions to Israel'. Pilger didn't explain what this had to do with the economic and social impact of building a large shopping centre in a deprived part of London. Rather, it acted as an identity marker for the *New Statesman*'s left-wing readers, informing them that Westfield is politically suspect, while also echoing older antisemitic ideas of cosmopolitan Jews and global finance undermining authentic local culture and business.[15]

Wilby's apology for the 2002 front cover is worth revisiting, because it said something else about left-wing attitudes to anti-semitism. Wilby wrote:

> Racism against white people is of no consequence because it has no historical resonance ... Given the distribution of power in our world, discrimination by blacks or Asians against whites will almost always be trivial. Jews are a different case. They no longer routinely suffer gross or violent discrimination; indeed, in the US and Europe at least, Jews today are probably safer than most minorities. But the Holocaust remains within living memory, as do the language and the iconography used by the Nazis to prepare the way for it. We have a special duty of care not to revive them.[16]

The implication is that antisemitism is a museum piece of historical interest but with little immediate potency beyond the neo-Nazi fringe. Wilby urges people to resist its revival, but doesn't consider that there may be other forms of antisemitism – in Muslim majority countries, say, or in parts of the left – that are thriving. Jews do not fit with his idea of racism, because they are not poor, powerless or excluded from society. It leaves the impression that his front cover was a political *faux pas* rather than anything more substantial.

The marginalisation of antisemitism in left-wing understandings of racism is also part of the generational shift from Old Left to New Left. In the debates over race relations, whether in Parliament during the 1960s or during the NUS No Platform debate of the 1970s, Jews were repeatedly held up as 'paradigmatic victims of racism' because of the Holocaust. Even though race relations legislation was intended to address problems faced by more recent Commonwealth immigrants, the legacy of Nazi genocide provided the historical backdrop and justification for legal measures against racial discrimination. But while the Old Left that lived through the wartime struggle against fascism instinctively saw the Holocaust as justification for the creation of Israel, the younger New Left was shaped by anti-colonialism rather than by the Second World War and had a different view of Zionism. The Holocaust became a political inconvenience rather than a formative event; and, as left-wing opposition to Israel and Zionism has strengthened, it has been accompanied by sustained efforts to revise the left's understanding of the Holocaust and its relationship to Israel.[17]

The crudest and most common version of this re-evaluation of the Holocaust is to compare Israel's treatment of the Palestinians to Nazi treatment of the Jews, and to argue that Zionism and Nazism are sibling ideologies, both born of European racial supremacy and with genocidal potential. This equation of Zionism and Nazism has Soviet origins, as seen in previous chapters, and it burst into life on the British left during the 1982 Lebanon War. That was the conflict that inspired Ken Livingstone's *Labour Herald* to publish its cartoon of Israeli Prime Minister Menachem Begin as a Nazi officer. The Socialist Workers Party's newspaper *Socialist Worker* published an article a few days after the Israeli invasion that claimed 'the true heirs of the Nazis are the present leaders of Israel. They've borrowed the Nazi argument of racial purity and applied it to themselves.' This became a staple of the party's coverage of the war. Two weeks later, a full-page article was titled: 'Holocaust Begin Style'. It included a cartoon showing a pair of Israeli soldiers holding two men, wearing striped clothing, at gunpoint. One Israeli soldier is saying to the other: 'It's funny how well those old uniforms of your granddads [*sic*] fit these P.L.O. terrorists'. The Socialist Workers Party's theoretical journal *Socialist Review* turned the traditional Trotskyist critique of Zionism as a misguided strategy against antisemitism on its head, by claiming that the war 'confirms something that we have always argued – that Zionism leads directly to the concentration camps. Only this time it is not the Jews on the receiving end of this genocide.'[18]

By the time of the Second Intifada and Israel's more recent conflicts with Hamas and Hezbollah, this comparison had become completely banal. In 2002, Portuguese writer and Nobel Laureate José Saramago claimed that Israel was evoking 'the spirit of Auschwitz' in its West Bank policies. In 2003, Oona King (then a Labour MP) wrote that Gaza was 'a hell similar in its nature' to the Warsaw Ghetto. Former Pink Floyd musician Roger Waters has said that 'The parallels with what went on in the 1930s in Germany are so crushingly obvious.' In 2013, then Liberal Democrat MP David Ward wrote:

> Having visited Auschwitz twice – once with my family and once with local schools – I am saddened that the Jews, who suffered unbelievable levels of persecution during the Holocaust, could within a few years of liberation from the death camps be inflicting atrocities on Palestinians in the new State of Israel and continue to do so on a daily basis in the West Bank and Gaza.

During Israel's conflict with Hamas in 2009, George Galloway (then a Respect MP) drew a direct comparison between the Israeli Army and the SS units that liquidated the Warsaw Ghetto:

In April and May of 1943, the Jews of the Warsaw Ghetto were surrounded by barbed-wire fences, by the occupiers of Poland, and they faced a choice, in the words of the song of the partisans: 'They could die on their knees or they could live forever'. And they chose to rise up against their occupier, to use their bodies as weapons, to dig tunnels, to fight, not to die in ones and twos of hunger and typhus, but to die as free men and women. Today, the Palestinian people in Gaza are the new Warsaw Ghetto, and those who are murdering them are the equivalent of those who murdered the Jews in Warsaw in 1943.[19]

Some of the organisers of that 2009 demonstration had even produced placards for their supporters proclaiming 'Stop the Holocaust in Gaza'. Comparing the plight of the Palestinians with the Holocaust performs several functions. Its political goal is to undermine the idea that the Holocaust provided a moral justification and a practical need for the creation of a Jewish state. The comparison has shock value that is bound to get a response in a way that other historical analogies might not. It claims historical insight by binding the two events together in a pseudo-analytical way, even though they are profoundly different. It removes the moral basis of Israel by suggesting that whatever status and privileges Jews had as victims has been lost. And it reduces European guilt for the Holocaust by claiming that its primary victims are actually no better than their persecutors. It is a powerful charge precisely because the Holocaust and Israel are linked by their shared Jewish features.

Beyond this crude equation, some on the left have tried different, more thoughtful, approaches. Two plays at the Royal Court Theatre in London, twenty-two years apart, usefully illustrate how ideas have changed as Holocaust education and remembrance have become increasingly embedded in British public life. The first play was called *Perdition*, written by a Trotskyist TV script writer called Jim Allen and directed by Ken Loach. It was a fictionalised account of a real libel trial in Israel in the 1950s involving Rudolf Kasztner, a Zionist official in Budapest in 1944 who negotiated for over 1,600 people, including many of his family and friends, to leave Hungary and escape the Nazi deportations to Auschwitz. Kasztner's actions have always been controversial. For some, he is a hero who rescued Jews; for others, he did so at the expense of the hundreds of thousands of Hungarian Jews who died. Kasztner brought a libel trial against a survivor called Malchiel Gruenwald, who accused him of collaboration. Kasztner lost the trial on most counts but the verdict was overturned on appeal. In between the two trials, though, he was assassinated in Israel by extreme right-wing Zionists. Allen used this case as the basis for a more general assault on the Zionist leadership during the war, accusing them of readily sacrificing European Jews in exchange for pursuing the goal of a Jewish state. He drew heavily on Lenni Brenner's *Zionism in the Age of the Dictators*: the same book that Livingstone cited in 2016 when he claimed that Hitler had 'supported Zionism'. Brenner (and, by extension, Allen) relied on a highly selective reading of negotiations between parts of the Zionist movement and Nazi Germany to imply that Zionist leaders were morally culpable for the deaths of millions of their fellow Jews in the Holocaust. Allen's script was brutal. His play accused American Jewish leaders of standing silent while Hungarian Jews were slaughtered, and local Zionists of actively helping: 'First you placed a noose around the neck of every Jew in Hungary, then you tightened the knot and legged it for Palestine.' Hungarian Jews 'were murdered not just by the force of German arms, but by the calculated treachery of their own Jewish leaders'; the result was that Israel was 'coined in the blood and tears of Hungarian Jewry'. It was similarly harsh in its verdict on Israel, a 'racist state' and 'a nation built on the pillar of Western guilt and subsidized by American dollars' that has become 'the most dangerous place on earth for a Jew'. The Israeli government 'commits outrageous crimes and then silences its critics by invoking the Holocaust'.[20]

The Royal Court commissioned historian David Cesarani to review the text of the play before it was prepared for production. He pointed out numerous historical inaccuracies and several changes were made before the final version was ready for staging. Some changes had less to do with historical accuracy and more to do with the antisemitic resonance of the script. In his original text, Allen had described the alleged

collaboration as 'the Zionist knife in the Nazi fist' and castigated rich American Jews in 'fur-lined dug-outs' on Park
Avenue. Despite these changes, a huge outcry from across the
Jewish community and well beyond it greeted the play when
it was announced by the theatre. The Royal Court's artistic
director Max Stafford-Clark decided to cancel the planned
performances – turning it into a *cause célèbre* about artistic
freedom. Allen blamed 'the Zionist lobby' for the cancellation,
something denied by Stafford-Clark. Historian Martin Gilbert
added to Cesarani's concerns about the historical inaccuracies
in the play, but more pertinent was its political purpose. Allen
described his play as

> the most lethal attack on Zionism ever written, because it
> touches at the heart of the most abiding myth of modern
> history, the Holocaust. Because it says quite plainly that privi
> leged Jewish leaders collaborated in the extermination of their
> own kind in order to help bring about a Zionist state, Israel,
> a state which is itself racist.

Loach and Allen were both angry that their play, which they
insisted was anti-Zionist but not antisemitic, had been cancelled by the Royal Court. 'I hadn't tangled with the Zionist
lobby before,' Loach told the Workers Revolutionary Party's
newspaper, and 'What is amazing is the strength and organisation and power of their lobby.' The 'Zionists', he claimed, 'want

to leave intact ... the generalised sense of guilt that everyone has about the Jews so that it remains an area that you can't discuss'. He was particularly angry with another playwright, Caryl Churchill, who publicly defended Stafford-Clark: 'the behaviour of people who would call themselves to be on the left has been unprincipled', Loach complained.[21]

Twenty-two years later, it was Churchill who found herself accused of antisemitism for a play about Israel and Jews at the Royal Court Theatre. Churchill's play was called *Seven Jewish Children: A play for Gaza*, and was her 'response' to a three-week conflict between Israel and Hamas in Gaza and southern Israel in December 2008 and January 2009. The play comprises a short series of conversations in which unidentified adults discuss what to tell, or not tell, their children about various scenarios drawn from Jewish and Israeli history. The scenarios are not identified but they seem to relate to the Holocaust, post-war emigration to Israel, settlement of the new state, the occupation of the West Bank and Gaza, and finally the 2008–09 conflict itself. The script consists almost entirely of short, contradictory sentences beginning 'Tell her' or 'Don't tell her', which taken together suggest ongoing and unresolved anxiety about death and displacement, endured first by Jews at the hands of the Nazis or other antisemites, and then by Palestinians at the hands of Jews. This culminates in a monologue that appears to be an appeal to tell the truth, and this is the section that critics of the play claimed was antisemitic:

Tell her, tell her about the army, tell her to be proud of the army. Tell her about the family of dead girls, tell her their names why not, tell her the whole world knows why shouldn't she know? Tell her there's dead babies, did she see babies? Tell her she's got nothing to be ashamed of. Tell her they did it to themselves. Tell her they want their children killed to make people sorry for them, tell her I'm not sorry for them, tell her not to be sorry for them, tell her we're the ones to be sorry for, tell her they can't talk suffering to us. Tell her we're the iron fist now, tell her it's the fog of war, tell her we won't stop killing them till we're safe, tell her I laughed when I saw the dead policemen, tell her they're animals living in rubble now, tell her I wouldn't care if we wiped them out, the world would hate us is the only thing, tell her I don't care if the world hates us, tell her we're better haters, tell her we're chosen people, tell her I look at one of their children covered in blood and what do I feel? Tell her all I feel is happy it's not her.

Don't tell her that.

Tell her we love her.

Don't frighten her.[22]

Those two lines – 'tell her we're chosen people, tell her I look at one of their children covered in blood and what do I feel? Tell her all I feel is happy it's not her' – became the subject of much criticism. The Jewish theological concept of 'chosen people' has long been abused by antisemites to (inaccurately) suggest that

Jews have a sense of racial superiority. The idea that Jews delight in the killing of non-Jewish children is central to the medieval charge of the 'blood libel'. Howard Jacobson called this passage 'The old stuff. Jew-hating pure and simple.' Churchill, a patron of the Palestine Solidarity Campaign, dismissed Jacobson's assessment as 'the usual tactic' of calling Israel's critics anti-semitic. The Royal Court insisted that 'While *Seven Jewish Children* is undoubtedly critical of the policies of the state of Israel, there is no suggestion that this should be read as a criticism of Jewish people. It is possible to criticise the actions of Israel without being anti-Semitic.' Some critics (including this author) pointed out that this defence was undermined by the fact that the play was called *Seven Jewish Children*, while the words 'Israel', 'Israelis', 'Zionism' and 'Zionist' do not appear in the script. Whatever the rights and wrongs of the argument over the play's alleged antisemitism, everybody agreed on its main theme: that the psychological and emotional trauma of the Holocaust and antisemitism was playing out via Israeli violence and oppression towards the Palestinians. The Jews, in other words, had not learned the correct lessons of the Holocaust and as a result had now become perpetrators where once they were victims.[23]

It may not be a coincidence that the trend on the left of comparing Israel's actions to those of Nazi Germany, or accusing Zionists of collaborating with Nazism, or lamenting an alleged failure of Jews to learn the lessons of their own genocide, has grown in parallel with a general increase in public discussion and awareness of the Holocaust in Britain. Historian Tony Kushner, in his book *The Holocaust and the Liberal Imagination*, has shown just how limited awareness of the Holocaust was before the 1980s. During and after the war, British public and political opinion struggled to absorb the particular Jewish aspects of the Holocaust even while showing sympathy for its victims. Until the 1980s, there was little or no education in schools and universities about the Holocaust, and public commemoration, even by the Jewish community, was on a small scale. This changed in the 1980s as Britain moved from a narrow version of tolerance for minorities that emphasised assimilation, to a more diverse, pluralist society. Since 1990, Britain has passed legislation to prosecute Nazi war criminals, made Holocaust education part of the national curriculum, takes students from every school in the country to Auschwitz on government-funded trips, introduced a national Holocaust Memorial Day and is, at the time of writing, planning a national Holocaust monument and education centre to be sited in central London.

As the Holocaust has become a more familiar reference point in British public life, so it has also become a common reference point for Israel's opponents, particularly those who do not think that Israel should exist. In their telling, it is the Palestinians, not Jews, who are the ultimate victims of Nazism and to whom Europe owes a debt. Mick Napier of the Scottish

Palestine Solidarity Campaign (a separate organisation from the main Palestine Solidarity Campaign) wrote to *Socialist Worker* in 2007 that Holocaust commemoration was used 'to "justify" the mass murder and expropriation of the Palestinians. An accurate understanding of the Nazi Holocaust is essential to grasp modern Israeli savagery towards the Palestinian people.' Napier wrote this to explain his decision to organise readings of *Perdition* to mark Holocaust Memorial Day that year. A fellow Scottish Palestine Solidarity Campaign member, while criticising Napier's decision, agreed with him that 'The Zionists have certainly controlled the discourse about Holocaust remembrance for many years, and have aggressively quashed the truth about Zionist collaboration with Nazis.' It is this battle to 'control the discourse' about the Holocaust, Israel and Zionism that leads some on the left to reject mainstream Holocaust remembrance.[24]

The contrast between *Perdition* and *Seven Jewish Children* is a useful way to understand the impact this growth of Holocaust education and commemoration has had on how Israel's opponents relate to the Holocaust. These two plays, both addressing British audiences at the same theatre two decades apart, took very different routes to the same political goal. Knowledge of the Holocaust was still relatively thin in Britain when *Perdition* was written, but left-wing hostility to Israel and sympathy for the Palestinians were intense after the 1982 Lebanon War and were fuelled by the relative strength of Trotskyist groups on the left at that time. This political environment was conducive to the production of such an ideological play, but few potential theatre-goers would have known much about the historical events it described. By the time *Seven Jewish Children* was written, the Holocaust had become a much more familiar episode, even if detailed knowledge of its different aspects and features is often lacking. In particular, its primary role has become an educational one. Lessons from Auschwitz is a programme set up by the Holocaust Educational Trust in 1999 to educate sixth-form students about the Holocaust. Over 28,000 students have taken part so far in a programme that is funded by grants from the UK and Scottish governments. When then Communities Secretary Eric Pickles announced a new tranche of funding in 2011, he pledged: 'We must ensure that the lessons from the Holocaust are taught today and to future generations.' Beyond the basic history of the Holocaust itself, these lessons are generally taken to be universalist ones to guard against prejudice, discrimination and hate. *Seven Jewish Children* turns this educational function of the Holocaust back onto Israel and Zionism, by suggesting that Jews – in their modern national form in Israel – have actually learned quite different lessons from the Holocaust. Instead of teaching their children to avoid prejudice and hatred, according to the play, they bring them up in ways that replicate and justify those negative values. Where *Perdition* uses ideology to damn Israel, *Seven Jewish Children* turns the Holocaust into a morality play about Jewish identity.

In the end, though, the political message of both is the same: Jews do not deserve to be treated as victims in the left's division of the world into oppressors and oppressed.[25]

What these different anti-Zionist approaches to the Holocaust have in common is that none of them are capable of engaging with the Jewish experience and memory of genocide. The Holocaust was, unsurprisingly, a transformative event in modern Jewish history. The collective Jewish memory of boycotts, deportations, ghettos and mass murder, often carried out with the cooperation of local, non-German, police forces and other state authorities across Nazi-occupied Europe, casts a permanent shadow under which all Jewish politics now takes place. It is not possible to understand why most Diaspora Jews relate to Zionism and to Israel in the way that they do without grasping this essential point.

The universal lessons of the Holocaust are regularly invoked by European leaders to justify and promote values of equality, tolerance and diversity. In a speech to the Holocaust Educational Trust in 2013, former Prime Minister David Cameron said, 'The horror of the Holocaust is unique but the lessons we learn from it are absolutely applicable right across our society at home and abroad … against anyone, any group and in any form.' French President François Hollande, speaking at the opening of a new memorial centre in 2012, said, 'Our work is no longer about establishing the truth … Today, our work is to transmit. That is the spirit of this memorial. Transmission: there resides the future of remembering.' When European Education Ministers decided in 2002, via the Council of Europe, to introduce a Day of Remembrance for the Holocaust in member states' schools, their declaration made no mention of Jews or of antisemitism. Instead, the decision was explained as a way of fulfilling the council's goals to 'strengthen mutual understanding and trust between peoples' and to 'seek to prevent repetition or denial of the devastating events that marked the last century'.[26]

Others, drawing on the anti-colonial aspects of post-war anti-racism, prefer to recommend the legacy of European colonialism as a way to shape Europe's present. In 2000, the Runnymede think tank produced a report on the future of multi-ethnic Britain, following a two-year research project chaired by academic (and now Lord) Bhikhu Parekh. The report called on 'multicultural Britain' to develop a new sense of national identity based on 'post-war migration but also devolution, globalisation, the end of empire, Britain's long-term decline as a world power, moral and cultural pluralism, and closer integration with Europe'. Academic and writer Paul Gilroy suggested that 'frank exposure to the grim and brutal details of my country's colonial past should be made useful … in shaping the character of its emergent multicultural relations'. Britain's 'multicultural future', he argued, depends on facing up to 'the hidden, shameful store of imperial horrors' in the country's past. Gilroy does not object to commemorating the Nazi genocide (although he views the creation of Holocaust Memorial Day as a cynical, empty act), but he asks why Britain places such emphasis on the collective memory of wartime victory against Hitler, while showing no interest in addressing its colonial history. The Second World War, he argues, is 'the favoured means to find and even to restore an ebbing sense of what it is to be English ... On the other hand, the mysterious evacuation of Britain's postcolonial conflicts from national consciousness has become a significant cultural and historical event in its own right.'[27]

These two alternatives of using either Holocaust memory or anti-colonialism as a foundation for building a pluralist, multicultural society needn't be contradictory. There are genocidal episodes in the history of colonialism, and both can be used to encourage the same values of anti-racism and diversity. It might be expected that left-wing anti-racists would have a particular motivation to combine the two, in order to add greater weight to their campaigns. However, some on the left now appear to see the Holocaust and colonialism as competing, or even opposing, historical legacies; and for many, it is their attitude to Israel that stands between them and mainstream Holocaust commemoration. Those who believe that Israel is a colonial settler state and Zionism is a racist, colonial ideology – and bearing in mind the formative role of anti-colonialism in left-wing anti-racism – conclude that to be anti-racist requires opposing colonialism and therefore opposing Israel.

On the other hand, Israel's supporters claim that Israel was not a colonial enterprise but was a refuge for Holocaust survivors, and therefore that the Holocaust provided the moral justification for the creation of Israel. This leaves some on the anti-Zionist left feeling that mainstream Holocaust commemoration should be shunned as an implicit endorsement of Zionism. Mick Napier sees Holocaust commemoration as a hypocritical veil to protect both Israel and ongoing Western racism in general:

> Increasingly, Holocaust commemoration has become a travesty, devoid of any moral compass that condemns today's mass killing of brown-skinned people for oil or strategic goals. Holocaust commemoration has been embraced by our Government, currently involved in the genocidal occupation of Iraq, and Zionists who defend Israel's ethnic cleansing of Palestine. The Israeli Declaration of Independence claims the Holocaust as a justification for this apartheid state. Tony Blair's ministers attend Holocaust commemorations one day and then the next day they ratchet up the rhetoric against asylum seekers and immigrants that the extreme right, including the Nazi BNP, are feeding on.[28]

A more common complaint is that the Holocaust gets more attention than colonialism, slavery or other crimes of Europe's past. 'Quite rightly, the Holocaust is remembered as genocide against Jewish people,' Jeremy Corbyn wrote in 2002, but 'Why is the slave trade not remembered in the same breath or the genocide of native Americans by the European armies and settlers who came to grab land and wealth using their advantage of technology and weaponry?' The controversial French comedian-cum-political activist Dieudonné M'Bala M'Bala, who has a string of convictions for antisemitic hate speech, made a similar argument in more resentful terms. Why, he asked, is there 'a community that gets all the public attention and exclusively lays claim to the image of the victim, when there is another entire community that no one cares about what happened to it – it's not studied in history lessons, and its experience is ignored by everyone.' In 2010, veteran black activist Lee Jasper, speaking at a 'Genocide Memorial Day' event, gave a talk about the impact of slavery and colonialism on African and Asian diaspora communities today, before claiming that Israel in Gaza 'seeks to do to others exactly that which was done to them by the Nazis'. The event Jasper was speaking at was organised by a fiercely anti-Zionist Muslim organisation, the Islamic Human Rights Commission, as an alternative to Holocaust Memorial Day. Those who question mainstream Holocaust commemoration on the basis that it privileges Jews at the expense of other minorities tend to be people of the left who are politically opposed to Europe's elites. This fits within what Shulamit Volkov called the New Left's 'cultural code' of anti-Zionism, anti-Americanism and anti-colonialism.

The merging of anti-Zionism with anti-Americanism and anti-colonialism, Volkov argued, has the potential to make Jews a general symbol of Western values. The denigration of Holocaust commemoration then becomes a way to reject those Western establishment values, with Jewish sensitivities a casualty along the way.[29]

Israel and its supporters in European Jewish communities sit on the fault line of these competing narratives of anti-racism. If Europe's values of diversity and pluralism are based on penance for its colonial past, and if Israel is a colonial state and Zionism is a form of racism, then Europe should oppose Israel too as part of its commitment to an anti-racist future. On the other hand, if Europe's modern identity is drawn from its memory of the Holocaust, and if Zionism is the legitimate national movement of the Holocaust's primary victims, then Europe should support Israel as part of its future commitment to the Jewish people. The left is divided between those who identify with the Jewish aspiration for nationhood and oppose antisemitism as part of their anti-racism, and those who oppose Israel and Zionism for exactly the same reason. The separation of antisemitism from anti-racist politics that has occurred since the 1960s makes this possible; the anti-colonial and anti-apartheid origins of left-wing anti-Zionism make it likely. Denigrating Holocaust memory as a way to attack Israel is its most obvious, and most objectionable, expression.

The moral consequences of this way of thinking can be

repugnant. In 2002, at the height of the second Palestinian Intifada, the *Morning Star* published a letter from a long-standing reader and veteran Communist that read:

> Israel, and all that Israel has done and is doing, is an affront to all those millions who fought and died fighting fascism before, during and after the war against fascism … An Italian partisan, fighting the German invaders in Italy, survived a year in Dachau. A few years ago, he committed suicide. He left a note saying that the good Jews were all killed in the concentration camps.[30]

'The good Jews were all killed in the concentration camps': linger for a moment on that line, published in Britain's leading communist newspaper; the newspaper for which Jeremy Corbyn wrote a column for several years before becoming leader of the Labour Party. It is a newspaper that is still read widely in the Labour movement that once enjoyed the support of many Jews who looked to the left as their natural home. The sentiments behind the letter are nauseating. The fact that it was deemed fit to publish is chilling. Worst of all, the attitudes and the political logic that lead to it are no longer surprising. It is an extreme example of a way of thinking about Jews, Israel and Zionism that is all too common across the left. These attitudes, this way of thinking, are the reason for the left's Jewish problem.

CHAPTER SEVEN

ANTISEMITISM UNDER CORBYN

O n 12 September 2015, Jeremy Corbyn was elected leader of the Labour Party and the political world tilted on its axis for British Jews. For the first time in recent history, one of Britain's two main political parties would be led by somebody who had no relationship with, or real understanding of, the main bulk of British Jewry; somebody who was, at best, a fierce critic of Israel, and at worst had actively campaigned against its very existence; and who came into office dogged by allegations that he, personally, had associated with and even supported antisemites, Holocaust deniers and terrorists. For Jews who were used to the Labour Party of Gordon Brown, who littered his speeches to Jewish audiences with childhood memories of his father imbuing him with a love for the land and people of Israel, or for older Jews who remembered the Labour Zionism of Harold Wilson, Eric Moonman and Ian Mikardo, this was a jolting change. And, most of all, this was no longer the Labour Party of Tony Blair, who built a cadre of Jewish donors to fund the revival of the Labour Party in the 1990s and attracted back many Jewish voters who had been drawn to Margaret Thatcher's Conservatives in the 1980s. That party was very much over.

Two questions have framed Jewish concerns about the Labour Party's new direction since Corbyn's leadership victory. The first asks whether the various examples of antisemitism that have emerged from the party are just one-off, random cases that reflect nothing more than the existence of antisemitism in wider society, or whether, more troublingly, they indicate something deeper: a way of thinking on the left about Jews, Israel and Zionism that has allowed unpleasant, hostile and even antisemitic attitudes to become part of acceptable opinion in Labour Party circles. In other words, does the Labour Party have a problem of a few antisemites, or has an antisemitic political culture developed within its ranks? Is it just a few bad apples in an otherwise anti-racist barrel, or is there something rotten about the barrel itself?

The second question concerns Corbyn's personal role in this story. Most of the allegations, scandals and stories about antisemitism in the Labour Party that have emerged since he became leader have not involved Corbyn directly, but they began with concerns about people he had associated with in his long years on the backbenches. A month before becoming leader, when polls showed he was destined to win the race to

succeed Ed Miliband, the *Jewish Chronicle* ran a front-page editorial that set out seven questions for Corbyn to answer lest he
'be regarded from the day of his election as an enemy of Britain's
Jewish community'. The range of organisations and people the
Jewish Chronicle asked about, all of whom Corbyn had come into
contact with or expressed support for in the course of his pro-
Palestinian activities, gives a sense of just how eclectic Britain's
pro-Palestinian movement is, and just how much it has failed to
police its own borders. It included an organisation called Deir
Yassin Remembered and the person who runs it, a Jewish man
called Paul Eisen, who was accused of being a Holocaust denier;
a Church of England vicar, Stephen Sizer, who had linked from
his own website to antisemitic conspiracy sites; the terrorist
organisations Hamas and Hezbollah; the involvement of the
Stop the War Coalition in Britain's Al Quds Day rally, an annual
pro-Iranian, anti-Israel demonstration; and an Israeli Islamist
leader called Sheikh Raed Salah who had repeated the medieval charge of blood libel, which claims that Jews murdered
Christian children and use their blood for religious rituals. Nor
was this the full list of allegations circulating around Corbyn at
the time: there was also his association with Dyab Abou Jahjah,
a Belgian Hezbollah supporter who had published Holocaust
denial cartoons on his website. Corbyn spoke alongside him at
a Stop the War Coalition event in 2009 and even – according to
Abou Jahjah – wrote to the Home Secretary on his behalf when
he was banned from re-entering the UK.[1]

Corbyn's support for Raed Salah highlights the difficulty in answering the question of whether he was simply ignorant of the antisemitic views around him; was complicit in excusing them; or whether, consciously or not, he actually shares some of them. Salah is the leader of the northern branch of Israel's Islamic Movement, which is the closest thing Israel has to a domestic version of the Muslim Brotherhood. In June 2011, Salah arrived in the United Kingdom as a guest of Middle East Monitor, a UK pressure group that is broadly supportive of the Muslim Brotherhood and of Hamas. His visit to the UK featured various speaking engagements, including one in the Houses of Parliament that was organised by the Palestine Solidarity Campaign and hosted by Jeremy Corbyn. Salah had previously been convicted in Israel in 2005 for his involvement with organisations that were accused of providing money to Hamas. At the time of his visit to the UK he was facing indictments in Israel for inciting antisemitism and inciting violence in a speech he gave in Jerusalem in 2007. This 2007 speech, which was followed by rioting amongst Salah's supporters, included the following reference to the antisemitic blood libel:

> We have never allowed ourselves, and listen well, we have never allowed ourselves to knead the bread for the breaking of the fast during the blessed month of Ramadan with the blood of the children. And if someone wants a wider explanation, you should ask what used to happen to some of the

children of Europe, whose blood would be mixed in the dough

of the holy bread. God all mighty, is this religion? Is this what

God wants? God will confront you for what you are doing...²

Medieval blood libels began in Norwich in 1144 and spread throughout England and across Europe for centuries afterwards. They alleged that Jews kidnap and murder Christian children and drain them of their blood for use in religious rituals (it is also known as a 'ritual murder' charge). In the Middle Ages this entirely spurious allegation was widely believed, and unexplained deaths of children were often blamed on local Jews, who would be tortured until they 'confessed'. Blood libels sometimes led to massacres and expulsions of Jewish communities or their forced conversion to Christianity. They often coincided with Passover and Easter, a time of year when the idea that Jews bear eternal guilt for the death of Jesus fuelled surges in antisemitism (sometimes it was claimed that the blood was used to make matzo, the unleavened bread eaten by Jews during Passover). This was not a fringe phenomenon: several cases reached widespread and enduring popularity. Hugh of Lincoln, a young boy whose death in 1255 was erroneously blamed on local Jews, was buried in Lincoln cathedral and his grave became a shrine for pilgrims. Dozens of local Jews were put on trial and executed. Hugh was even mentioned in Geoffrey Chaucer's *Prioress's Tale* – 'O yonge Hugh of Lyncoln, slayn also / With cursed Jewes, as it is notable' – and it was only in the 1950s that the cathedral removed the shrine and replaced it with a notice acknowledging the antisemitic nature of the Hugh of Lincoln myth. Blood libels spread to the Middle East in the nineteenth century as a cultural export of European colonialism. There was even a blood libel-related massacre of Jews in Europe after the Holocaust, when over forty Jews were murdered by a Polish mob in Kielce, Poland, in 1946, after it was rumoured that they had kidnapped a local boy. The murderous history of blood libels and their recurring presence in European culture mean that a blood libel charge is not something that is easily done by mistake, or as a misguided expression of anger towards Israel. It is a charge that lies deep in the heart of European antisemitism and assumes that Jews are unimaginably cruel, deceitful and conspiratorial. All the historic allegations and charges of blood libel and ritual murder were baseless and entirely fabricated; but in 2007, at the time when Salah made his speech in Jerusalem, a mini-scandal had erupted in Israel because a prominent Israeli scholar, Professor Ariel Toaff, had published a book suggesting that some of the blood libel allegations in fifteenth-century Italy might be true. This is likely to be what Salah had in mind when he referred to the blood libel in his speech.

The gravity of Salah's blood libel comments did not prevent Jeremy Corbyn, Middle East Monitor, Palestine Solidarity Campaign and Salah's other British supporters from rising up in fury when the then Home Secretary, Theresa May, tried to have Salah deported and excluded from the UK. Nor was their conviction dented when it was reported that Salah had apparently repeated an antisemitic conspiracy theory about the 9/11 terrorist attacks, allegedly writing in October 2001 that 'a suitable way was found to warn the 4,000 Jews who work every day at the Twin Towers to be absent from their work on September 11, 2001, and this is really what happened! Were 4,000 Jewish clerks absent [from their jobs] by chance, or was there another reason?' Salah and his supporters first denied that he had made the blood libel comments at all; then admitted he had said them but denied that he faced charges for it in Israel; then admitted he had been indicted but wrongly claimed he had been acquitted; then said that his reference to mixing 'the blood of the children' in 'holy bread' had nothing to do with Jews or the blood libel at all. All these defences fell apart one by one, but still Salah's supporters gave him the benefit of the doubt and refused to entertain the notion that such a prominent Palestinian leader, whose cause they considered to be just, could also be an antisemite. Instead, some of his supporters invoked conspiratorial language to explain why British Jews might protest about his presence in the UK. According to Salah's Islamic Movement, 'Since Salah received the invitation to come to Britain, the Jewish lobby went crazy and did everything in its power to prevent the visit, so that the Zionist narrative remains the only narrative.' Middle East Monitor published an article blaming the affair on 'Israel's British hirelings' and 'Israel's lackeys in Britain', who 'have shown themselves to be even more extreme than their paymasters in Tel Aviv'. Salah challenged the Home Secretary's attempt to deport him and eventually won his legal battle, but even the immigration tribunal that ruled in his favour concluded that his speech could only be a reference to the antisemitic blood libel (although the tribunal said that this was not sufficient grounds on which to deport him). This was completely overlooked by his supporters, including by Jeremy Corbyn. Two days after the news emerged that Salah had won his legal case, Corbyn, sitting alongside Salah's lawyer Tayab Ali, accused Theresa May of acting on 'prejudice rather than fact', called Salah an 'honoured citizen' who 'represents his people extremely well' and renewed his invitation to Salah to take 'tea on the terrace' of Parliament. It was as if, for Corbyn, Salah's blood libel speech and the criminal charges arising from it had never happened or were completely irrelevant (Salah was subsequently tried and convicted on those charges in Israel in 2014). Instead, when Ali called for a public inquiry into 'the government's relationship to the pro-Israeli lobby' and the possibility that prominent British Jews who donate to the Conservative Party 'are able to directly influence government policy', Corbyn immediately backed the idea. He 'strongly supported' Ali's suggestion, Corbyn said, because only a public inquiry could uncover 'what's going on in the Home Office and the way the government makes decisions'.[3]

Corbyn's record – of which the Salah case is just one example – is the reason why the baggage he brought with him into the leader's office went much further than simply his lifelong opposition to Israel; and it explains why, when evidence of antisemitism in Labour started to emerge, there was a lack of trust in his efforts, such as they were, to root it out. This began in Oxford in February 2016, when Alex Chalmers resigned as co-chair of the Oxford University Labour Club, citing the allegedly antisemitic behaviour of some of its senior members as the reason. In a Facebook post announcing his resignation, Chalmers explained:

> Whether it be members of the Executive throwing around the term 'Zio' (a term for Jews usually confined to websites run by the Ku Klux Klan) with casual abandon, senior members of the club expressing their 'solidarity' with Hamas and explicitly defending their tactics of indiscriminately murdering civilians, or a former Co-Chair claiming that 'most accusations of antisemitism are just the Zionists crying wolf', a large proportion of both OULC and the student left in Oxford more generally have some kind of problem with Jews.

The final straw for Chalmers was the decision of the Labour Club to endorse the forthcoming Israel Apartheid Week. He further claimed that Jewish students were routinely ridiculed and denounced, while Chalmers himself (who is not Jewish) was called a 'Zionist stooge'. Other allegations subsequently emerged from members of the university Jewish Society, including that Labour Club members mocked the victims of the January 2015 terrorist attack on a kosher supermarket in Paris when their funerals were on television, and that one member called Auschwitz a 'cash cow'.[4]

Revelations of other apparently antisemitic comments by Labour Party members, activists and officials around the country began to flow. This book has space for only a few examples. Vicki Kirby, the vice-chair of Woking Constituency Labour Party, was accused of tweeting 'Who is the Zionist God? I am starting to think it may be Hitler #FreePalestine'. Beinazir Lasharie, a Labour councillor in Kensington and Chelsea, allegedly posted a video on Facebook called 'ISIS: Israeli Secret Intelligence Service' and wrote another post saying, 'I've heard some compelling evidence about ISIS being originated from Zionists!' Khadim Hussain, a Labour councillor in Bradford and former Lord Mayor of the city, had apparently written on Facebook: 'Your school education system only tells you about Anne Frank and the six million Zionists that were killed by Hitler.' Other material on his Facebook page endorsed the conspiracy theory that Israel and/or the United States were behind ISIS. Salim Mulla, a Labour councillor in Blackburn and former mayor of the town, was alleged to have written that 'Zionist Jews are a disgrace to humanity' and posted conspiracy theories suggesting that Israel was behind ISIS terrorist attacks in Europe and school shootings in America. Ilyas Aziz, a Labour councillor in Nottingham, was accused of posting material on social media from the conspiracy theorist David Icke. Shah Hussain, a Labour councillor in Burnley, appeared to have tweeted to the Israeli footballer Yossi Benayoun: 'you and your country doing the same thing that hitler did to ur race in ww2'. A party member and veteran Trotskyist called Gerry Downing posted an article on his own website on 'Why Marxists must address the Jewish Question'. Some, like Downing, were thrown out of the party; others, like Mulla and Aziz, were allowed to remain as members after a short suspension, while Khadim Hussain resigned from the Labour Party but retains his seat on Bradford Council as an Independent.

These attitudes came from a wide range of Labour Party members, in different parts of the country, writing at different times and in response to different events, but they revealed a pattern of thinking. This was not, on the whole, an old-fashioned, overt dislike of Jews. Rather, it was a mélange of ideas that had particular appeal to people on the left: conspiracy theories about 'Zionists' or Israel controlling Western politicians or being behind 'false flag' terrorist attacks; other conspiracy theories about the Rothschilds controlling the world banking system; comparisons of Israel to Nazi Germany; and a general sense that Israel and its supporters are so inhuman as to be uniquely cruel, racist and murderous. As a set of ideas, they are a modern representation of the types of anti-Zionism that developed in parts of the British left from the 1960s onwards. Soviet antisemitic conspiracy propaganda, combined with the idea that the creation of Israel was itself a consequence of a Western colonial plot, mixed with older antisemitic versions of socialist anti-capitalism, added to contemporary resentment about the legacy of the Holocaust and the assumption that Jews and Zionism are part of today's networks of power, all find their current expression through social media memes about wars fought for the Rothschilds and ISIS being an Israeli creation. It is a far cry from the Marxist class theories of Matzpen or the human rights campaigning of Palestine Action. Most of these posts and comments were made before Corbyn became party leader, underlining the fact that this was a problem that had been growing on the left for years, rather than one that had suddenly appeared from nowhere. Ideas that had festered, largely ignored, on the fringes of the left for years were dug up by right-wing newspapers and blogs as a way to attack Corbyn; and the attacks stuck because people from those fringes were increasingly attracted to the Labour Party under Corbyn's leadership. Several of the alleged offenders denied bearing any malice towards Jews, and, in their own minds, they may well be right, but their language and thinking was nonetheless antisemitic. Conspiracy theories about Zionists or Israel, for example, only exist in the way that they do because they mimic, almost exactly, the conspiracy theories about Jews that have circulated in European culture for more than a century. Internet memes about Rothschild bankers controlling the world's financial system draw on Nazi-era antisemitism for their cultural resonance. The comparison of Israel to Nazi Germany is so offensive and hurtful precisely because it plays on the Jewishness of both the victims of the Holocaust and the State of Israel to carry its emotional punch. The moral implication of the comparison is that the Jews of today in Israel (and their supporters in Diaspora communities) are no better than their Nazi persecutors of yesterday – and therefore should stop going on about the Holocaust quite as much as they do.[5]

This rising tide finally swamped the Labour Party at the end of April 2016, when first Naz Shah MP and then Ken Livingstone were suspended from the party. Before becoming an MP, Shah had been prominent in pro-Palestinian campaigning in Bradford during the conflict between Israel and Hamas in the summer of 2014, which resulted in the deaths of over 2,000 Palestinians, many of them civilians, and seventy-three Israelis, most of them soldiers. This war saw extensive anti-Israel protests and a rise in antisemitic hate crimes in the UK, and it was not uncommon for Israel's critics to express views that went well beyond reasonable criticisms of actual Israeli actions and veered into antisemitism. Shah's offending Facebook posts, calling for Israel to be 'relocated' to the United States and for people to defeat 'the Jews' in an online poll about the conflict, happened during that period. At the time, they went unnoticed in the mass of angry online debate about the conflict, but, like so many antisemitic comments by Labour Party members that summer, they would be unearthed two years later by the right-wing Guido Fawkes blog to shattering effect.

Before then, however, Shah was herself the target of a bizarre anti-Zionist campaign by George Galloway when they faced off against each other in the Bradford West seat during the 2015 general election. Galloway had won the seat for the Respect Party in 2012 and Shah was Labour's choice to challenge him. This was a nasty campaign, characterised by legal threats and personal slurs, and perhaps the most extraordinary part of it was that Galloway tried to cast Shah, a local Muslim woman with a record of pro-Palestinian campaigning, as an Israeli stooge. Three weeks before polling day, Galloway tweeted an image of Israeli Prime Minister Benjamin Netanyahu, smiling with his arms outstretched, captioned with 'Thank you Bradford West for electing Naz Shah! Our campaign worked!' Half an hour later he posted a second tweet that juxtaposed crowds of celebrating Israelis and celebrating Palestinians, dancing in public and waving, respectively, Israeli and Palestinian flags. The Israelis were captioned with 'Thank you for electing Naz Shah'; the Palestinians with 'Thank you for electing George Galloway'. The message in both tweets was obvious: Shah would serve the interests of Israel, and Galloway would stand up for the Palestinians. There was no factual basis for this claim, which was a brazen attempt by Galloway to mobilise anti-Israel sentiment against his opponent. After Galloway lost his seat to Shah, he said in his concession speech, 'The venal, the vile, the racists and the Zionists will all be celebrating.' It is an example of how, for some on the left, 'Zionist' and 'anti-Zionist' have become general political labels that are no longer about whether somebody supports or opposes Israel, but are used as moral indicators to show whether a person is considered to be friend or foe. It was particularly ironic, then, that Shah was herself suspended from Labour a year later for making antisemitic comments arising from her own opposition to Israel.[6]

Shah apologised and intuitively grasped that the fact that her posts had caused such offence meant she lacked a basic understanding of modern antisemitism. She used her three-month suspension from the party to educate herself through a genuine dialogue with her local Jewish community and with national Jewish organisations. She later acknowledged to the BBC that her comments were antisemitic and offensive, but she insisted this was a result of ignorance and 'subconscious biases' rather than conscious hatred of Jewish people. This question, of whether the people in the Labour Party who express antisemitic views are actually antisemites or are just ignorant, is never straightforward. People might not even be honest with themselves about whether they harbour what is still, in the anti-racist, anti-fascist moral universe of the left, a grievous sin. Sometimes the strongest clue can be found in how people respond when they are accused of expressing racist or antisemitic views. And while Shah, once her antisemitic comments became publicly known, behaved like somebody who had spoken from genuine ignorance rather than knowing prejudice, the opposite can be said for the Labour grandee who rode to her defence.[7]

Ken Livingstone is a veteran of the far left's battles with Britain's Jewish community. From his days editing *Labour Herald* in the early 1980s, through his time at the Greater London Council and then as Mayor of London, he knows where the community's pressure points lie and exactly what kind of language evokes an angry, pained response from British Jews. The day after Shah was suspended by the party, Livingstone was interviewed about it on BBC radio and said:

> I've been in the Labour party for forty-seven years. I've never heard anyone say anything antisemitic. I've heard a lot of criticism of Israel and its abuse of the Palestinians, but I've never heard someone be antisemitic ... Let's remember, when Hitler won his election in 1932, his policy then was that Jews should be moved to Israel. He was supporting Zionism. [He then] went mad and ending up killing six million Jews ... There has been a very well-orchestrated campaign by the Israel lobby to smear anybody who criticises Israeli policy as antisemitic ... Frankly, there has been an attempt to smear Jeremy

Corbyn, and his associates, as antisemitic from the moment he became leader.[8]

Livingstone's claim that Hitler was 'supporting Zionism' by allowing German Jews to leave for Palestine in the 1930s suggests that Zionism is nothing more than the belief that Jews should leave Europe because they can't live in non-Jewish societies. This narrow, negative view of Zionism underpins Livingstone's misrepresentation of history. Hitler did want to rid Europe of its Jews and initially tried to achieve this via mass emigration rather than genocide, but he certainly did not support the Zionist goal of Jewish empowerment through national self-determination. Zionism was a movement to help Jews escape from antisemitism and give them control over their own future through the structure and sovereignty of a nation state. No longer would Jews be at the mercy of antisemitic politicians and subject to the whims of potentially hostile societies, so the thinking went, because they would create their own society in Israel governed by Jewish politicians. Hitler wanted the opposite: he made antisemitism and the destruction of the Jewish people the defining characteristics of Nazi Germany. To claim that Hitler ever supported Zionism is to traduce Zionism and diminish Hitler's antisemitism. Livingstone must have known that associating Hitler with Zionism in the way he did would arouse a furious reaction. He compounded the offence by claiming that 'anybody who criticises Israeli policy' is smeared as antisemitic and, further, that this is not spontaneously done but is the deliberate product of a 'well-orchestrated campaign'. This added the charges of conspiracy and dishonesty to that of Nazi collaboration. Livingstone later told the Parliamentary Home Affairs Select Committee:

> If I had said something that was untrue and it caused offence, I would apologise. What I said was true. What caused offence was a group of embittered old Blairite MPs running around lying about what I had said ... the MPs who smeared me about antisemitism have been criticising Jeremy Corbyn and stabbing him in the back for the last nine months on a whole series of issues.[9]

As a keen student of twentieth-century history, Livingstone is likely to know that Germany's defeat in the First World War was widely attributed by German nationalists to its alleged betrayal by internal enemies, chiefly Jews and communists, who were said to have stabbed Germany in the back. Hitler fiercely believed in this 'stab in the back' myth and it became a central part of Nazi propaganda. Whether Livingstone's use of this same metaphor to claim that Corbyn is the victim of similar treachery was a conscious reference to this antisemitic myth is, again, something that only Livingstone will know for sure.

As the row over his comments rumbled on into 2017,

Livingstone added further outrageous claims: that the Zionist movement collaborated with Nazi Germany by agreeing to buy German goods, thereby undermining an international boycott; that the SS set up training camps for Zionist Jews in Germany; that the 'Zionist flag' was the only flag, other than the swastika, that was allowed to be flown in Nazi Germany; and that Nazi Germany armed the Zionist underground in British-controlled Mandate Palestine. These were all either complete fabrications or such wild distortions of the truth as to be completely misleading. The suggestion that on the eve of the Holocaust, the SS, which was directly responsible for the extermination of the Jewish people in Europe, would train and arm the very people they sought to destroy is tantamount to Holocaust denial. Unlike Shah, Livingstone has never retracted his comments or accepted that they were antisemitic. He still insists they were historically accurate, even though several expert historians of the Holocaust, including Professor Timothy Snyder, Professor Yehuda Bauer, Professor Rainer Schulze and Professor Deborah Lipstadt, have all said otherwise. But historical accuracy was not Livingstone's aim: he simply sought, as he has for decades, to denigrate Israel and Zionism by associating them as closely as possible with Nazism. The consequence has been to make alleged relations between Hitler, Nazism and the Zionist movement a subject of heated and largely ignorant debate amongst people who know little of the actual history and are motivated primarily by factional politics. One example was the Haavara Agreement, previously a document of significant interest to historians of Nazi Germany but to few others, which suddenly became a live political issue in the 21st-century Labour Party thanks to Livingstone. This agreement was struck between German Zionists and the Nazi regime in 1933, to allow German Jews to leave the country with some of their possessions rather than losing absolutely everything. Around 60,000 Jews were saved through this agreement, but at the time it was criticised by other Jewish organisations who wanted a total boycott of Nazi Germany. In the 1930s, these debates were between desperate people who shared a common goal of saving Jews from the Nazis. In 2016, Ken Livingstone ensured it would be just one more thing for people in and around the Labour Party to argue about in their increasingly bitter struggle for the future of their party; and those people who want to defend Labour and Corbyn from the charge of antisemitism now do so by claiming that Hitler supported Zionism. Livingstone was eventually found guilty of bringing the party into disrepute with his comments about Hitler and Zionism, but was given the mildest of punishments: a two-year suspension from being allowed to hold an internal party office (such as conference delegate or chair of his constituency party), one year of which he had already served while waiting for his hearing.[10]

The whole affair was hugely damaging for the Labour Party's image in the Jewish community. A week after the suspension of

Shah and Livingstone, the *Jewish Chronicle* published an opinion poll showing that just 8.5 per cent of British Jews would vote Labour if there were a general election then, compared to 18 per cent who had voted Labour in the 2015 election. The poll also showed that 66 per cent of British Jews felt Corbyn had not done enough to tackle antisemitism and 38 per cent felt that Labour had a 'high' level of antisemitism. The growing disconnect between British Jews and Labour's grassroots was shown by the fact that a separate poll, conducted at around the same time, found that only 5 per cent of Labour Party members thought antisemitism was a bigger problem in Labour than in other parties, while 49 per cent thought that 'the Labour Party does not have a problem with antisemitism and it has been created by the press and Jeremy Corbyn's opponents to attack him'. This rose to 62 per cent amongst those members who had voted for Corbyn in the 2015 leadership election. Over half thought that Livingstone's comments were not antisemitic and that he should not be expelled from the party (although only slightly fewer thought Labour was right to suspend him). Nevertheless, as the media looked more closely at the story of antisemitism in the Labour Party, a cottage industry of bloggers and Twitter accounts sprang up to look for more examples of antisemitic comments, primarily on social media, by Labour supporters, members and activists. As they dug, more and more cases emerged. In Bradford, Nasreen Khan was shortlisted to be a Labour council candidate despite apparently writing on Facebook in 2012: 'It's such a shame that the history teachers in our school never taught us this but they are the first to start brainwashing us and our children into thinking the bad guy was Hitler. What have the Jews done good in this world??' Khan was subsequently dropped from the shortlist. In Birmingham, Labour councillor Zafar Iqbal was spared disciplinary action after he claimed to have no idea why his Facebook account had shared an antisemitic video by the American white supremacist leader David Duke. Andy Slack, a Labour councillor in Chesterfield, retained his place in the party and his council seat after he allegedly shared an image on Facebook that showed an antisemitic caricature of a hook-nosed Jew in army uniform, blood dripping from his hands and mouth, with the slogan 'Israel was created by the Rothschilds, not God... And what they are doing to the Palestinian people now is EXACTLY what they intend for the whole world.' Billy Wells was dropped as a council candidate in Great Yarmouth after he was accused of writing on Facebook, 'It's the super rich families of the Zionist lobby that control the world. Our world leaders sell their souls for greed and do the bidding of Israel.' Terry Couchman, a council candidate in Wiltshire, was suspended after comments about 'the ZioNazi storm troopers of IsraHell' and 'fake Jews of IsraHell and the USA' were found on his Facebook page. Renfrewshire Labour councillor Terry Kelly was suspended and then reinstated by the party following articles on his blog claiming that the Oscars are rigged by the 'powerful Jewish lobby' and that 'the American Jewish Lobby is extremely powerful and it has its boot on Obama's neck'. After his suspension was lifted, he blamed it on 'the Zionist "powers that be" in Israel'. Roy Smart, a Labour council candidate in Tunbridge Wells, was suspended by Labour and dropped as a candidate after the *Daily Mirror* found Holocaust denial material and conspiracy theories about the 'Rothschilds' Jewish mafia' on his Facebook page. The sheer number of cases threatened to overwhelm the party's understaffed compliance unit, which was used to handling a relatively small number of disciplinary cases each month, usually in relation to the suitability of election candidates, and was now being deluged with antisemitism cases to investigate. In March 2018, the Labour Party revealed that 300 cases of antisemitism had been reported since Corbyn became leader, of which somewhere between 75 and 200 had still not been dealt with. This might still be an underestimate: one campaign group, Labour Against Antisemitism, claimed to have reported over 1,000 cases to the party.[11]

The number of antisemitism cases, and the repeated pattern they revealed of conspiracy theories, Holocaust abuse or denial and obsessive hatred of Israel, points towards a culture of antisemitism in the party rather than a random scattering of unrelated bigotries. The virtual petri dishes in which this culture has grown are the new alt-left media blogs that have become the favoured source of news for many of Corbyn's supporters, and the unofficial Facebook groups that sprang up to back Corbyn's campaign for the Labour leadership and became the political watering holes for his grassroots support. These new sources of information, news and political advocacy are popular precisely because the media is so distrusted across the left. It is taken for granted that the Labour Party is handicapped in elections due to the right-leaning editorial line of most national newspapers in Britain: according to a poll in August 2016, 69 per cent of Labour voters thought that 'the mainstream media as a whole has been deliberately biasing coverage to portray Jeremy Corbyn in a negative manner'. This goes up to 97 per cent amongst party members who supported Corbyn in that summer's leadership election, compared to 44 per cent of those who supported his challenger, Owen Smith MP. This idea is taken a step further by many on the left who see the media as an integral part of the elite that controls the levers of power in society and which, therefore, will always promote the establishment view rather than giving publicity to insurgent or radical politics.[12]

This frustration has led to the embrace of alternative sources of information and new media outlets. The rise of overseas TV channels like Iran's Press TV, Russia Today (later rebranded as RT) and Qatar's Al Jazeera offered one alternative for those who do not trust the British media. While several MPs of all parties have appeared as guests on Russia Today, Corbyn, Livingstone and George Galloway actually presented their own shows on Press TV. It is certainly true that Press TV, an arm of Iranian state broadcasting, gives space to voices and opinions that cannot get a hearing in the mainstream British media, but this goes well beyond left-wing backbench MPs. Press TV has a record of giving a platform to far-right voices, including Peter Rushton, a leading figure on the British far right for over twenty years, and Holocaust denier Michèle Renouf. In 2008, Press TV published a lengthy article by another British Holocaust denier, Nicholas Kollerstrom, that argued that 'the alleged massacre of Jewish people by gassing during World War II was scientifically impossible'. When Press TV was fined by Ofcom in 2011 for broadcasting an interview of jailed Iranian-Canadian journalist Maziar Bahari that was obtained under duress during his imprisonment, the channel responded by publishing, on its website, an article that quoted from the notorious antisemitic hoax *The Protocols of the Elders of Zion*. Having cited *The Protocols*' claim that most of the media is in the hands of a Jewish conspiracy, the article proudly declared: 'Press TV of Iran is one of the "few exceptions" to The Lobby's control of global print and electronically transmitted news and analysis.'[13]

While some prefer to watch Press TV or RT to the BBC, it is the emergence of alt-left media blogs like The Canary, Skwawkbox and Evolve Politics that have transformed the media landscape for the British left. These blogs attract a large, loyal readership with a regular diet of stories about Labour successes, Tory misdeeds and media bias, all told in hyperbolic language and with varying degrees of accuracy. Their output is unashamedly partisan in support of Corbyn's leadership. Kerry-Anne Mendoza, founder and editor of the biggest alt-left site, The Canary, admits that 'we are absolutely biased … We're in this as an issue-driven organisation.' Matt Turner of Evolve Politics concurred, saying, 'The way we write is not without its biases but it presents an alternate point of view which is legitimate.' They justify this by insisting that newspapers and broadcasters are just as biased and committed to their own political interests but pretend otherwise. At least these pro-Corbyn blogs are open about their political motivations, so the thinking goes, and they see themselves as integral to the success of the Corbyn project. Mendoza explained that 'we set up The Canary precisely because of the one-sided reporting already happening in the mainstream media – we are presenting the other side of that story … Our mission is to disrupt the hateful messages of the right-wing UK press.'[14]

These sites are remarkably popular amongst Corbyn supporters. An investigation by BuzzFeed News found that, during the 2017 general election campaign, their articles repeatedly garnered larger readerships on social media than anything from national newspapers. Research by Oxford University's Reuters Institute for the Study of Journalism in 2018 found that Canary readers trust it as a news source more than readers of the *Daily Mail, The Sun,* the *Daily Mirror* and *The Independent* trust those news outlets. They have a symbiotic relationship with large, unofficial Facebook groups where supporters of Corbyn's Labour gather online. These groups take much of their content from the alt-left blogs, and in turn provide much of the blogs' traffic. Research during the 2015 Labour leadership campaign found that 57 per cent of Corbyn supporters took most of their news from social media, compared to 32 per cent amongst the general population. The scale of this online political ecosystem is impressive: according to an investigation by the *Sunday Times* in early 2018, the twenty largest pro-Corbyn Facebook groups had a combined membership of 400,000 people. While most of the content posted in these groups is the usual stuff found in everyday political conversations – posts about the NHS, schools or housing, for example – when the discussion turns to Jews, Israel or antisemitism, all too often it generates comments that are antisemitic, alongside denials that there is any significant antisemitism to be found in Corbyn's Labour Party and allegations of a smear campaign by Zionists, Blairites or the right-wing media. The *Sunday Times* found thousands of posts endorsing antisemitic conspiracy theories, denying the Holocaust or calling for violence against Corbyn's political opponents across various different groups during their investigation. Several members of Corbyn's own staff and that of shadow Chancellor John McDonnell MP were members of some of the groups. There is no suggestion that any of them had posted anything antisemitic, or even seen the antisemitic posts and comments, but that is not the point. Antisemitic attitudes and language are part of the grassroots political culture of the mass movement that propelled Corbyn to the party leadership and has subsequently been absorbed into the Labour Party.

Conspiracy theories are an integral part of this political culture. One opinion poll in August 2015 found that 28 per cent of Corbyn supporters believe the world is controlled by a secretive elite, compared to 13 per cent of the general population. Another poll in August 2016 found that 55 per cent of those supporting Jeremy Corbyn in that summer's Labour leadership contest thought MI5 had been working to undermine Jeremy Corbyn, compared to only 11 per cent of those who supported his challenger, Owen Smith. This difference was reflected in other ways: 50 per cent of those who had joined since September 2015, when Corbyn became leader, agreed with the suggestion about MI5, compared to 28 per cent of those who had been members before the May 2015 general election. Fully 35 per cent of Corbyn supporters even thought that some Labour MPs had been secretly planted in the party by the Conservatives to undermine the Labour left. Mendoza has appeared as a guest on the online radio show of Richie Allen, a leading conspiracy theorist based in Manchester whose show is hosted on the website of Britain's top conspiracist David Icke. She did not object when Allen claimed that 'if we put Jeremy Corbyn and John McDonnell in tomorrow, it won't make a blind bit of difference; central bankers, Rothschild-controlled central banks control the world', or when he said that 'Israel has no right to exist.' At the end of the interview Mendoza told Allen, 'The thing that really I love about your show, I love about you, is that you're passionately engaged and you really care and everything that you say comes from a place of wanting to make the world a better place.' A few weeks before interviewing Mendoza, Allen had hosted Holocaust denier Nicholas Kollerstrom on his show on Holocaust Memorial Day to discuss 'the myths and realities of the Holocaust'. Mike Sivier, who edits another alt-left blog called Vox Political, has also appeared as a guest on Allen's show. Sivier has repeatedly insisted that complaints about antisemitism in Labour are a smear and that Ken Livingstone should not have been disciplined by the party. The Canary takes a similar line. When Livingstone was suspended for claiming that Hitler supported Zionism, The Canary warned that the 'media madness surrounding Ken Livingstone's comments' was a 'trap' to trick people into confusing anti-Zionism with antisemitism. A week later, it published an editorial, written by Mendoza, arguing that it is 'wholly legitimate, and indeed urgent' to compare modern Israel to Nazi Germany and Gaza to the Warsaw Ghetto.[15]

One of the main unofficial Labour Facebook groups is called Labour Party Forum and has around 16,000 members, nine of whom are administrators for the group. If antisemitic material is posted, it should be reported to the administrators for removal – but often it was the administrators of the group who were posting the antisemitic material. One of the administrators of Labour Party Forum posted an article from the American far-right website Veterans Today that claimed the 'pagan Holocaust religion exalts the primacy of Jewish suffering'. Another posted a meme from David Icke about 'Rothschild Zionist Israel'. A third wrote to a Jewish person on the group that 'of course the persecution of the Jews was a terrible thing but like an abused child you have now become the abusers'. When it was brought to this particular administrator's attention that there was Holocaust denial material in the group, he called the complainant a 'frothing Hasbara troll' ('hasbara' is the name for pro-Israel public relations campaigns) and then wrote two hashtags: #StopIsrael and #FreePalestine. This belief that complaints of antisemitism can be rebutted by assertions of support for Palestine is reflected in Labour Party Forum's Position Statement, posted at the top of the group's page. After declaring that 'we resolutely support a two state solution with secure viable borders for both sides', the statement then sets out the group's opposition both to antisemitism and to Israel; and declares that anybody posting either antisemitic content or 'support of Israel's actions' will be blocked. In reality, it is people who argue against antisemitism, rather than those who post it, who are much more likely to be forced out. One academic study of antisemitic language in a different unofficial Labour-supporting group with a similar name, The Labour Party Forum (which had approximately 40,000 members), found that 'the TLPF membership was effectively being purged of many of those who argued most effectively against the sorts of [antisemitic] repertoires mobilised in the data we have seen, while those who mobilised such repertoires were protected'.[16]

However, the Facebook group that brought this problem to Corbyn's doorstep was not one with his name on, nor one set up to support the Labour Party. It was a pro-Palestinian Facebook group called Palestine Live, whose membership included many of the leading and best-known activists in Britain's pro-Palestinian movement. Set up in 2013 and with over 3,000 members, this was a secret Facebook group, meaning that the existence and content of the group was known only to members; it did not show up in Facebook searches and only people chosen by the group's administrators could join. Jeremy Corbyn was a member, as were fellow Labour MPs Chris Williamson and Clive Lewis, former Liberal Democrat peer Baroness Tonge and former Lib Dem MP David Ward. In March 2018, David Collier, an independent blogger who writes about antisemitism and extremism in the pro-Palestinian movement and who had infiltrated Palestine Live, published a 290-page report showing numerous examples of antisemitism within the group. This went much further than simply over-heated commentary about Israel and Palestine, and included

Holocaust denial and conspiracy theories taken from far-right, antisemitic websites. It was a distillation of the antisemitism that had been growing in parts of the left for decades.

The antisemitism in Palestine Live was not incidental. All three of the group's administrators regularly posted antisemitic material. The group's founder and one of its administrators, Elleanne Green, posted material from the far-right site Veterans Today and The Ugly Truth, whose strapline was 'intelligent "antisemitism" for thinking Gentiles'. Other posts by Green included conspiracy theories linking Israel to the 9/11 terrorist attacks and to ISIS terrorism in France. When one member posted Holocaust denial articles in the group, Green replied, 'We don't usually do all the Holocaust questioning stuff in here … there are other places for that.' Green even posted an article that quoted approvingly from Hitler's memoir *Mein Kampf*, alleging that 'the Jews again slyly dupe the dumb Goyim' and that Israel would be 'a central organization for their international world swindle'. Another administrator of the group, Tony Gratrex, is a veteran pro-Palestinian activist from Reading. He posted several articles in the group alleging that Israel was behind 'false flag' terrorist attacks in the UK, the US and Europe. A Holocaust denial article posted by Gratrex claimed that 'somewhere between 100–150 thousand people perished in Auschwitz mainly as a result of disease and starvation, which was not a deliberate act on the part of the Germans but rather the outcome of Allied carpet-bombing of Germany's infrastructure', and dismissed 'the

Zionists' pre-meditated fictional account of six million dead Jews'. The third administrator, Carol Foster, posted an apparently self-penned poem called 'The Jewish Lobby', which read:

> The Jewish Lobby it's plain to see
> Is full of people unlike me
> They're bigoted and full of bile
> Their talk is cheap and rather vile
> From what they say it's really clear
> They are everything that they most fear
> So it's really clear now is the hour
> To rob these demons of their power[17]

To quantify the antisemitism in Palestine Live, Collier looked more closely at all the posts in the group in the first two weeks of February 2018. He found that nearly two thirds were from group members who had several examples of antisemitism, such as conspiracy theories, classical antisemitic tropes or Holocaust denial, on their personal Facebook pages. When he removed posts by Jewish anti-Zionists from his sample, the proportion of active members who had antisemitic content on their own Facebook pages went up to nearly three quarters during that period. In other words, the most active members of the group were also the most antisemitic; and because they were the most active group members, they inevitably shaped the tone and direction of debate in the group.

Members of Palestine Live reacted to this antisemitism in different ways. Deborah Fink, a Jewish anti-Zionist, chose to advise fellow group members to swap references to Jews for references to Zionists, apparently believing this would remove the antisemitism from the ideas they were expressing. In one exchange, she explained to somebody who wrote, 'It's all over for the Jewnazi' that 'I prefer ZioNazi to Jew Nazi', because not all Jews support Israel. Another member, Thomas Tallon, took an alternative approach, leaving the group in protest at what he considered to be 'Nazi-grade, unequivocal racism', and posting a statement in the group condemning the antisemitism it contained. In his view, 'Anyone who joined around or after the summer of 2014 will assuredly have been perfectly aware of what he was getting into.' Having said that, people can be added to Facebook groups without their knowledge and never visit them; or they can drop into groups occasionally and not see anything amiss. Simply being a member of Palestine Live is not evidence that a person is either antisemitic themselves or aware of antisemitism from others. This was Corbyn's explanation of his involvement, telling the media:

> I replied by Facebook message to a couple of things about
> a suggestion on the vote on recognising Palestine, which I
> supported, and inviting a doctor to speak at an event. I have
> never trawled through the whole group. I have never read all
> the messages on it. I have removed myself from it. Obviously,

any antisemitic comment is wrong. Any antisemitism in any
form is wrong.

However, Corbyn's involvement in the group is revealing in
other ways. He was repeatedly tagged in posts by other users,
particularly by Green, and sometimes replied. He also sometimes interacted with posts where he hadn't been tagged,
suggesting that, at least occasionally, he proactively looked at
the group's content. In October 2014, when Corbyn was still a
backbencher, his office helped other activists in Palestine Live
to organise an anti-Israel meeting in Parliament at which visiting American writer Max Blumenthal was the guest speaker.
Blumenthal had contacted Green to ask her to set up a meeting for him to speak, and Green asked other members of the
group for help. She specifically tagged Corbyn and Tonge to
ask them if they would organise a meeting in Parliament, and
one of the other group members followed this up with an
email to Corbyn's office. The end result of this networking was
that one of Corbyn's aides helped the members of Palestine
Live to book a room in Parliament for Blumenthal to speak.
In fact, Blumenthal turned up late on the night in question,
so an impromptu speech was given by James Thring, a veteran
far-right activist who was present. The following day, Corbyn
wrote a comment on Palestine Live thanking his aide for helping to organise the meeting and apologising that he couldn't
attend in person. Later that week he 'liked' another post he

had been tagged in, about a different meeting that Blumenthal spoke at in London. The following week, Corbyn responded positively to another request from Green, this time to organise a meeting in Parliament for Norwegian doctor and pro-Palestinian activist Mads Gilbert. Perhaps Corbyn did only dip in and out of Palestine Live, as he claims, and never looked long enough to see the antisemitism it contained. Elsewhere on Facebook, though, Corbyn seemed to enjoy spending time interacting with other pro-Palestinian activists and commenting on their posts, on subjects as wide-ranging as Israel's security barrier ('like a great serpent running through the land'); David Miliband's talents and flaws ('David's problem is not his ability, he has bags of it, but his perception of the world'); Rupert Murdoch's takeover bid for BSkyB (Murdoch will 'hugely profit and forever damage our sources of information and right to know what is happening in the world'); and the BBC's coverage of the 2011 uprising in Egypt ('Does the BBC "analysis" really matter. Aljazeera have been giving a far more realistic coverage all day and their experts all come from the region.')[18]

If the Palestine Live Facebook group brought the issue of antisemitism uncomfortably close to home for the Labour leader, the next scandal to emerge featured Corbyn squarely at the centre of the action. In 2012, American graffiti artist Kalen Ockerman, also known as Mear One, painted a large mural on a wall in Tower Hamlets, east London, an area known for impressive and imaginative street art. Ockerman's mural was a visual conspiracy theory about global inequality. It showed six old, white men, obviously wealthy, playing Monopoly on a board that rested on the backs of darker-skinned, crouching, faceless people: a representation of the downtrodden. Above them was an eye in a pyramid, which is a symbol commonly associated by conspiracy theorists with the Illuminati, Freemasons or other secret societies. Behind them was a scene of industrial dystopia, full of machinery and chimneys belching fiery smoke into the atmosphere. A protestor stood to the side, clenched fist aloft, holding a placard that read 'The New World Order is the Enemy of Humanity'. Not only was this an obvious conspiracy piece, but some of the men sat around the table – the bad guys in the scene – looked like Jewish caricatures complete with big noses. Ockerman described it as 'a mural that depicted the elite banker cartel known as the Rothschilds, Rockefellers, Morgans, the ruling class, elite view, the Wizards of Oz'. He later clarified that the banker figures were a mixture of 'Jewish and white Anglos' and insisted that it was a critique of 'class and privilege', not of Jews.[19]

The mural caused a huge fuss locally. It was denounced as antisemitic by political figures on all sides in Tower Hamlets, as well as by people from the Jewish community, and was subsequently removed. The then Mayor of Tower Hamlets, Lutfur Rahman, was in no doubt this was the right course of action, saying, 'Whether intentional or otherwise, the images of the

bankers perpetuate antisemitic propaganda about conspiratorial Jewish domination of financial and political institutions.
Where freedom of expression runs the risk of inciting racial
hatred ... then it is right that such expression should be
curtailed.' Ockerman protested with a post on Facebook complaining that 'they want to buff my mural' – in other words,
to remove it – and Corbyn found his way onto Ockerman's
Facebook page to sympathise. 'Why?' he asked. 'You are in
good company. Rockerfeller [*sic*] destroyed Diego Viera's [*sic*]
mural because it includes a picture of Lenin.' This is presumably a reference to *Man at the Crossroads*, a 1930s fresco by the
Mexican artist Diego Rivera that was commissioned for the
Rockefeller Center in New York and then destroyed before it
was completed. The comparison can only have been meant as a
compliment: Rivera was a friend of Trotsky and exactly the kind
of Latin American socialist romanticised by Corbyn's brand of
leftism. Nobody paid much attention to Corbyn's expression
of support at the time, but it had not gone completely unnoticed. In November 2015, after Corbyn became Labour Party
leader, the *Jewish Chronicle* asked his office about it but did not
receive a reply. In February 2017, a Labour supporter called
Sam Shemtob made a formal complaint to the party, but again,
nothing seems to have been done. Then, in March 2018, two
weeks after the news had broken about Corbyn's membership
of Palestine Live, Labour MP Luciana Berger saw images of
the mural and Corbyn's supportive comment for the first time,

and asked Corbyn's office for an explanation. Berger is Jewish and has been the target of antisemitism from both far right and far left since becoming an MP. Once she made her query public (having had no response initially), Corbyn's account of his thinking six years earlier was haphazard to say the least. First he claimed to have been 'responding to concerns about the removal of public art on grounds of freedom of speech', but acknowledged that the mural was antisemitic and should have been removed. When people pointed out this meant that Corbyn had knowingly supported an antisemitic mural on free-speech grounds, he issued a second statement clarifying that in 2012 he was only making 'a general comment about the removal of public art on grounds of freedom of speech', but that he now supports the removal of Ockerman's mural and 'I sincerely regret that I did not look more closely at the image I was commenting on'. In neither statement did he apologise. Nor, more importantly, did he explain how he could have known enough about the controversy around the mural to go to Ockerman's Facebook page to write a supportive comment, but not be aware that it was being removed because it was accused of being antisemitic.[20]

Many found Corbyn's explanations unconvincing. *Jewish Chronicle* editor Stephen Pollard accused him of lying when he claimed not to have noticed that the mural was antisemitic. Novelist Howard Jacobson asserted that if Corbyn did not realise the mural was antisemitic, it can only be because he shares, at some level, the antisemitic view depicted in the mural: 'In the end there is only one conclusion we can reach: if he saw nothing exceptionally offensive in this mural it can only be because it mirrored an image of the Jew as bloodsucker he was already carrying in his head.' A more charitable view would be that Corbyn was blinded by the left-wing view of racism as a phenomenon defined by skin colour and power. If racism is defined by rich, powerful, white men oppressing poor, powerless people of colour, then Ockerman's depiction of the bankers in his mural cannot possibly be antisemitic; on the contrary, it is the faceless workers in the mural who are the victims of racial exploitation. But this begs another question: if Corbyn is so incapable of recognising antisemitism – not just antisemitic forms of anti-Zionism, but old-fashioned, conspiracist, Jews-with-big-noses antisemitism, what is the value of his claim to oppose something he can't recognise?[21]

This turned out to be the moment the dam burst. All the anger, frustration and sheer disbelief in the Jewish community, in the Parliamentary Labour Party, and amongst many journalists that the festering sore of antisemitism in the Labour Party had been allowed to grow for so long poured out. The difference this time was that the mural was not about the Israeli–Palestinian conflict. Nor was Corbyn being condemned for the views of somebody else he had once met or spoken alongside. This was a mural featuring the hoariest of antisemitic images – rich Jewish bankers with big noses conspiring to dominate the world – and Corbyn had personally written a message in its support. Three days after Berger's tweet, with mounting media coverage, numerous condemnations from Labour MPs and a public apology from Labour's deputy leader Tom Watson, the Jewish community's main representative organisations, the Board of Deputies of British Jews and the Jewish Leadership Council, published an unprecedented open letter to the Leader of the Opposition. 'Enough is Enough', it read, and then listed the charge sheet against Corbyn:

> When Jews complain about an obviously antisemitic mural in Tower Hamlets, Corbyn of course supports the artist. Hizbollah commits terrorist atrocities against Jews, but Corbyn calls them his friends and attends pro-Hizbollah rallies in London. Exactly the same goes for Hamas. Raed Salah says Jews kill Christian children to drink their blood. Corbyn opposes his extradition and invites him for tea at the House of Commons. These are not the only cases. He is repeatedly found alongside people with blatantly antisemitic views, but claims never to hear or read them. Again and again, Jeremy Corbyn has sided with antisemites rather than Jews.[22]

The next day, 2,000 people gathered to protest outside Parliament – the first time anybody present could remember the Jewish community demonstrating against one of Britain's main political parties on the grounds of antisemitism. Around forty Labour MPs attended to show their support, some of whom spoke alongside Jewish community leaders. Corbyn wrote a public letter to the Board of Deputies and Jewish Leadership Council that, for the first time, accepted that antisemitism 'has surfaced' in Labour and should not be 'dismissed as simply a matter of a few bad apples'. He acknowledged that the left has its own forms of antisemitism and that 'newer forms of antisemitism are sometimes woven into criticism of Israeli governments', including comparisons of Israel to Nazi Germany, and he pledged he would be a 'militant opponent' of antisemitism in the party. He also apologised for his comment about the antisemitic mural. The significance of this letter should not be missed. Until this point, while consistently saying he opposed and condemned antisemitism, Corbyn had always rejected complaints directed at him or at people in his political orbit. He had never described the comparison of Israel with Nazi Germany, utterly ubiquitous in pro-Palestinian circles, as antisemitic. Nor had he accepted that the left has its own kind of antisemitism. His new line was backed by Momentum, the left-wing activist movement that was created out of Corbyn's 2015 leadership campaign after he had won. Momentum issued a statement warning that 'accusations of antisemitism should not and cannot be dismissed simply as right-wing smears nor as the result of conspiracies', and spoke of 'unconscious bias which manifests itself in varied, nuanced and subtle ways and is more widespread in the Labour Party than many of us had understood even a few months ago'. For the Jewish community and for the Labour Party, this felt like a decisive moment.[23]

Except amongst Corbyn's supporters on the left of the party, on the alt-left blogs and in the pro-Corbyn Facebook groups, things carried on as normal. Polling in the days following the demonstration found that only 11 per cent of Labour members thought antisemitism was worse in Labour than in other parties and 23 per cent thought there was no problem to speak of at all (for comparison, a different poll found that 22 per cent of the general population thought Labour had a worse problem than other parties, and 34 per cent thought that Corbyn was personally antisemitic). Skwawkbox claimed that media coverage of the mural was a sign of the establishment's 'desperation, hypocrisy and dishonesty', to help the Tories in the forthcoming local elections. The Canary urged readers to join a counter-protest, organised by the small far-left group Jewish Voice for Labour, to oppose the main Jewish community demonstration at Parliament. Those Labour MPs who attended the Jewish community demonstration started to receive abuse on social media; some were threatened with deselection by activists in their local constituency parties. One MP, Thangam Debbonaire, was summoned to a meeting of her local party in Bristol West to 'explain her actions'. A motion of censure included the suggestion that antisemitism exists because 'when people see inequality, ecological disaster and war alongside the accumulation of unprecedented wealth, in the private hands of a few, it is reasonable that they seek out explanations' (it was voted down by 108 votes to 84). Debbonaire left the meeting visibly upset after being heckled from the floor. That same day, Jennie Formby, the newly appointed general secretary of the Labour Party and a Corbyn ally, wrote to all constituency Labour parties warning them that 'tackling antisemitism in the party is a central priority' and 'criticism of any individual or organisation who has expressed concern about antisemitism would be deeply unhelpful to that process'.[24]

As media coverage of the mural and the demonstration snowballed, the Facebook pages of The Canary and Skwawkbox filled up with comments about 'right-wing media hysteria', claiming 'More ridiculous, vile and false antisemitism smears', 'Wealthy Jewish [sic] prepared to slander Corbyn', 'The "Friends of Israel" Zionists are having a field day', 'This is about the illuminati/world bankers/Rothschild's [sic] who happen to majority Jewish [sic] and happens to be true of what is happening to our planet', 'Just more shit from the 1% global elite who really make the decisions on what effects [sic] our lives', 'Zionists run the BBC', 'This is what happen's [sic] when Zionist Jews control our government!', 'Maybe a number of very rich people who live in our country are Jewish, so they are concerned they will have to pay more tax'. And so on. In the We Support Jeremy Corbyn Facebook group (the biggest of the pro-Corbyn Facebook groups, with 68,000 members), a Labour Party member called Frances Naggs posted an 'open letter to Jeremy Corbyn' the day after the Jewish community demonstration, which read:

> Yesterday we witnessed the full onslaught of a very power-ful special interest group mobilising its apparent, immense strength against you. It is clear this group can employ the full might of the BBC to make sure its voice is heard very loudly and clearly ... and no special interest group, regardless of their history or influence, can be allowed to dictate who the rest of us can vote for or how we vote ... We know that any politician who stands for the many and not the few will have very many powerful enemies and it is expecting an awful lot of a person to put up with the pressures that are put on you. But thank-you, thank-you for your inspiration and steadfast-ness and be sure you still have my support.

Within a day and a half, 2,000 members of the Facebook group had liked the letter, it was shared hundreds of times and nearly 1,000 had asked for their names to be added to it. This response contrasted with that of the shadow Chancellor John McDonnell, who described the letter as deploying 'an antisemitic stereotype that undermines not supports Jeremy and his determination to unite our communities'. Elsewhere in the We Support Jeremy Corbyn group, Jonathan Arkush, the President of the Board of Deputies of British Jews, was described as a 'Zionist Jewish thug', a 'c***', a 'f****** Tory', a 'Zionist prick', as a rat and as vermin.[25]

It was as if the new line coming from the top of the party, that antisemitism is a genuine problem in Labour that needs to be addressed, and that it is not a smear to say so, was not being heard amongst Corbyn's grassroots supporters. People who had spent years comforting themselves that allegations of antisemitism on the left, or in the pro-Palestinian movement, were a cynical trick designed to stop them criticising Israel, were unsurprisingly resistant to the message that this was not the case. That this was coming from Corbyn, McDonnell and others who for years had themselves dismissed or minimised allegations of antisemitism in the pro-Palestinian movement added to the disbelief. The antisemitic culture that had grown on the fringes of the left for decades, moved into the mainstream of the Labour Party, and now shaped the discourse about Jews, Israel and Zionism in Corbyn's movement had taken on a life of its own.

CHAPTER EIGHT

WHY CHAKRABARTI FAILED

The growth of an antisemitic culture in the Labour Party and its association with history's oldest and most enduring racial prejudice has, at times, been intensely discomforting for Jeremy Corbyn, and damaging to the image of the party. They would claim, with justification, that they have not ignored the problem and have taken measures to address it; and their critics would claim, also with justification, that those measures have been half-hearted, cosmetic and ineffective. In the two years following Jeremy Corbyn's election as Labour leader, the party held three different inquiries into antisemitism, introduced new rules governing the use of antisemitic language by members and began an overhaul of its disciplinary processes. Yet these efforts, for various reasons, have failed to have the desired effect, and their failure has further damaged the party's image in the eyes of most British Jews. The reasons they failed show just how deeply this antisemitic culture, and in particular the culture of denial about the existence and nature of antisemitism in the party, has become embedded in parts of the British left.

The first of Labour's three inquiries was launched by Labour Students following Alex Chalmers' resignation as chair of Oxford University Labour Club. It looked solely at the allegations of antisemitism at Oxford and was completed within a week. Labour Students passed their report to the national party, who, instead of publishing it or acting on its findings, decided to hold a second inquiry of its own. The party's National Executive Committee – its highest governing body – asked Baroness Jan Royall of Blaisdon, a veteran of Labour's front bench in the House of Lords, to lead it. After hearing all the available evidence and taking submissions from a range of Jewish organisations, she came to the conclusion that, although Oxford University Labour Club did not suffer from institutional antisemitism, it did have a 'cultural problem' that meant 'some Jewish members do not feel comfortable attending the meetings, let alone participating'. She added, 'It is clear to me from the weight of witnessed allegations received that there have been some incidents of antisemitic behaviour and that it is appropriate for the disciplinary procedures of our party to be invoked.' In mid-May, three months after Chalmers's resignation, Labour's NEC decided to only publish the executive summary of Royall's report and to withhold the main text. This meant, conveniently for Labour, that Royall's verdict that there was no evidence of institutional antisemitism was published, as that was in the executive summary, but her other comments regarding the culture of the Labour Club and the evidence of antisemitic behaviour, all of which were in the main body of her report, were not. This only became clear in August when the *Jewish Chronicle* obtained a leaked copy of the full report and published it on their website. Royall herself seemed displeased by this partial suppression of her findings. She wrote in May, when the NEC decided not to publish her report in full, of her 'disappointment and frustration that the main headline coming out of my inquiry is that there is no institutional antisemitism in Oxford University Labour Club'. That conclusion is 'only part of the story', she went on, because 'there is a cultural problem which means that Jewish students do not always feel welcome'. In January 2017, it emerged that the NEC had decided to ignore Royall's recommendation that two members of the Labour Club be put forward for disciplinary action. The investigation into their behaviour was dropped, and to this day nobody in Oxford University Labour Club has been disciplined, either by the party or by Oxford University, for the antisemitism that Royall found.[1]

By the time the executive summary of Baroness Royall's report was published, it had already been superseded by a third inquiry, which became the best-known and most controversial of the three. Led by Shami Chakrabarti – now herself a Labour peer – the way it was conceived, executed and published illustrates perfectly why, after more than two years of scandals and controversies, the Labour Party has failed to fully address the problem of antisemitism in its ranks or to win back the trust of so many British Jews. The Chakrabarti Inquiry was set up by Labour in response to the storm around the suspensions of Naz Shah and Ken Livingstone. According to the journalist and former *Jewish Chronicle* political editor Martin Bright, the idea for an inquiry came mainly from the office of John McDonnell and was, initially, resisted by some within Corbyn's circle. Bright suggested to a contact in McDonnell's office that they hand the job to Shami Chakrabarti, who had recently stepped down as director of the human rights pressure group Liberty, as she was 'an honest broker, whose reputation has too much to lose from a whitewash'. The irony of this assessment would, in time, become starkly apparent. The inquiry attracted an extraordinary amount of attention but there were indications from the start that all might not be as it seemed. Firstly, its terms of reference established that it would look at 'antisemitism and other forms of racism, including Islamophobia' – even though it was a direct response only to complaints of antisemitism and there had been no similar concerns aired about racism or Islamophobia in the party. This broadening of the inquiry's focus was in line with Corbyn's personal habit of condemning antisemitism together with racism and anti-Muslim hatred, rather than addressing it on its own. Secondly, on the day Chakrabarti accepted the role of inquiry chair she also joined the Labour Party, having previously been a 'Labour voter and supporter' but not a member. She explained in her report that she joined because 'I wanted to be clear with everyone and especially with Labour members and supporters, that my Inquiry would be conducted, and any recommendations made, in the Party's best interests'. She went on:

> If you worry about whether you still belong in your instinctive political home, please read on. Equally, if you feel that antisemitism or other racism is going to be manipulated by a hostile media, or by political rivals to silence your legitimate concerns about the world, this Report and our work is for you.

The message was unmistakeable: anybody hoping the inquiry would provide genuinely independent scrutiny of the reasons why antisemitism was rising in one of Britain's main political parties, or of Labour's performance in dealing with that problem, was going to be disappointed. Where the party's interests clashed with those of the Jewish community, the party would come first.[2]

Over eighty organisations contributed to the inquiry through either written submission or meetings, including Jewish and pro-Israel groups, pro-Palestinian campaign groups, Muslim community organisations, Labour Party and trade union branches and anti-racist organisations. Many Jewish organisations and activists submitted lengthy statements outlining not just the antisemitism they had experienced and witnessed in and around the Labour Party, but why they thought that anti-semitism was present in the first place. Several insisted that the party's problems were part of a broader culture of anti-semitism in parts of the left, rather than simply being a case of individuals making ill-judged remarks. Dr David Hirsh, a soci-ology lecturer at Goldsmiths, University of London, a Labour Party member and a long-standing campaigner against anti-semitism on the left, explained in his submission that the type of antisemitism found in the party should be understood as a case of 'institutional and cultural racism', involving 'racist ways of thinking, racist outcomes, racist norms and practices, discrimination and structural power imbalances' rather than individuals who consciously dislike Jews simply on account of their being Jewish. There is, he explained, a connection between the 'broad culture of emotional, disproportional and irrational hostility to Israel' that exists on the left and the cases of antisemitism that had emerged from Labour Party members. Presciently, he warned that administrative fixes or the policing of language alone will not cure the problem, as people will simply find a more euphemistic form of words to express the same antisemitic views: saying 'Israel lobby' rather than 'Jewish lobby', for example. Instead, Hirsh argued, 'polit-ical change' is necessary: 'If the party leadership cannot move Labour back into the mainstream democratic consensus on Israel and on antisemitism then this issue will continue to throw up crisis after crisis and it will continue to alienate most of the Jewish community; no doubt it will alienate many swing voters too.'[3]

The Chakrabarti Inquiry took a different view. Unlike Baroness Royall's report, it did not address the question of whether the Labour Party is institutionally or culturally anti-semitic and ignored all the evidence and argument it received on this question. Chakrabarti's only nod in this direction was to assert that the Labour Party is 'not overrun by antisem-itism, Islamophobia, or other forms of racism'. Instead, most of the body of the report, and thirteen of its twenty recom-mendations, concerned changes to the party's disciplinary and educational processes. Some of the suggestions actually risked weakening the party's powers to deal with antisemitic members. It was often unnecessary and disproportionate to suspend people while they were under investigation for anti-semitism, she wrote, and if they were suspended it shouldn't be publicised. Another recommendation was for some cases to be dealt with informally with no disciplinary sanction at all, and there should be no lifetime bans.

The report is not entirely without merit. It recommends that the abusive epithet 'Zio' should be banned, that 'racial or reli-gious tropes and stereotypes about any group of people should have no place in our modern Labour Party' and that compari-sons of Israel to Nazi Germany should be avoided. The fact that it took a two-month inquiry for such basic recommendations to be made shows how damaged the party's internal discourse about Jews, Israel and Zionism had become. Worse, though, is that the Chakrabarti Report did not ask, much less answer, the question of why Labour Party members use this language at all, beyond putting it down to personal insensitivity and 'incivility of discourse'. There was no investigation of antisemitic politics in general, or the history of antisemitism on the left, or the reasons why intense anti-Israel campaigning can foster antisemitic ways of thinking and acting. The Chakrabarti Report acknowledged that stereotypes about Jews being 'wealthy or interested in wealth or finance or political or media influence' are present in the Labour Party, but seemed not to wonder whether this antisemitic stereotype may have a particular appeal in a party that sets itself against the concentration of wealth and power in the hands of the few. Even when the report recommended that 'Zio' and Nazi comparisons should be banned by the party, it did not call either of them antisemitic. Instead, they should be banned to help promote 'kindness, politeness or good advocacy' and 'constructive debate'. The reason the Chakrabarti Report was so superficial is because its author wrongly treated the antisemitism found in the Labour Party as a discursive problem rather than a cultural one: people choosing the wrong words, rather than having the wrong ideas.

Chakrabarti also refused to address the question of who Corbyn and others had shared platforms with in the past, even though this was the behaviour that had first triggered concerns about antisemitism under his leadership. It was as if the report was designed to place a *cordon sanitaire* around the leader and his politics, to prevent the party's problem of anti-semitism contaminating him personally. Yet, as so often in this story, the focus returned to Corbyn, this time at the report's dramatic, and at times farcical, launch event. Representatives of Jewish community organisations, journalists from Jewish and national media, Members of Parliament and party activ-ists gathered in a plush conference room overlooking the river Thames to hear first Corbyn, and then Chakrabarti, present the findings of the report. It took place at a volatile moment in British politics. The week leading up to the launch had seen the country vote to leave the European Union, the resignation of Prime Minister David Cameron, the resignation of almost the entire shadow Cabinet in protest at Corbyn's leadership, and an overwhelming vote of no confidence in Corbyn by Labour MPs while thousands of party members rallied in his support outside Parliament. Two weeks previously, Labour MP Jo Cox had been murdered by a neo-Nazi terrorist while campaigning in her Yorkshire constituency. The atmosphere in the room was more akin to a political rally than a sober report launch. Corbyn was cheered when he entered the room; journalists were booed when they asked questions about his leadership. A veteran left-wing activist called Marc Wadsworth was hand-ing out press releases calling for 'traitor' MPs to be deselected. He refused to give one to Ruth Smeeth, a Jewish Labour

MP, who was instead handed a copy by a nearby journalist, Kate McCann of the *Daily Telegraph* – a detail that would later become crucial. Many of the party activists in the room appeared to have no idea what they had been invited to: 'It was, literally, a rent-a-mob,' according to Mark Gardner, who was present on behalf of the Community Security Trust. When the journalists from the *Jewish Chronicle* turned up, they were asked by one attendee, 'Do you know what this event is? I've turned up to support Jeremy. I've heard Jeremy is Jewish. Not that I mind or anything, but is he?'[4]

The incongruity of Corbyn speaking at the launch of a supposedly independent report into his own party was magnified by what he actually said, and by what he didn't say. He began his speech by accusing Conservative and UKIP politicians of using racist language during the EU referendum campaign, before addressing the actual subject at hand. Labour will aim to set the 'gold standard' for anti-racism, he promised. Zio is a 'vile epithet', stereotyping is wrong, and – in a striking choice of words – 'Our Jewish friends are no more responsible for the actions of Israel or the Netanyahu government than our Muslim friends are for those of various self-styled Islamic states or organisations.' Many took this to imply an equivalence between Israel and ISIS, although Corbyn later denied it. Then Marc Wadsworth spoke up: 'I saw that the *Telegraph* handed a copy of a press release to Ruth Smeeth MP, so you can see who's working hand in hand.' This direct attack on a

Jewish MP and the suggestion that she was conspiring with the media led to uproar. Shouts of 'How dare you!' rang out while Smeeth left the room in tears. 'Antisemitism at the launch of an antisemitism report,' Kevin Schofield of PoliticsHome commented with some amazement as he watched the scene unfold. Corbyn had earlier said, when asked, that he disliked the use of the word 'traitor' in Wadsworth's press release, but he did not intervene on Smeeth's behalf and later left the event chatting happily with Wadsworth. Smeeth later called on Corbyn to resign and 'make way for someone with the backbone to confront racism and anti-Semitism in our party and in the country'. Any hope Corbyn and Chakrabarti had that their report would draw a line under the party's problem of antisemitism and put a stop to the negative headlines was shattered. It was, in the words of the *Jewish Chronicle*'s Marcus Dysch, 'the political equivalent of running into a burning building with a can of petrol and liberally chucking the fuel over anything you could find'. Within five weeks of publishing her report, Corbyn had made Chakrabarti a Baroness; a few weeks after that she was in his shadow Cabinet. The Board of Deputies of British Jews called it a 'whitewash for peerages' scandal.[5]

At the heart of the report was a glaring reluctance to accept that what the party was dealing with was actually antisemitism, or that it justified expulsion from the party. Instead, antisemitic remarks have been repeatedly described in euphemistic terms: as offensive, or unhelpful, or upsetting for Jews, or saying the wrong thing – anything to avoid accepting that veteran activists of the left might be capable of holding or expressing antisemitic views. The report calls the comparison of Israel to Nazi Germany 'insensitive and incendiary', but not antisemitic; After Ken Livingstone was found guilty of bringing the party into disrepute with his claims that Hitler supported Zionism, Corbyn said that his old comrade had been 'grossly offensive' and 'caused deep offence and hurt to the Jewish community' – but did not call his comments antisemitic. Len McCluskey, general secretary of Unite and Corbyn's main trade union backer, said Livingstone's comments were 'extraordinary and bizarre', but insisted that Livingstone is not an antisemite. More recently, Baroness Chakrabarti has called for Livingstone to be expelled from the party for remarks that are 'incendiary' and an 'insult' – but, again, didn't say they were antisemitic. Corbyn was pressed on this point by David Burrowes MP when he appeared before the Home Affairs Select Committee as part of an inquiry they held into antisemitism in 2016, and he seemed determined to avoid giving a view one way or the other:

> Corbyn: Ken Livingstone made remarks that are wholly unacceptable and totally wrong. They were drawn to the attention of the party compliance unit very rapidly. A decision was made within a very few hours to suspend his party membership. He is now – the remarks are now being investigated by the party and due process will take place.

[...]

Burrowes: On what basis do you condemn Ken Livingstone's remarks as being wrong and unacceptable?

Corbyn: The use of the Hitler comparison on the issues of Zionism in Germany in the 1930s – the historical parallel that he drew.

Burrowes: So on the basis that they are racist and antisemitic.

Corbyn: I think it is a wrong comparison to draw, but his remarks are subject to investigation and there is a due process going on within the party. I think we must let that process take place; it is not for me to comment on a process that is going on.

Burrowes: But you have done. You have made a judgement that you have condemned it—

Corbyn: No, I made a point about the remarks, and I think we should allow them to be investigated.

Burrowes: You have made a judgement that they are wrong and unacceptable. Should Ken Livingstone—

Corbyn: We made a judgement that he should be suspended.

[...]

Burrowes: So you won't at this stage, despite condemning it and saying it is wrong and unacceptable, tell us that and make it clear, as others have done? Let's look at the list – we've got the Chief Rabbi, the Board of Deputies, the Holocaust Education Trust, the Jewish Labour Movement and many other Jewish people in my constituency and no doubt yours, who regard it as racist. Why don't you agree with them?

Corbyn: There is due process taking place on Ken Livingstone. I condemn the remarks that he made. That is why I and others were consulted on this and he was suspended from party membership. Due process is taking place.

[...]

Burrowes: You don't need to be prompted to say it as it is, that Ken Livingstone was racist and antisemitic.

Corbyn: Look, I have made my views absolutely clear on what Ken Livingstone said—

Burrowes: OK, you're not willing to say it.

Corbyn: Sorry, can I finish? There is a due process. He is part of that due process that is taking place at the present time in our party. I would suggest that other parties also look at due process for themselves when their members make racist remarks.

This exchange was interrupted by the bizarre sight of Shami Chakrabarti, who accompanied Corbyn at the hearing and was sat directly behind him, passing notes to her leader and prompting him with his answers. This hearing took place four days after the launch of the Chakrabarti Report, and her behaviour confirmed that neither she nor her report were going to hold Corbyn personally to account for anything.[6]

Corbyn's explanation at the time was that he risked prejudicing Livingstone's disciplinary case if he expressed a view as to whether Livingstone's comments were antisemitic or whether he should be expelled. This is difficult to credit, given that Livingstone was not charged with antisemitism but rather with bringing the party into disrepute, and Corbyn was prepared to say that Livingstone's comments were unacceptable and wrong. Nor did he take the opportunity to clarify his view once Livingstone's case was over, even though many Labour MPs and other prominent figures, including Mayor of London Sadiq Khan, Andy Burnham MP (now Mayor of Greater Manchester) and Labour's deputy leader Tom Watson, have all described Livingstone's comments as antisemitic. When Livingstone eventually decided to resign from the party in May 2018 to prevent a second disciplinary case reaching its conclusion, Jeremy Corbyn said his resignation was 'sad after such a long and vital contribution to London and progressive politics', but 'the right thing to do'.[7]

The assumption that left-wing people could not, by definition, be antisemitic is compounded by the long-standing and widespread belief that allegations of antisemitism on the left or in pro-Palestinian circles are usually made in bad faith to silence critics of Israel. This phenomenon was named the Livingstone Formulation by David Hirsh, after Livingstone had written in 2006 that 'for far too long the accusation of anti-Semitism has been used against anyone who is critical of the policies of the Israeli government, as I have been'. The implication is not just that Israel and its supporters get it wrong about where the boundary lies between legitimate criticism of Israel and antisemitism: it is that they deliberately and maliciously invent claims of antisemitism, in a coordinated and knowing way, to shield Israel and intimidate its critics. It is itself a conspiracy theory that accuses Jews of dishonesty and manipulation, and it is endemic on the left. Amongst Corbyn's supporters, this has expanded into the allegation of a smear campaign against Corbyn to derail his project to reshape the Labour Party. According to Skwawkbox, when Labour MP Ruth Smeeth demanded that Corbyn should address the antisemitic abuse she had received, she was acting from 'ulterior motives' to promote 'an anti-Semitism slur against Jeremy Corbyn and his supporters' because she is 'right-wing' and a 'defender of Israel's awful human rights record'. Another Skwawkbox article warned that 'the Establishment and right wing will not hesitate to use antisemitism smears to try to get their way'. The Canary took a similar line, arguing that 'the Labour right, the Conservatives, and supporters of Israeli apartheid' are deploying 'bogus antisemitism smears against Jeremy Corbyn'. 'Media pundits, pro-establishment Labour MPs and the Israeli lobby have a common aim', another article claimed: to topple 'anti-establishment leader and critic of the State of Israel, Corbyn'. A Canary editorial written by Kerry-Anne Mendoza argued that there was a 'coordinated effort' by a coalition of 'Blairites within the party and the media, along with their conservative peers and the pro-Israel lobby', to conduct a 'sickening smear campaign' against Corbyn because he supports Palestinian rights.[8]

This belief in a smear campaign extends all the way into Corbyn's inner circle. Seumas Milne, while appearing on George Galloway's show on RT in 2015, said, 'They're trying to smear Corbyn, by association, with anti-Semitism.' Len McCluskey said that the suggestion that Labour has a problem of anti-semitism is 'mood music that was created by people who were trying to undermine Jeremy Corbyn'. Diane Abbott, speaking as shadow International Development Secretary in 2016, told the BBC, 'It's a smear to say that Labour has a problem with anti-semitism. It is something like a smear against ordinary party members.' Filmmaker Ken Loach wrote that 'exaggerated or false charges of anti-Semitism have coincided with the election of Jeremy Corbyn as leader'. Corbyn himself described as 'utterly disgusting subliminal nastiness' a 2016 column by Jewish journalist Jonathan Freedland in *The Guardian* that noted: 'No one accuses [Corbyn] of being an antisemite. But many Jews do worry that his past instinct, when faced with potential allies whom he deemed sound on Palestine, was to overlook whatever nastiness they might have uttered about Jews.' Two years later, Corbyn's public line had changed. In March 2018, when the Board of Deputies of British Jews and the Jewish Leadership Council made broadly the same allegation as Freedland, accusing Corbyn of repeatedly siding 'with antisemites rather than Jews', Corbyn apologised for the 'pain and hurt' caused to Jewish party members and accepted that he and the party had made mistakes; but a lot of damage was done in those intervening two years.[9]

The narrative that allegations of antisemitism are being mobilised not just to defend Israel, but now to obstruct Corbyn's path to power, has evolved further, with a new, more insidious variant of the Livingstone Formulation. This new version claims that it is the prospect of socialism itself, and a more equal and just future for the people of the UK, that is motivating the supposed smear campaign. According to journalist and Corbyn supporter Paul Mason, Corbyn is being 'smeared as an anti-Semite' by a combination of right-wing media and 'a group of up to thirty Labour MPs who just cannot reconcile themselves to the idea of a socialist party that fights for socialism'. David Rosenberg of the Jewish Socialists' Group wrote that the Jewish community leaders who organised the demonstration outside Parliament are 'a socially conservative force in the Jewish community … led and dominated by supporters of the Tory Party' who 'pursue a relentless anti-left agenda'. Radical Jewish group Jewdas, who hosted Corbyn at a Passover Seder meal a few days after the demonstration, claimed it was 'a malicious ploy to remove the leader of the opposition and put a stop to the possibility of a socialist government'. An article in the *Morning Star* claimed it was an attempt to obstruct 'Corbyn's alarming progress towards mobilising the many against the few and his unswerving support for Palestinian rights'. Thus the Livingstone Formulation has developed an anti-capitalist strand to sit alongside its anti-Zionist one. The original version implies a dual loyalty charge, that British Jews who complain about antisemitism on the left are doing so in the service of a foreign power, while the newer form links back to older forms of socialist antisemitism that imagine Jews as part of the capitalist elite, protecting their interests at the expense of the masses.[10]

Those people on the left who want to reassure themselves that allegations of antisemitism are either completely invented or exaggerated have been encouraged by a small but noisy cadre of Jewish leftists who are opposed to Zionism and to Israel and are largely detached from the mainstream of Jewish communal life. Jewish anti-Zionism might sound like an oxymoron, but Zionism has always had its opponents within Jewish politics who felt that Jews should continue to strive for equality within the societies in which they lived rather than moving en masse to create a new society elsewhere. In the early years of political Zionism during the late nineteenth and early twentieth centuries, when its vision of a Jewish national home in what was, at the time, part of the Ottoman Empire seemed hopelessly utopian, its Jewish opponents far outnumbered its supporters. However, as antisemitism grew in Europe in the 1920s and 1930s and a new Jewish society began to take shape in what would become Israel, Zionism became increasingly popular amongst Jews. It offered an escape from growing oppression, combined with the positive vision of a new future for the Jewish people in their historic homeland. The Holocaust and the establishment of Israel in 1948 transformed the Jewish world. The old Jewish heartland of Eastern Europe, for centuries the cultural and religious centre of the Jewish world, was swept away by the Nazi genocide, and within a few years a new Jewish civilisation began to flower in Israel. European Jewish communities were slowly rebuilt after the Holocaust, although in many cases only as a faint shadow of their former size and vitality, but the Zionist argument that the Jewish people as a whole should never again rely on others for its survival was unanswerable after their near-extermination at the hands of the Nazis and their collaborators across Europe. At the same time, the idea that Jews should seek their freedom and safety via the universal promise of socialism lost credibility following the Soviet Union's pact with Nazi Germany in 1939, antisemitic campaigns by Stalin and his Soviet bloc allies after the Second World War, and the persecution of Jews in the Soviet Union until its collapse in 1989. As Israel has grown in size and self-confidence, it has come to rival, and in many cases outdo, American Jewry as the focus of global Jewish life. It is understandable that support for Israel's existence has become the default position for the overwhelming majority of Jews. Nevertheless, there remains a rump of Jewish leftists who cling to the politics of pre-war Jewish socialism and reject Zionism as a fateful wrong turn down the morally corrupting path of military power and national chauvinism. In Britain, many of these Jewish leftists are long-standing members of the Labour Party or smaller parties and factions of the hard left, and have campaigned alongside Corbyn, Livingstone and other veterans of the Labour left for, in many cases, decades. And when Corbyn's Labour was accused of harbouring antisemitism, they invoked their Jewish identity to defend their leader.

Jews For Jeremy was the name adopted by some Jewish supporters of Corbyn during his 2015 Labour leadership campaign. It was formed in August 2015 by Julia Bard and David Rosenberg of the Jewish Socialists' Group in direct response to allegations that Corbyn had previously been associated with people who had expressed antisemitic views. 'The smear campaigns against Jeremy Corbyn aimed at dissuading voters in the Labour leadership election from backing him has been led by an undeclared alliance of Blairites, a swathe of right-wing and liberal media commentators, and self-appointed leaders and protectors and "spokespersons" of the Jewish community,' wrote Rosenberg not long after the group was formed. It was superseded in April 2016 by a new group called Free Speech on Israel, launched 'to counter the manufactured moral panic over a supposed epidemic of antisemitism in the UK'. Free Speech on Israel had a narrower focus, as its name suggests. This group's purpose was to argue that claims of antisemitism were only raised 'to discredit Israel's critics' and 'to suppress criticism of Israel and undermine freedom of speech for Palestinians and their supporters'. In their view, this is not done by mistake, or because people have an honestly held, but erroneous, view of what antisemitism is: rather, these are 'exaggerated and falsified allegations', 'mischievous or false charges' and a 'lie' born of deliberate calculation. The group's vice-chair, Jonathan Rosenhead, has even speculated that antisemitic social media posts by people claiming to support Corbyn might be the product of 'false flag operations' by the Israeli government designed to discredit the Labour leader.[11]

Sometimes the enthusiasm of Jewish anti-Zionists for spreading these claims has gone too far, even for the Labour leadership. In January 2017, Al Jazeera broadcast a four-part exposé of pro-Israel lobbying in the UK, based on extensive secret filming by an undercover reporter. The series caused some embarrassment for the Israeli embassy in London, as one of its junior staff, Shai Masot, was filmed boasting that he was going to 'take down' Foreign Office minister Sir Alan Duncan due to his perceived sympathies for the Palestinians. Masot was sent home to Israel and the Israeli ambassador apologised. This was enough for the British government but not for the Labour Party, who – echoing Corbyn's support for Raed Salah five years earlier – called for an inquiry into 'improper interference in our democratic politics'. Al Jazeera also suggested, with little or no evidence, that Israel and its supporters were behind false claims of antisemitism in the Labour Party. The chair of Free Speech on Israel, Mike Cushman, took this as an opportunity to air his own conspiracy theories about Israeli or Zionist influence in British politics. 'Most senior members of both main parties, with the exception of Corbyn and his close associates, and the Liberal Democrats, [are] part of the network of Israeli influence,' he wrote. Prime Minister Theresa May supports Israel 'as reciprocity for previous career assistance from the Israelis', and 'the Labour Party has become a pawn of Zionist organisations that place loyalty to Israel's interests above advancing the Labour Party'. This article, which first appeared on the Free Speech on Israel website, was republished on the websites of the Labour Representation Committee and its sister publication, Labour Briefing. These two factions have played an important role in the Labour left since the 1980s; John McDonnell was chair of the Labour Representation Committee until he became shadow Chancellor, and since then has been its honorary president. Complaints that they had endorsed an obviously antisemitic article led to hurried discussions amongst the officers of the Committee and the Briefing and they decided, at McDonnell's insistence, to remove the article from their websites (it remains available on the Free Speech on Israel site). Only a minority in either group thought the article was antisemitic, but McDonnell's influence held sway. McDonnell later claimed, in relation to a different allegation of antisemitism, that he 'plays no role in the content or decision-making process' of the Committee, but his central role in having Cushman's article removed suggests otherwise. Despite this, Cushman, a Labour Party member, was not subject to any disciplinary measures by the party, and the Labour Representation Committee and Labour Briefing websites both still carry other articles arguing that 'false accusations of anti-Semitism are being used against the Left'; that Ken Livingstone should not have been suspended; that 'the Tory Jewish lobby' is conducting a 'political onslaught' against Labour; that Corbyn is victim of 'the malicious use of allegations of antisemitism as a political weapon'; and that antisemitism is 'the baseball bat of choice for internal as well as external attacks on Jeremy Corbyn and his project'. Dave Osler, the former Trotskyist student who had been involved in the failed move to ban City of London Polytechnic's Jewish Society over thirty years earlier, resigned from the Labour Representation Committee and Labour Briefing in 2017 in protest at their weak stance against antisemitism, but few others appear to see a problem.[12]

One challenge for Jewish anti-Zionists in Labour is that the party already has a formal Jewish affiliate which represents its traditional Labour Zionist position. This is the Jewish Labour Movement, previously known as Poale Zion (Hebrew for 'Workers of Zion'), which has a history, size and formal status in the Labour Party that cannot be matched by any of the newer and smaller Jewish anti-Zionist groups. The Jewish Labour Movement, and Poale Zion before it, have played an integral role in the party's relations with its sister Labor Party in Israel, and managed to build a working relationship with Corbyn's leadership team. Two of the Jewish Labour Movement's leading figures, Jeremy Newmark and Mike Katz, were selected as Labour Party candidates in heavily Jewish north London constituencies for the 2017 general election (both failed to win their seats), and the Movement later received an award from the party, presented by Corbyn himself, in recognition of their efforts 'engaging and mobilising the Jewish community in support of Labour campaigns'. Inevitably, the Jewish Labour Movement became a target for anti-Zionist groups. Free Speech on Israel described them as 'defenders of apartheid in Israel'. At Labour Party conference in 2016, leaflets were handed out describing them as 'a representative of a foreign power, Israel' – invoking the old antisemitic 'dual loyalty' allegation that Jews are not loyal to their own country. Calls were made repeatedly for the Jewish Labour Movement to be thrown out of the Labour Party, presumably so an anti-Zionist, or non-Zionist, Jewish group could take its place. Just such an organisation, called Jewish Voice for Labour, was created in 2017 specifically to campaign within the Labour Party as an alternative to the Jewish Labour Movement. Sharing many of Free Speech on Israel's members, officers and views, Jewish Voice for Labour consistently argues that antisemitism allegations are a smear against the party and its leader. Glyn Secker, the secretary of both Jewish Voice for Labour and Free Speech on Israel, wrote on the Jewish Voice for Labour website, 'We have always claimed that the campaign inside the Labour Party of false allegations of antisemitism has a dual purpose: to attack on the left [*sic*] and the rise of Corbyn, and to silence criticisms of Israel's human rights abuses.'[13]

The 2017 Labour Party conference showed how these groups' unremitting desire to attack Israel, and their insistence that it is a smear to suggest the party has a problem of antisemitism, can interfere with the party's efforts to repair its image with British Jews. The conference began positively, with Jeremy Corbyn, on the main conference stage, presenting the Jewish Labour Movement with their award. It also saw the adoption of a new disciplinary rule, jointly supported by the Jewish Labour Movement, the National Executive Committee and Momentum, that, for the first time, made antisemitism and other forms of hate speech explicit offences in the party rulebook. This should have heralded a new chapter in the party's efforts to deal with antisemitism. But despite this rule change receiving near-unanimous support in terms of votes, the mood on conference floor was quite different. Two of the biggest ovations of the entire conference were given to activists from Jewish Voice for Labour and Free Speech on Israel when they hit back at allegations of antisemitism. Leah Levane received a standing ovation when she complained about people being accused of antisemitism 'every time you criticise the despicable behaviour of the State of Israel towards the Palestinian people'. Naomi Wimborne-Idrissi, after giving an unremarkable speech in support of the Palestinian cause, received loud cheers and applause when she concluded with the line, 'Conference, I am not an antisemite and this party does not have a problem with Jews!' Elsewhere at the same conference, a guest speaker at the

Free Speech on Israel fringe meeting appeared to suggest that Holocaust denial is an acceptable part of political argument, saying, 'This is about free speech, the freedom to criticise and to discuss every issue, whether it's the Holocaust: yes or no; Palestine; the liberation; the whole spectrum. There should be no limits on the discussion.' The controversy was ratcheted up further when Ken Loach refused to condemn this comment, telling the BBC that 'history is there for us all to discuss'. Jewish Voice for Labour's official launch event at the conference drew a big crowd that included Loach, McCluskey and Tosh McDonald, president of the rail union ASLEF. McCluskey and McDonald both donated money and McCluskey in particular was bowled over by what he heard. 'I listened and thought my God – the speakers are saying everything I believe in!' he later recalled, and promised to support them in future. While many express regret at the divisive nature of rows over antisemitism, McCluskey seemed to welcome it: the launch of Jewish Voice for Labour 'transforms the discussion into one of left vs right as it should be', he said.[14]

The extent of grassroots resistance to Labour's efforts to discipline people for alleged antisemitism was exposed when veteran Israeli Marxist Moshé Machover, one of the original activists for Matzpen in the 1960s, was suspended by the party for an article he wrote for a group called Labour Party Marxists (widely believed to be linked to the Communist Party of Great Britain). They gave out a newspaper at the conference that featured a two-page article by Machover titled 'Anti-Zionism does not equal anti-Semitism'. The article began by claiming that 'the whole campaign of equating opposition to Zionism with anti-Semitism has, in fact, been carefully orchestrated with the help of the Israeli government and the far right in the United States'. It followed this conspiracy theory by quoting senior Nazi Reinhard Heydrich, one of the architects of the Holocaust, writing in 1935 that 'national socialism has no intention of attacking the Jewish people in any way ... The government finds itself in complete agreement with the great spiritual movement within Jewry itself, so-called Zionism.' Machover quoted Heydrich because he was trying to demonstrate that Zionism shared 'an area of basic agreement' with Nazism, but in so doing he lent credence to a piece of Nazi propaganda denying the antisemitism that led to the Holocaust. Labour Party Marxists also circulated a voting guide informing conference delegates that the 'Anti-Semitism scandal' was 'entirely fabricated' and encouraging them to vote against the new rule change because it 'is supported by the Jewish Labour Movement, which already tells you that you should probably oppose without even having to read it'. Machover was suspended from the party, not for antisemitism, but for supporting a rival party. This provoked a widespread grassroots campaign in his support. Dozens of party branches passed motions calling for his membership to be reinstated. Hundreds of party members signed an open letter from Free

Speech on Israel condemning his expulsion and claiming it was the result of pressure 'from supporters of Israel (not excluding the Israeli Embassy) to act against critics of Israel and of Zionism'. As many pointed out, if writing for a communist publication is an offence, then Jeremy Corbyn, for several years a *Morning Star* columnist, was as guilty of it as anyone. Indeed, copies of the *Morning Star* were handed out free to delegates at that party conference, sponsored by various trade unions. By the end of October, Machover had been reinstated, a move that was welcomed by Corbyn's office. Laura Murray, Corbyn's stakeholder manager (and daughter of Stop The War Coalition's Andrew Murray) wrote to complainants, 'We are very much aware of the public support for Moshé Machover and the distress and anger caused by his auto-exclusion ... I am glad that he is now a Labour Party member again.' With Machover, as with Livingstone and several other cases of alleged antisemitism in the party, the Labour leadership appear to find it impossible to accept that people they have known for so many years, and have always viewed as anti-racists, could have said or written anything antisemitic.[15]

Jewish opponents of Zionism have benefited from these personal and political loyalties, but sometimes this can cost the left and the Labour Party dear. With their self-declared Jewish identity and their long record of left-wing activism, Jewish anti-Zionists and non-Zionists could have built a bridge between the mainstream Jewish community and the Corbynite left;

instead, they seem determined to burn every bridge that anyone else tries to build. At every stage, leading activists in Free
Speech on Israel and Jewish Voice for Labour have encouraged the Labour Party to treat allegations of antisemitism as
a malicious smear or a gross exaggeration. This is part of their
own opposition to Israel and the mainstream Jewish community, but it has encouraged others on the left down a path that
was only ever going to damage their relations with the Jewish
community as a whole. Nor is their role limited to denying
that antisemitism is a serious issue: sometimes, their hostility
towards Zionism and the mainstream of the Jewish community reaches such a pitch that they cause the problems in the
first place. At the 2017 Labour Party conference, it was the
speeches, articles and meetings of Jewish anti-Zionists that
created the negative headlines about antisemitism and over-
shadowed the positive steps the party took by working with the
Jewish Labour Movement. One of the longest-running cases of
antisemitism in the Labour Party involved Tony Greenstein,
the veteran Jewish anti-Zionist who had campaigned alongside
Corbyn in the Labour Movement Campaign for Palestine in
the 1980s. Greenstein was eventually expelled from the Labour
Party in February 2018, almost two years after being suspended,
for directing antisemitic, sexist and racist abuse towards fellow Labour Party members. In March 2018, when the Board
of Deputies of British Jews and the Jewish Leadership Council
held their demonstration outside Parliament, Jewish Voice for

Labour held its own, much smaller, counter-protest in a corner of Parliament Square. Amongst the counter-protestors were former Labour Party members who had already been expelled, like Greenstein and Gerry Downing, plus the founder of the Palestine Live Facebook group, Elleanne Green. They held placards with the slogan 'Jews for Jez' and a Holocaust-style yellow star. This resulted in the bizarre situation of people who had been thrown out of the Labour Party for antisemitism protesting, ostensibly in Corbyn's defence, against a Jewish community demonstration opposing antisemitism, on the very day when Corbyn publicly acknowledged, for the first time, that the Labour Party had a significant problem of antisemitism that it had failed to deal with properly. Two days later, Corbyn described Jewish Voice for Labour as 'good people' who 'are committed to fighting antisemitism and making sure there is a Jewish voice in the party'. He refused to say that they should not have held their counter-protest against the main Jewish community demonstration.[16]

The failure of many on the left to recognise antisemitism as an equal form of racism to the type of concrete discrimination that affects other minorities means that, if the person accused of antisemitism is black, arguments over antisemitism and racism can turn even more toxic. Jackie Walker is a black woman of part-Jewish heritage and a long-standing Labour Party activist who has held senior positions in Momentum and the Labour Representation Committee. She has known

Corbyn for many years. Walker was first suspended from the party in early May 2016 after a Facebook discussion in which she asked, 'What debt do we owe the Jews?' Then, when somebody replied, 'The Holocaust,' Walker wrote:

> I hope you feel the same towards the African holocaust? My ancestors were involved in both – on all sides and as I'm sure you know, millions more Africans were killed in the African holocaust and their oppression continues today on a global scale in a way it doesn't for Jews … and many Jews (my ancestors too) were the chief financiers of the sugar and slave trade which is of course why there were so many early synagogues in the Caribbean.

Walker followed this with another post in which she asked, 'What do you think the Jews should do about their contribution to the African holocaust? What debt do they owe? Shall we open an account? The Jewish holocaust does not allow Zionists to do what they want.' The implication that today's Jews are responsible for the alleged wrongdoing of Jews who lived centuries ago is problematic enough, but the central complaint about Walker's post focused on her claim that 'many Jews' were the 'chief financiers' of the slave trade. This claim is a modern antisemitic myth that was first published in coherent form by Louis Farrakhan of the Nation of Islam in a 1991 book called *The Secret Relationship Between Blacks and Jews*.

Farrakhan has been banned from the UK, partly for his antisemitic views. It is true that some Jews were involved in the slave trade, but not in disproportionately high numbers, not as its driving force, and those who were involved did not act 'as Jews' or in the name of all other Jews (as is suggested by the idea that 'the Jews' of today owe a debt as a result).[17]

When Walker was suspended, she, her friends and supporters were outraged. Momentum organised a campaign to have her reinstated. Labour Party branches, including those in Corbyn's and Abbott's constituencies, passed motions calling for her suspension to be dropped. McDonnell's Labour Representation Committee organised an email campaign for its supporters to protest against the 'spurious' charges. Left Futures, the website of Momentum founder Jon Lansman, called it a 'frenzied witch-hunt'. The *Morning Star* claimed her suspension was the result of a cynical right-wing effort to undermine Corbyn. The fact that Walker had campaigned against UKIP in Thanet was held up as evidence that her comments about Jews and the slave trade couldn't possibly be antisemitic. By the end of May, the case was dropped and Walker was readmitted to the party. She qualified her original comments by saying she should have written that Jews were 'amongst' the chief financiers of the slave trade, but also described herself as a victim of 'increasing convergence between Zionists, the right of the Labour Party, the Tories and our right-wing media', designed to undermine Corbyn and the left so that 'Israeli propagandists and their fellow travellers' can 'get on with their dirty work'. She even hinted at a deeper conspiracy, asking, 'Is it coincidence that Sadiq Khan, new London Mayor, full of his new found fame, has already met with the Israeli Ambassador for talks that it is suggested may lead to greater trade links with Israel?' Antisemitism is not a big problem in the party, she wrote; a bigger problem is that Zionists and right-wingers can get people like her suspended.[18]

Four months later, Walker was suspended once again. This time it was for comments she had made at a training session on antisemitism that was run for the party by the Jewish Labour Movement at the 2016 Labour Party conference. Walker attended the training, which had been recommended by Baroness Royall's report into antisemitism at Oxford University Labour Club, with a group of fellow activists including Wimborne-Idrissi, Secker and Rosenhead. They all made comments and asked questions that were, to say the least, unhelpful, but Walker's drew a furious reaction. She complained that Holocaust Memorial Day does not commemorate other genocides (which is not true); argued that there is no particular terrorist threat to Jewish schools or nurseries; and said, 'I still haven't heard a definition of antisemitism that I can work with.' The combination of the offence caused by her comments, particularly in relation to Holocaust commemoration, and the disruption to the training session was embarrassing for the party and, again, derailed what should have been a constructive event. Walker apologised 'if offence has been caused', but this time she did not benefit from the same level of support. Momentum removed her as its vice-chair – although she remained on its steering committee – and there was no chance of her suspension being quietly dropped by the party.[19]

Walker has no doubt that she is the victim of a racist witch-hunt and that Jews have privilege and power that is denied to black people or Muslims. 'There is a hierarchy of race,' she said in a Facebook video a few days after the Jewish community demonstration outside Parliament. 'We all know it. We all know there are some groups that are seen as more important than others. We all know that there are some groups who can get to the media more than others.' Black voters support Corbyn in the hope of change, she said, and

> to see those people, those shameful people, standing in Parliament, in their privilege, in their privilege, attacking the only hope many of us, as oppressed people, have seen … in that demonstration I saw again and again people who I knew who were absolute enemies of people of colour, enemies of Muslims, enemies of our tolerant society.

She appears to believe that complaints about her allegedly antisemitic comments are comparable to the racist lynchings of black people in America; a comparison that would place British Jews complaining about antisemitism in the role of the Ku Klux Klan. Walker has turned her experience into a one-woman show called *The Lynching*, which she first performed at the Edinburgh Festival in August 2017 and has since toured to small but enthusiastic audiences around the country. Her use of the imagery of the racist lynching of black people in America is deliberate. Walker's website promoting the show gives a potted history of this practice before connecting it directly to allegations of antisemitism in Corbyn's Labour Party: 'In recent years, lynching black people has been replaced by other methods – the police killings of black people, the metaphorical lynching of destroying a person's public and social credibility. The purpose is always the same – to silence, control and oppress.' Her show features a black female doll, clearly intended to represent Walker, dangling from a noose at the side of the stage while Walker tells her life story. This divisive narrative of privileged Jews silencing black voices in the Labour Party received a further boost with the suspension and eventual expulsion of Marc Wadsworth for his comments and behaviour at the launch of the Chakrabarti Report. The idea that there is a general witch-hunt against people on the left of the party, particularly targeting those who are vocal supporters of the Palestinians, has gained currency more widely. In October 2017, Walker, Greenstein, Wadsworth and others formed Labour Against the Witch-Hunt to campaign against suspensions and expulsions. Their demands include abolishing the party's internal compliance unit that processes its disciplinary cases and an end to 'the outrageous cull of left-wing party members on fake charges'. The group has both prominent and grassroots supporters: Loach is one of its sponsors, as are the well-known barrister Michael Mansfield QC and Noam Chomsky. An open letter from Labour Against the Witch-Hunt to Corbyn in early 2018 warning against 'a cynical alliance between those who wish to deflect criticism of Israel and Zionism, and the right-wing in the Labour Party and the news media, who oppose your wider politics', drew nearly 6,500 signatures in two months. Chris Williamson, Labour MP for Derby North, is the most visible parliamentary supporter of this campaign and has spoken alongside both Walker and Wadsworth in their support. In March 2018, he described the suspensions of Walker and Livingstone as 'ridiculous ... grotesque and unfair' while speaking alongside Walker at a Momentum meeting in Peterborough. It was a 'real pleasure and a privilege' to share a platform with her, he said.[20]

Sometimes, this idea of a smear campaign combines with the drive to protect factional interests within Labour, to create institutional processes and outcomes that fail Jewish party members. Since Corbyn became leader, every part of the party, from Parliament to the national party machine to the selection of council candidates and local party officers, has been subject to a power struggle between the left and right of the party, and between the different sub-factions of the left. One consequence is that people in Labour's decision-making structures are less likely to take strong action against somebody for anti-semitism if doing so would weaken their side in this factional struggle. 'It's all about control: control of the party and con-trol of the processes,' one source from the party was quoted as saying. An internal assessment of Labour's disciplinary process in May 2018 warned, 'There is a perception that cases are not dealt with in a consistent manner due to political forces influ-encing decisions with particular respondents – particularly at the NEC Disputes Panel stage of the process.' Leaked minutes from a meeting of the party's NEC in March showed how left-wing NEC members voted as a bloc to minimise or prevent disciplinary action in three cases of alleged antisemitism. These NEC members included key figures on the left of the party who had spoken publicly about the need to expel antisemites but argued exactly the opposite in private. That NEC meet-ing was chaired by Christine Shawcroft, who lost her job later that month as chair of the NEC's disputes panel – the body charged with hearing antisemitism cases – because she lobbied the party's compliance unit to drop charges against Alan Bull, a council candidate in Peterborough who was accused of posting a range of antisemitic material on Facebook. One post on Bull's page included a Holocaust denial article titled 'International Red Cross Report Confirms the Holocaust of Six Million Jews is a Hoax' in which the infamous 'Arbeit Macht Frei' sign over the gates of Auschwitz had been changed to 'Muh Holocaust'. Another Facebook post, redolent of antisemitic conspiracy theories, described David Miliband as 'a jew he is paid by Rothschild who owns Israel and also controls mossadd [*sic*] who kill people for Israel and Zionism ... people like JFK john smith robin cooke Diana Kelly'. A third suggested that Israel is allied to ISIS. Bull claimed all the posts were doctored. He had first been reported to the party in July 2017, but in October he was selected as a candidate for the May 2018 council elections. Various people, including two sitting Labour councillors in Peterborough, Richard Ferris and Matthew Mahabadi, made further complaints, but still nothing was done. Frustrated with the lack of action, Ferris and Mahabadi even turned up to a council meeting in March 2018 wearing T-shirts bearing the slogan 'Labour Councillors Against Antisemitism' and started a Twitter account of the same name where they publicised Bull's case. The *Jewish Chronicle* reported on it the following day – at which point Bull was suspended within hours.[21]

This was the point at which Shawcroft, who is also a director of Momentum, took up Bull's case. She circulated an internal email, copying in several left-wing members of the NEC, including Lansman and the party's new general secretary Jennie Formby, arguing that Bull's suspension for antisemitism was imposed for 'political reasons' as part of 'partisan disputes' and that he should be reinstated to prevent Labour losing a winnable council seat. This emerged only when her email was leaked to *The Times*; Shawcroft resigned shortly afterwards. Shawcroft insisted that she had not seen Bull's Facebook posts before defending him and that she would not have supported him if she had done, but this hardly makes things any better. She knew he had been accused of antisemitism, but automatically dismissed it as part of the 'shenanigans around council selections' without any investigation. For the person in charge of the panel hearing Labour's antisemitism cases, this was an extraordinary confession. It was as if the judge in a forthcoming trial had urged the prosecution to drop all charges without having seen any of the evidence, just because the defendant had an important job to do. Whether Shawcroft did so because, like so many on the left, she assumes that any allegation of antisemitism is likely to be unfounded, or whether she did it out of factional, party or personal loyalty, only she will know. In some ways her personal motivations are irrelevant. Like her colleagues at that March NEC meeting, she was acting in her capacity as a party official and therefore her attempt to suppress action against antisemitism reflected on the Labour Party as an institution. Shawcroft was the author of her own downfall but she still tried to reverse the roles of victim and offender by claiming that 'this whole row is being stirred up to attack Jeremy, as we all know'. As for Ferris and Mahabadi, they got the kind of treatment familiar to many whistleblowers in institutions with something to hide. The local Constituency Labour Party secretary attacked them for 'damaging the Labour Party' in an email to all local members, and their fellow Labour councillors investigated them for 'bullying and intimidating behaviour'. Too often in today's Labour Party, it is easier to be antisemitic than to be the person actively opposing antisemitism.[22]

Shawcroft's doomed attempt to save Bull from suspension pales into insignificance alongside the party's abject failure to expel Ken Livingstone. The way his disciplinary hearing unfolded in March and April 2017 revealed all the flaws – procedural and institutional – in the party's process for dealing with antisemitism. A panel of three members of the party's National Constitutional Committee sat for the best part of three days while two big beasts of the legal world, Clive Sheldon QC and Michael Mansfield QC, squared off on behalf of the Labour Party and Livingstone respectively. A procession of witnesses for both sides took the stand before Livingstone himself gave evidence. At times, the three panel members struggled to keep up with the legal sparring of Sheldon and Mansfield. At one point, in a surreal exchange that shows just how much Livingstone has perverted internal Labour Party discourse about Jews and Israel, the two barristers had a lengthy discussion, taking up twelve uninterrupted pages of the hearing's transcript, about whether or not, and to what extent, Hitler supported Zionism. One of the panel members, Russell Cartwright – who was nominated by Unite to sit on the National Constitutional Committee – was clearly sympathetic to Livingstone. He described Naz Shah's posting calling for Israel to be relocated to America as an attempt at satirical humour and claimed that the interviews that got Livingstone suspended were largely conducted by Tory-supporting interviewers.

Livingstone called five witnesses, all Jewish opponents of Israel, who insisted that nothing he had said was antisemitic or even offensive. 'Nothing you could say about Israelis is antisemitic,' said Jenny Manson, co-chair of Jewish Voice for Labour. 'It might be nasty to say nasty things about the Israelis,' she went on, 'but Israelis are a group of Jews. They are not all Jews.' Manson also said that Livingstone's claims about Hitler supporting Zionism were 'true', that Shah's Facebook post calling for Israel to be relocated to the United States was 'quite funny', and called for 'much more freedom of speech than we are currently having on the subject of Israel and the Jews'. Naomi Wimborne-Idrissi was even more dismissive of the idea that there is any antisemitism in the party, saying, 'I have asked people in the Labour Party, "Where are these Jews who are offended by these things?" because I've not met them ... Who are they? Show them to me. I haven't met them. And I've asked people and they have failed to introduce me to any of these people.' She then claimed that 'the Zionist movement has successfully occupied the minds of Jews worldwide since the Holocaust', that Israeli Prime Minister Benjamin Netanyahu was 'delighted' about the terrorist attacks at the *Charlie Hebdo* office and a kosher supermarket in Paris in January 2015, and warned that 'Jews have to take responsibility' for Israel being, in her view, a 'racist endeavour'. None of the panel members, or anybody else at the hearing, challenged these comments. Wimborne-Idrissi was not the only person to conflate Jews with Israel during the hearing. When Mansfield was discussing Shah's Facebook post that said 'the Jews are rallying to the poll', which Shah had posted in relation to an online newspaper poll in July 2014 on the question of whether Israel was committing war crimes during that summer's conflict in Gaza, he appeared to treat British Jews as if they are Israelis. 'I'll be careful,' he said, as if to suggest that he was weighing his choice of words, and then explained:

> A lot of elements of the Jewish community would no doubt be upset, and some might be more than upset, by being accused – their government – some of their government being accused of war crimes in this way. And the government of Israel – make no mistake about it; if you accuse them of a war crime, they think you're antisemitic.

Later in the hearing he returned to the subject and again excused Shah's language by explaining, 'What is she supposed to say in this post in the middle of this onslaught, with this article? "Oh, some members of the Jewish community are" or "Only a certain synagogue is"?' Mansfield appeared to be suggesting that if Shah had referred only to some Jews rather than 'the Jews' as an opponent to be defeated, her post would have been fine. The irony is that some of Livingstone's witnesses grasped the problem much more clearly by pointing out that Shah should have written 'supporters of Israel', rather than conflating that category with 'the Jews' or bringing synagogues into it. Meanwhile Shah had long ago accepted that her post was antisemitic and apologised for it.[23]

When Livingstone took to the stand, he appeared to treat the entire event as a joke. He introduced himself to one witness as 'Boris Johnson, the international war criminal' and adopted a flippant air throughout. He said that he was not operating independently when he spoke to the media, but was effectively acting as an outrider for Corbyn himself. During the 2015 Labour leadership campaign, Livingstone was in 'pretty much daily contact' with Corbyn's campaign team, whose manager, Simon Fletcher, had worked for Livingstone when he was Mayor of London. After Corbyn became leader, Livingstone spoke regularly to Fletcher and Seumas Milne to discuss Livingstone's media appearances and agree what he should say. Corbyn's office even ran Livingstone's Twitter account on his behalf and wrote tweets in his name. When Shah's Facebook posts became the latest thing for which Corbyn was being attacked, Livingstone just did what he was supposed to do: he went on the radio and TV, probably having discussed it with Fletcher and Milne first, as he usually did, and defended his leader. He told the tribunal that he couldn't remember even looking at Shah's posts beforehand (he claimed never to have looked at a tweet in his life) but this didn't matter because 'I didn't go on the radio to defend Naz Shah. I went on the radio to defend the Labour Party from accusations of antisemitism and Jeremy Corbyn from being accused of being soft on antisemitism.' Crucially, nobody from the Labour Party told Livingstone to stop talking about Hitler and Zionism. 'If I'd been asked,' he told the hearing, 'I would have done it, but no one from the general secretary's office or the press office got in touch.' Later that day, Corbyn's office did contact Livingstone – to tip him off that he was going to be suspended. Livingstone was in no doubt that he was the victim of an orchestrated campaign by Labour MPs, who, he claimed, 'had been smearing the Labour Party as antisemitic deliberately, in the hope that this would undermine our results at the May elections' and thereby trigger a leadership challenge against Corbyn. 'Why did the Labour Party suspend me for telling the truth,' he asked the hearing, 'but not suspend those Labour MPs who deliberately lied and smeared me?' In an extraordinary climax to his evidence, Livingstone threatened the panel members, and through them the Labour Party, warning:

> If you vote to expel me, that is biased, it is rigged, and I will go for judicial review. Do you really want a repeat of what's happened here today out in public? It would be very damaging to the Labour Party. It would expose rules and a way of conduct which is contrary to British justice, even just by

excluding the press and public. I mean, you should talk to your lawyer privately afterwards about how damaging this would appear in an open court where a judge considers the way you conduct your business.

The following day, the panel returned with a guilty verdict, but decided that, due to 'the substantial and lengthy contribution that Mr Livingstone has made to the Labour Party', his punishment would be only a two-year suspension (one of which he had already served) from holding internal party office or from activities outside his local branch. After that he could resume full membership of the party. The consequences of this verdict were shattering. The party's highest disciplinary body decided that a party member can be found guilty of bringing the party into disrepute by repeatedly and deliberately abusing the memory of the Holocaust to wind up the Jewish community, while defending antisemitic comments by others, and ultimately remain a party member. This cannot easily be dismissed as an error of judgement. It was the result of over two days of evidence and legal arguments, which itself followed months accumulating evidence, interviewing witnesses and building the party's case. The staff in the party's compliance unit did their job, but this was an institutional decision, produced by the Labour Party's institutional processes and attitudes, and as such it scars the party as a whole.

The mix of conspiracy theories, assumptions of bad faith,

factional loyalties, disregard for mainstream Jewish sensibilities, repeated failure to act decisively, publicly and consistently against antisemitism, provocative interventions from anti-Israel activists and a bullying approach to political debate sometimes creates an environment that Jewish party members find intolerable. Baroness Royall wrote in her report of Jewish members of the Oxford University Labour Club who refused to attend meetings because of the behaviour and language they found there. Joe Goldberg, a Labour councillor in Haringey until 2018, said that 'it has become impossible to operate as a Jewish councillor in the Haringey party without having your views and actions prejudged or dismissed in terms that relate to your ethnicity'. Philip Rosenberg, a Jewish member of Hampstead and Kilburn Constituency Labour Party and a Labour councillor until 2018, wrote that his local branch's obsessive 'singling-out' of Jews and Israel and 'the nauseating cacophony of jeers and heckling against anyone who dares question the "permitted groupthink"' amounted to institutional antisemitism. Rosenberg warned that 'the effect on most Jews will be a clear sign that this is no safe space for us'. Another Jewish member in Hampstead and Kilburn has described the 'monomania' of people whose sole reason for being in politics is not to build a better economy or improve the NHS but purely to pursue their obsessive anti-Zionism. These activists tend to be older people who left the Labour Party under Tony Blair or Neil Kinnock, spent the past decade or more in the smaller groups of the far left and re-joined under Jeremy Corbyn. It is usually these 'retreads', not the younger members who have joined Labour for the first time under Corbyn, who bully local party officers and dominate debates. In Hampstead and Kilburn this got so bad that the local party chair imposed a moratorium on all discussion of Israel, Palestine and anti-semitism at the beginning of 2017. It didn't take long for things to return to normal the following year. In May 2018, a meeting of Hampstead and Kilburn's General Committee debated a motion condemning the shooting of Palestinians on the Israel–Gaza border. The initial vote drew an overwhelming show of hands in favour of the motion, but some at the meeting wanted to proceed with the votes against the motion and abstentions: not because they would affect the outcome of the vote, but just so they could publicly identify anyone who had dissented from the anti-Israel line. The consequence of all this behaviour is to create a toxic environment for Jewish members who cleave to a traditional Labour Zionist position. 'Jewish members are left wondering what is coming next,' a local member said.[24]

One Jewish Labour Party member, Cathy Ashley, has even taken out a formal complaint against her entire Constituency Labour Party because of its 'hostile environment for main-stream Jews'. Ashley is a lifelong party member, a former councillor and spent six years as chair of the Holocaust Memorial Day Trust. Her complaint arose from a meeting of Dulwich and West Norwood Constituency Labour Party, in south London, when a debate on antisemitism following Livingstone's suspension turned so hostile that she walked out to the sound of abuse from some of her fellow party members. One person gave a speech in Livingstone's defence, saying it was 'an inconvenient truth' that Hitler supported Zionism – the same views for which Livingstone had already been found guilty of bringing the party into disrepute – then sat down near Ashley and, in the words of a witness, 'leaned into her and was pointing aggressively' while pressing on with his defence of Livingstone. Ashley later recalled, 'I clearly found it distressing. He continued to press his case. I did not raise my voice but I responded that his argument was a form of Holocaust denial.' The motion condemning Livingstone was put to the vote and defeated to cheers from some people. Visibly distressed, Ashley left the room to loud jeers and applause from a group that included Livingstone's old *Labour Herald* comrade Ted Knight. Ashley was contacted in the days following the meeting by various people to express their support and sympathy. One councillor who had been at the meeting wrote to the local party chair to complain that the support for Livingstone was 'revisionist and offensive' and warned that 'some of my local members have resigned their membership altogether because of the tone of discussion on anti Semitism [*sic*] within the wider party'. Despite this, a formal complaint was lodged against Ashley because her comment that Livingstone's views were a form of Holocaust denial was deemed to be harassment of the member who had given a speech in favour of Livingstone. An emergency meeting of the local party's executive committee was hastily called at which it was decided that Ashley should apologise and 'give a commitment to handle emotive issues better in the future or to absent yourself if you feel you would be unable to do so'. Ashley was not invited to this meeting even though the rules stated she should have been; nor was she shown the complaint against her or given the opportunity to defend herself. Her guilt was simply assumed and she was also pressured to step down from the role of political education officer, which she held at the time. She refused to apologise and the entire experience left her 'devastated and exhausted'. This is not the first, time, she wrote in her complaint, that she has 'been targeted for being a Jew who reflects the views of the great majority of the Jewish community on the matter of anti-Semitism'. In her opinion, one factor 'that gives licence to this and helps to create such a toxic atmosphere is the anti-Zionist and anti-Jewish Labour Movement obsession' of Jewish Voice for Labour, which has strong support in Dulwich and West Norwood Labour Party. She concluded that 'there is no place for any Jew, who is part of the wider Jewish community, to hold office within DAWN Labour Party or participate in the meetings or the structures of the party, unless they are willing unemotionally to stand by in the face of Holocaust denial'. In February 2018, Ashley lodged a formal complaint with the national party against her own

Constituency Labour Party. By definition, her allegation is one of institutional, not personal, antisemitism. It is made up of the initial, allegedly antisemitic comments by one individual; multiplied by the behaviour of a group of like-minded members at the meeting; legitimised by the subsequent decisions of local party officers; and compounded by the patronising instruction to a Jewish member not to react in an 'emotional way' to perceived antisemitism. At the time of writing, four months after submitting her complaint, she is yet to hear whether the party will even lay charges.[25]

The problems in Dulwich and West Norwood, in Hampstead and Kilburn, and in other local branches around the country, are the Labour Party in microcosm. The kind of antisemitism that is expressed mixes hatred of Israel and Zionism with older traditional antisemitic tropes, Holocaust revisionism and wild conspiracy theories. It is facilitated by the swirl of social media, conducted in a bullying atmosphere and often defended for factional reasons or through personal loyalty. Key activists from the hard left or Jewish anti-Zionist groups seek to shape the party's response and obstruct action against antisemitism. Generic condemnations of antisemitism and assurances that it has no place in the Labour Party are rarely followed through. The idea that allegations of antisemitism are part of a manufactured, malicious smear campaign is widespread. Those members, Jewish and not, who complain about antisemitism and the party's handling of it are either ignored or themselves victimised. These problems have got worse, not better, under Corbyn's leadership; and it is all done, rightly or wrongly, whether he likes it or not, whether he is aware of it or not, in the name of Jeremy Corbyn's Labour Party and for his favoured causes of socialism and Palestine.

CONCLUSION

INSTITUTIONAL ANTISEMITISM

The idea of institutional racism is best known for being levelled at the Metropolitan Police following the racist murder of Stephen Lawrence in south-east London in 1993. According to the report of the independent inquiry into the police failures following that murder, institutional racism can be 'detected in processes, attitudes and behaviour' of an organisation 'which amount to discrimination through unwitting prejudice, ignorance, thoughtlessness and racist stereotyping'. This discrimination is normalised and spread via an organisation's internal culture, which can be 'all powerful in shaping our views and perceptions of a particular community', and 'institutionalised in the way the organisation operates'. It is found not only in racist assumptions and stereotypes, but also in the inability or refusal to see racism when it is present. It is entirely possible, and indeed common, for individual members and

policies of the organisation in question not to be racist, but for
the organisation to still discriminate in how it treats particular
minorities. And, crucially:

> It persists because of the failure of the organisation openly and
> adequately to recognise and address its existence and causes
> by policy, example and leadership. Without recognition and
> action to eliminate such racism it can prevail as part of the
> ethos or culture of the organisation. It is a corrosive disease.[1]

Two years ago, when the first edition of this book was published, much was still in doubt about how the antisemitism that
existed in the Labour Party would play out. It was early days in
Jeremy Corbyn's leadership and, while antisemitism was clearly
a problem, there was still much debate about exactly what kind
of problem it was. Many people in the party argued that it was
nothing more than an accumulation of individual cases that
simply reflected the existence of antisemitism in wider society;
a natural, if unwanted, product of the party's rapid growth in
recent years rather than a sign of something deeper and more
systemic in the left. The party had held an inquiry, Baroness
Chakrabarti had made her recommendations, Ken Livingstone
had been suspended and the problem would ease, so this way
of thinking went. Others felt differently. Their view was that
the cases of apparent antisemitism in the party formed a pattern. From this perspective, the antisemitism was the product

of a particular mindset generated by hostile attitudes towards Jews, Israel and Zionism that had become acceptable in Labour Party circles. Labour's efforts to address it had been superficial and ineffective, and, having incubated on the fringes of the left for decades, it had become part of the institutional culture of the party. If so, Labour would not be able to rid itself of this problem quite so easily.

The evidence of the past three years suggests that the latter view is correct. Despite what too many people in the Labour Party still appear to believe, the allegation that Labour has a problem of antisemitism is not part of a plot to unseat Corbyn, or to prevent a socialist government, or to silence critics of Israel. Even Corbyn himself, after the Jewish community demonstration outside Parliament in March 2018, accepted that antisemitism in the party 'has too often been dismissed as simply a matter of a few bad apples'. The cases of antisemitism in Labour have not declined; on the contrary, they are so numerous that most are no longer newsworthy. Members of the party's NEC – its highest governing body – give the impression of resisting disciplinary action against people accused of antisemitism if it would damage their factional interests, rather than taking a genuinely 'zero-tolerance' approach. Dozens of CLPs pass motions supporting Marc Wadsworth and other Labour members who have been suspended or expelled. Ken Livingstone was found guilty of bringing the party into disrepute, but the disciplinary panel decided his conduct was still consistent with membership of the Labour Party. The Chakrabarti Inquiry failed in its mission to restore trust in Labour's ability to deal with antisemitism, and the Jewish community's confidence in the party is as low as it can go. Sometimes the antisemitism is naked and personal. Stephane Savary, a Labour and Momentum member from the left of the party, found that attitudes to him changed markedly when people discovered he was converting to Judaism. He was accused of infiltrating the left to damage Corbyn, of pretending to support Labour and of only caring about defending Israel. The fact he had joined Labour in 2009 and supported Corbyn in both leadership elections made no difference. More often, though, the antisemitism is found in the collective assumptions of Labour's organisational culture rather than the personal prejudices of its members. The discriminatory and marginalising experiences of Jewish members in some constituency Labour parties are the product of attitudes that are embedded in the political culture and decision-making processes of those local parties, rather than overt, individual hatred. It was institutional, not personal, antisemitism, that affected Jewish party members in Haringey, Dulwich and West Norwood, and Hampstead and Kilburn, and it is institutional antisemitism that explains the national party's inability to stop its antisemitism from continuing to grow.[2]

Of course, there are many people in the Labour Party who are not antisemitic or who actively oppose it. The party has rules against antisemitism and policies about how to deal with it. It still has many Jewish members (although an unknown number have resigned) and MPs, Jewish and not, who speak out repeatedly against antisemitism. However, similar things can be, and were, said about the Metropolitan Police in relation to colour-based racism in the 1990s. The charge of institutional racism does not mean that every person in an organisation is racist, or that the organisation itself sets out to deliberately discriminate. It refers instead to the way that the character of an institution is often shaped by its informal working culture rather than by its formal rules. It is this informal culture that creates the uncomfortable environment that many Jewish Labour Party members experience. Are Jewish people as welcome as everyone else in the Labour Party, or do other members suspect them of having ulterior motives or hidden loyalties? Are they sometimes forced to justify their presence by explaining their view of Israel in a way that nobody else does? Do antisemitic comments and statements always attract opprobrium and consistent, strong disciplinary action? Are Jewish complaints about alleged antisemitism treated with sensitivity, seriousness and respect? Does everyone in the Labour Party see the Jewish community as 'their people', whose interests the party seeks to represent and support? What kind of attitudes dominate the discussion when Labour members and supporters gather to discuss Jews, antisemitism or Israel, either at party meetings or on social media? And is there a culture of denial and suspicion when the issue of antisemitism is raised? It is in the answers to these questions, rather than in the formal policies and statements of the party and its leaders, that the place of Jews in Labour's institutional culture can be found; and too often, sadly, the answers are damning. This is why the Home Affairs Select Committee, in a report on antisemitism published in October 2016, warned that 'the failure of the Labour Party to deal consistently and effectively with antisemitic incidents in recent years risks lending force to allegations that elements of the Labour movement are institutionally antisemitic'. Those Jewish anti-Zionists who regularly speak up in defence of Corbyn and deny there is a problem of antisemitism would argue otherwise, but that only proves the point. Few in number but loud of voice, they feel at home in Corbyn's Labour Party partly because they are eager to distance themselves from the views of the overwhelming majority of their fellow Jews. They are the exceptions that prove the rule.[3]

In many ways this is a case of chickens coming home to roost for the part of the left where Corbyn has spent his entire political career and that now controls the Labour Party. The left has a long tradition of opposing antisemitism and fighting for equality, but it also has other traditions and trends that encourage or utilise antisemitism and have provided fertile soil for the Labour Party's problems. Since the 1960s, the idea has spread across the left that Zionism is a racist ideology and that Israel is a Western colonial implant in the Middle East. It is a short step from this to the idea that Israel should not exist and that its supporters in the West – which includes most Jews – are racists and therefore political opponents of the left. This New Left view that Israel and Zionism are illegitimate form a modern bridge to older Marxist theories that Jews are not an authentic people who should, as history progresses, disappear entirely. The emotional, historical and spiritual Jewish connection to Israel was at first ignored by this way of thinking and then later taken as evidence that Jews are complicit in Israel's alleged crimes. Conspiracy theories about Jewish, or Zionist, wealth, power and influence emerged from Soviet propaganda and have become worryingly common in the post-9/11 left. The Holocaust is either denigrated or turned against Israel via the most grotesque and offensive historical distortions. Underpinning all of this is the assumption that when Jews complain about antisemitism on the left or in the pro-Palestinian movement, then, unless those Jews are themselves anti-Zionists, they are likely to be lying to defend Israel. The word 'Zionist' has become a political insult, used in parts of the left to stigmatise and exclude those Jews who think Israel should exist and who feel a bond with it. This has become a moral question and one of political identity, rather than an objective analysis of Israeli or Palestinian policy and action. The Israeli–Palestinian conflict has been inflated to para-digmatic importance for many on the left and generates an emotional reaction that is unparalleled. Anti-Zionists may say that, because they believe Zionism is racist, they are perfectly entitled (or even obliged) to exclude Zionists from the left. Given that over 90 per cent of Jews say Israel is part of their Jewish identity, in practice this means excluding all but a fraction of British Jews. This doesn't seem to bother as many of Israel's opponents on the British left as it should. This means that, even though anti-Zionism may be anti-racist in theory, in practice it too often results in antisemitic political campaigns – as happened on British campuses in the 1970s and 1980s. Where anti-Zionism is concerned, the non-antisemitic theory rarely survives contact with the antisemitic reality.

At the same time, a type of anti-racist politics has developed that is blind to antisemitism if it doesn't come from the far right, and that sees Jews as part of the powerful, wealthy establishment in Western societies. It ought to be simple for left-wing people, with their anti-racist instincts and sensitivities for minority concerns, to identify and challenge antisemitism when it does appear within their movement, but unfortunately this doesn't happen often enough. The idea that antisemitism only comes from the right and that left-wing people are, by definition, anti-racist, inhibits this kind of self-reflection to a remarkable degree. The possibility that somebody might believe antisemitic things about Jews without feeling any personal animosity towards them is not considered. There is a much-studied phenomenon of 'antisemitism without Jews': countries where antisemitic attitudes are common amongst the general population or in government policies, but where few if any Jews actually live. Modern-day Iraq is one example, where, according to a 2014 opinion poll, 80 per cent of respondents said they have an unfavourable opinion of Jews. The British left today gives the impression of being a slightly different phenomenon: a place where there is antisemitism without antisemites. Unlike the time of Wilhelm Marr or Nazi Germany, nobody today admits to being an antisemite, and few concede the possibility that they may unwittingly harbour antisemitic prejudices or beliefs. Because of the insistence that antisemitism is a right-wing problem, to do so would place them outside the left. There are some exceptions. Naz Shah admitted after her suspension that her views on Israel had been based on ignorance and appealed for the Jewish community to educate her. However, for most, the unshakeable need to define oneself as anti-racist trumps everything. This instinct is commendable, but it obstructs any serious reflection about the nature and extent of the left's own problem of antisemitism.

It would be understandable if Labour Party members and supporters are personally affronted by the suggestion that their party is institutionally antisemitic. They might find it ridiculous that Labour, traditionally the party of anti-racism that prides itself on fighting discrimination and inequality, could even be thought of in those terms. It is a complete inversion of the party's own identity and sense of purpose; yet this would not be the only aspect of the Labour Party that has fundamentally changed since Corbyn became its leader. He did so thanks to a huge influx of new members and returning old members, and as part of a broader effort by activists from the far left to take control of the party. Three years on, this project has made significant progress. Anybody who assumes that Corbyn is just a different kind of leader of the same Labour Party as before needs to adjust their thinking: this is a different party from the one Corbyn took over, and part of this change is that it incorporates the kind of antisemitic political culture described in this book. What was once on the fringes of the left has now been placed front and centre in British politics. It will continue to churn out party members and activists making antisemitic statements, or making excuses for others who do so, as long as this culture remains untouched.

The impact on Jewish voters was made clear in the local elections in May 2018. Labour had identified Barnet Council, run by an unpopular Conservative group that had recently lost its majority, as one of its key targets in London, but Barnet happens to include Britain's largest Jewish community. Labour candidates in the area met a wave of hostility on the doorstep. According to Adam Langleben, a Labour councillor in Barnet with a strong record of challenging left-wing antisemitism, 'Throughout the campaign, in all of the wards that we were trying to win, candidates who knocked on doors met Jews and non-Jews who raised the anti-Semitism question.' Labour activists, many of whom were, like Langleben, Jewish themselves, were shouted at in the streets and called racists and antisemites, simply because they campaigned for Labour – supposedly the party of anti-racism. On election day, Labour failed to take the council, losing six seats to the Tories. Their vote share dropped in the six wards with the largest Jewish populations, but in none of these were Jewish voters the majority: it was Jewish and non-Jewish voters who turned away from Labour in Barnet. A similar pattern was seen in individual wards in Salford and Bury that are home to large numbers of Jewish voters. Corbyn visited Barnet once during the campaign for a quick photo opportunity with some local activists. He did not meet any of the sitting Labour councillors, or any members of the public, but the activist group he did meet included Jenny Manson, co-chair of Jewish Voice for Labour. A planned victory rally in Barnet for the day after the election was hurriedly cancelled. Langleben issued a public invitation to Corbyn to visit Barnet and find out for himself how Jewish Labour members, and the wider Jewish community, feel about the party's problems with antisemitism, but at the time of writing he has yet to take up this invitation. It stands as a metaphor for Corbyn's lack of understanding, engagement or interest in the Jewish community beyond those few leftist Jews he has known for years.[4]

It is not possible to change an organisational culture through procedural tweaks, or rule changes, or by hiring more staff to implement the same flawed processes. It requires education, personal example, sacrifice and a willingness to listen to and work with an organisation's strongest critics. It needs difficult self-reflection and open acceptance of the problem and, as the report of the Stephen Lawrence Inquiry pointed out, most of all it needs leadership; but in the midst of all this, the leader of the Labour Party has stood largely oblivious. In December 2017, speaking at a reception of the Jewish Labour Movement to mark the festival of Chanukah, Corbyn declared without irony that 'there is zero tolerance of antisemitism in the Labour Party and that is how it should remain'. The evidence repeatedly suggests otherwise. Elsewhere, Corbyn has said that 'no anti-Semitic remarks are ever done in my name', even though so much of the antisemitism reported to his own party, or highlighted by his own MPs, is done in Facebook groups that bear his name, or in tweets that use pro-Corbyn hashtags. By the middle of 2018, Corbyn had changed his public line, acknowledging that antisemitism was a genuine problem in starkly different terms from how he spoke about it two years earlier, but whether this was done out of genuine enlightenment or to try to stop negative headlines is questionable, as he still seems to lack either the understanding or the willingness to take the necessary steps to fix the problem. This relates directly to the question of whether Corbyn is personally antisemitic. There is no doubt that he strongly and genuinely believes that he opposes all forms of racism. There is also no doubt that he has Jewish friends and comrades on the left going back decades.

He repeatedly condemns antisemitism in generic terms and pledges to oppose it. Nevertheless, his behaviour since becoming leader raises troubling questions. It is hard to fathom how the leader of a political movement can be so slow to intervene and so apparently reluctant to take personal responsibility for solving the problem, if he is as personally disturbed by antisemitism as he claims. His public statements on the issue still suggest he sees this as a problem that affects other people, rather than something that has come from within his own political world. There is a lack of the political and moral urgency that characterises Corbyn's response to other injustices in the world.[5]

Then there is Corbyn's reaction to the antisemitic conspiracy mural in east London in 2012, which led some to suspect that he did not think the mural was antisemitic because he shares the prejudices it depicted. There are his repeated calls for an inquiry into 'pro-Israeli' influence in British politics. There is the underlying question of whether it is possible for Corbyn to have spent decades on the hard left alongside the likes of Ken Livingstone and Tony Greenstein, building campaigns and organising events with the kind of activists found in the Palestine Live Facebook group or, in years gone by, the Labour Movement Campaign for Palestine, without absorbing any of the hostile and prejudiced assumptions and stereotypes about Jews, Israel, Zionism and antisemitism found in those circles. At the very least, it seems that he spent many years in those circles without challenging the antisemitism he surely encountered. Ultimately, it is not possible to peer into somebody's soul and discover with any certainty what they really think and believe about Jews. Perhaps even Corbyn does not truly know or understand his own deepest thoughts and imaginings about the cultural and political figure of 'The Jew'. All that can be done, as with any politician, is to judge him by his words and actions – and by his lack of words and actions. By this measure he has been found repeatedly wanting. As the leader of the Labour Party, whose supporters have effective control of most of its decision-making roles and committees and who benefits from a huge army of loyal grassroots followers, Corbyn could lead the cultural change that the party and the broader left need to truly eradicate this antisemitism – if he chooses to do so. The question is not whether he has the power to do it or whether, in theory, he would want to. The question is whether, as a lifelong product and leader of that same political culture, he is even capable of recognising that this is the choice he needs to make.

ENDNOTES

Introduction

1. 'In our thousands...': Jeremy Corbyn, 'Gaza Flotilla Massacre: London Demo' (3 June 2010) https://www.youtube.com/watch?v=vQLYXJUH2uY; 'The great...': Seumas Milne, 'Palestinians have every right to defend themselves' (26 November 2012) https://www.youtube.com/watch?v=1EBjlQ-PI7g

2. 'Became...': Jeremy Corbyn, 'Feature – the role of empires: The continuing abuse of poverty-stricken Gaza', *Morning Star* (29 October 2008); 'Macabre...': Jeremy Corbyn, 'They don't get it; Our leaders can't see the real situation in Gaza', *Morning Star* (21 January 2009)

3. 'The European...': Colin Shindler, *Israel and the European left: Between Solidarity and Delegitimization* (New York: Continuum, 2012), p.243; 'A leading...': Reut Institute, *Building a Political Firewall against Israel's Delegitimization: Conceptual Framework* (March 2010)

4. 'Jews exploit...': L. Daniel Staetsky, *Antisemitism in contemporary*

Great Britain: A study of attitudes towards Jews and Israel (Institute for Jewish Policy Research, September 2017)

Chapter One: When the Left Stopped Loving Israel

1. Jane Degras, 'Crisis Management in the Russian Press, 1967', in *The Left Against Zion: Communism, Israel and the Middle East*, ed. by Robert S. Wistrich (London: Vallentine, Mitchell 1979) pp.106–13

2. James R. Vaughan, '"Keep left for Israel": Tribune, Zionism and the Middle East, 1937–1967', *Contemporary British History*, 27/1 (2013): 1–21

3. 'It can...': Philip Mendes, *Jews and the left: The Rise and Fall of a Political Alliance* (Basingstoke: Palgrave Macmillan, 2014), p.1; 'The history...': Nathan Weinstock, 'Introduction', in *The Jewish Question – A Marxist Interpretation* by Abram Leon (New York: Pathfinder Press, 1970)

4. Shirley Williams, interview (29 January 2014)

5. Frantz Fanon, *Black Skin White Masks* (London: Pluto Press, 2008); Frantz Fanon, *The Wretched of the Earth*, sixth edn (London: Penguin Classics, 2001)

6. Patrick Seale & Maureen McConville, *French Revolution 1968* (London: Penguin, 1968), p.40

7. Harry Hanson, 'Britain and the Arabs', *The New Reasoner*, 6 (autumn 1958): 3–14

8. 'Both against...': Stuart M. Hall, 'The new Conservatism and the old', *Universities & Left Review*, 1/1 (spring 1957): 21–4; 'The

fixing...': Claude Bourdet, 'The Way to European Independence', *The New Reasoner*, 5 (summer 1958): 13–24; Ali A. Mazrui, 'Moise Tshombe and the Arabs: 1960 to 1968', *Race & Class*, 10 (1969): 285–304 (p.298)

9. 'A European-American...': Fayez A. Sayegh, *Zionist Colonialism in Palestine* (Beirut: Palestine Liberation Organization Research Center, 1965); 'The concept...': Hasan Sa'b, *Zionism & Racism* (Beirut: Palestine Liberation Organization Research Center, 1968); 'A colonialism...': *Palestine 20 years after: FLN Position in 10 Points* (Front of National Liberation, 1968)

10. 'An ideology...': *Zionism: Instrument of Imperialist Reaction* (Moscow: Novosti Press Agency Publishing House, 1970); 'The formula...': Antony Lerman, 'Fictive Anti-Zionism: Third World, Arab and Muslim Variations', in *Anti-Zionism and Antisemitism in the Contemporary World*, ed. by Robert S. Wistrich (Basingstoke: Macmillan Press & Institute for Jewish Affairs, 1990), pp.121–38

11. Maajid Nawaz, 'Malia Bouattia is symbolic of the poison of the regressive left', *Jewish Chronicle* (20 April 2016)

12. 'Backed by...': Che Guevara, 'Vietnam must not stand alone', *New Left Review*, 1/43 (May–June 1967): 79–91; 'A tremendous...': 'Interview with Isaac Deutscher: On the Israeli-Arab War', *New Left Review*, 1/44 (July–August 1967), 30–45; 'A colon...': Tony Cliff, *The Struggle in the Middle East* (London: International Socialism, 1967); 'Africa today...': Christopher Fyfe, 'Book review: Burden of Empire – An Appraisal of Western Colonialism in Africa South of the Sahara', *Race & Class*, 10/2 (1968): 240–42

13. 'Except for…': Maxime Rodinson, *Israel: A Colonial-Settler State?* (New York: Monad Press, 1973), p.42; 'Can only…': Fawwaz Tra-bulsi, 'The Palestine Problem: Zionism and Imperialism in the Middle East', *New Left Review*, 1/57 (September–October 1969): 53–90; 'In terms of…': Karen Farsoun, Samih Farsoun, Alex Ajay, 'Mid-East Perspectives from the American left', *Journal of Palestine Studies*, 4/1 (autumn 1974): 94–119; 'The specifically…': Stephen Halbrook, 'The Class Origins of Zionist Ideology', *Journal of Palestine Studies*, 2/1 (autumn, 1972): 86–110

14. 'This one…': *Palestine Day Conference 1966* (London: General Union of Arab Students in United Kingdom and Ireland, 1966); 'Native British…': 'The Pro-Arab Lobby', *Jewish Chronicle* (24 May 1968)

15. 'Most American…': Norman Podhoretz, 'A Certain Anxiety', *Commentary*, 52/2 (August 1971): 4–10; 'One of…': The National Archives (TNA) FCO/17/1766, W. B. J. Ledwidge, 'Mrs Meir and British Jewry's Aid to Israel' (7 December 1972); 'A cata-lyst…': Robert Wistrich, 'Introduction: The post-war Jewish world', in *Terms of Survival: The Jewish world since 1945*, ed. by Robert S. Wistrich

Chapter Two: From Anti-Apartheid to Anti-Zionism

1. 'The deliberate…': 'Middle East Peace Process', Hansard, House of Commons Debate [hereafter HC Deb], 26 June 2007, vol. 462, col. 63WH

2. Jeremy Corbyn, 'Solidarity with humans; Jeremy Corbyn explains why we should all join the Palestine Solidarity Campaign', *Morning Star* (13 July 2005)

3. 'The global norm...': Håkan Thörn, *Anti-Apartheid and the Emergence of a Global Civil Society* (Basingstoke: Palgrave Macmillan, 2006), p.6

4. 'Help us...': Palestine Solidarity Campaign website http://www.palestinecampaign.org/vote-palestine/

5. 'Nowhere in...': Sayegh, *Zionist Colonialism in Palestine*; 'Israeli apartheid': 'The Arab Boycott and Apartheid', *Arab Outlook*, 1/2 (December 1963)

6. 'Lackey Israel...' & 'colonialism...': 'Messages', *Afro-Asian Bulletin* 4/1 (January/February 1962)

7. 'The peoples...': Bodleian Library, Oxford (BOD), Anti-Apartheid Movement Archive (AAM) MSS/AAM/1393 Papers of the International Conference In Support of the Peoples of Portuguese Colonies and Southern Africa (18–20 January 1969); 'The revolutionary...': George Clark, 'Leading Young Liberals Step Down', *The Times* (17 July 1968); 'There is...': Hugh Noyes, 'Young Liberals say: "Party irrelevant"', *The Times* (14 September 1968)

8. 'The hothouse...': Peter Hellyer, 'The Young Liberals and the Left 1965–70', *Journal of Liberal History*, 67 (summer 2010): 60–67

9. 'Boring': Peter Hellyer, 'Young Liberals: The "Red Guard" Era', *Journal of Liberal Democrat History*, 17 (winter 1997–98): 14–15

10. Peter Hain, interview (5 July 2012)

11. 'Sometimes...': London School of Economics Archive (LSE) KILOH/12 George Kiloh, *Forty Years Off: A Personal Account of the Young Liberals and the Liberal Party 1965–69*, p.10

12. 'To take...': Peter Hain, *Don't Play with Apartheid* (London: George Allen & Unwin, 1971), p.115

13. 'From being...': Hain, *Don't Play with Apartheid*, p.124

14. 'an enormous...': Hain, interview; 'non-violent...': LSE Liberal Party (LP) LP/1/7 Liberal Party Council minutes (21 February 1970)

15. 'One of...': Peter Hain, *Outside In* (London: Biteback Publishing, 2012), p.65; 'All sorts...': Hellyer, interview (18–20 June 2012), emphasis in original

16. All quotes BOD MSS/AAM/1393 Papers of the International Conference In Support of the Peoples of Portuguese Colonies and Southern Africa (18–20 January 1969)

17. 'Distorted picture...': Peter Hellyer, 'Impressions From My Visit to the Middle East', *The Arab*, 2/26 (March 1969): 2–3; 'Zionism is...': *Address by the Al-Fateh Delegation to the Second International Conference in Support of the Arab Peoples* (Cairo, January 1969)

18. 'Trying to...': Hellyer, 'Impressions from my visit to the Middle East'; 'Prompted a...': Hellyer, 'The Young Liberals and the Left'

19. 'A Western...': Michael Jefferson, 'The Case Against Zionism and the present state of Israel', *New Outlook*, 77 (April 1969); 'Anti-Zionist...': LSE Young Liberals (YL) YL/6 NLYL Executive minutes (1 June 1969) & LSE YL/5 NLYL International Newsletter no.2 (July 1969)

20. LSE LP/16/75 Jeremy Thorpe, 'Britain and the Middle East', Anglo-Israel Friendship League (4 April 1968)

21. *NLYL Annual Report Skegness 1970* & 'Palestine Solidarity Conference in Algiers', *Free Palestine*, 2/8 (January 1970)

22. 'Liked the...': Kiloh, *Forty Years Off*, p.87; 'Flair for...': Hain, interview; 'World opinion...': LSE YL/4 'Young Liberal News: Liberal Condemns Zionist Apartheid' (23 January 1970)

23. 'Liability': A. J. Travers, 'Liberals in Anti-Israel Storm', *Daily Telegraph* (27 January 1970), A. J. Travers, 'Young Liberal chairman "a liability"', *Daily Telegraph* (29 January 1970), 'Byers attacks Young Liberal', *The Guardian* (29 January 1970); 'The major...': LSE YL/4 Young Liberal News Press Release, 'Young Liberal Stands Firm on Middle East' (7 March 1970)

24. 'The expulsion...': LSE YL/4 Young Liberal News Press Release, 'Law and Order, The Middle East and The New Left' (16 March 1970); 'The creation...': LSE YL/10 'YL Policy Booklet: Middle East' (undated)

25. 'That the...': LSE YL/4 LPO Press Release (1 May 1970); 'Jews see...': Francis Boyd, 'Eaks row could hit Liberal Party funds', *The Guardian* (2 November 1970); Francis Boyd, 'Eaks episode rumbles on', *The Guardian* (3 November 1970)

26. 'Once the...': Phil Kelly, interview (22 January 2013)

27. 'The world...': Peter Hain, 'Palestine must win', *Free Palestine* (April 1973); 'A great...': Hain, interview; 'The common...': Kiloh, *Forty Years Off*, p.107; Sir Lawrence Freedman, interview (10 February 2010)

28. 'A core...': Freedman, interview; 'An imagined...': Thorn, *Anti-Apartheid*, p.193

29. 'A real...': Fenner Brockway, 'Peer's tribute', *Jewish Chronicle* (15 December 1978)

Chapter Three: Creating Palestine or Destroying Israel?

1. 'Campaigns for...': http://www.palestinecampaign.org/about/; 'A safe...': Jeremy Corbyn, 'Why I support the campaign for Palestinian human rights' (2 August 2015) http://www.stopwar.org.uk/index.php/news-comment/787-jeremy-corbyn-why-i-support-the-international-campaign-for-palestinian-human-rights; 'I think...': Asa Winstanley, 'Jeremy Corbyn backs boycott of Israeli universities involved in arms research' (2 August 2015) https://electronicintifada.net/blogs/asa-winstanley/jeremy-corbyn-backs-boycott-israeli-universities-involved-arms-research

2. 'Tried to...': Ghayth Armanazi, interview (28 February 2013); 'The parallels...': FOP advert, *Free Palestine* (November 1968)

3. 'Struggling for...': 'Undeserved Honour', *Free Palestine* (July 1968); '"Mr Big"...': Claud Morris, *The Last Inch: A Middle East Odyssey* (London: Kegan Paul International, 1996); 'The tragic...': 'Editorial: Our Aim...', *Free Palestine* (June 1968)

4. 'In the...': 'Despair', *Free Palestine* (July 1972); 'With interest...': Stan Newens, letter, *Free Palestine* (July 1974); 'Now is...': 'Editorial: No Pride in Violence', *Free Palestine* (July 1974)

5. 'Some young...': Colin Smith, 'Hit-and-run bombers', *The Observer* (31 August 1969)

6. 'The capitalist...': 'Palestine Solidarity Campaign', *Free Palestine* (May 1969)

7. 'Conservative...': Ibrahim Ali, 'Palestine: Guerilla [*sic*] Organisations', *International Socialism*, 36 (April/May 1969); 'The Palestine...': 'Introduction', *Black Dwarf* (2 May 1969)

8. Peter Hellyer, interview (26 December 2009)

9. 'British Students Visit al-Fatah', *Free Palestine* (September 1969)

10. 'The young...': Armanazi, interview

11. 'Help from...': Modern Records Centre, University of Warwick (MRC) MSS/152/1/4/4 Lil Power, 'Report on Palestine Solidarity Campaign & Conference' (undated); 'In view...': 'Mr Ghayth Nabib Armanazi', HC Deb, 6 February 1975, vol. 885, c. 597W. The Home Secretary declined the request. Reported in 'Protest over accreditation of diplomat', *Jewish Chronicle* (31 January 1975)

12. 'Despite...': Hain, 'Palestine Must Win'

13. 'An Anti-Apartheid...': LSE FAULDS/3/2/10 Louis Eaks correspondence to Andrew Faulds (28 April 1972); PHS, 'New Pals', *The Times* (5 June 1972)

14. 'The first...': Ghada Karmi, *In Search of Fatima* (London: Verso, 2002), p.394; 'Seminal...': Ghada Karmi, interview (1 February 2013)

15. Karmi, interview

16. 'This section...': 'Campaigning for Palestine', *Free Palestine*

(November 1974); 'an uphill...': Karmi, interview; Galal Maktari, interview (8 February 2013)

17. 'Israel: The Untold Story' advert, *The Times* (11 May 1973); 'The Libyan Arab Republic' advert, *The Times* (6 June 1973)

18. 'The Palestine Report', Part 1, *The Guardian* (14 May 1976) & Part 2, *The Guardian* (15 May 1976); Philip Kleinman, 'Money talks again', *Jewish Chronicle* (21 May 1976)

19. 'The Palestine Report', Part 1

20. 'One more...': Daphna Baram, *Disenchantment: The Guardian and Israel* (London: Guardian Books, 2004), p.141; 'our PLO...': Kleinman, 'Money talks again'; 'Perhaps...': Michael May, 'British Public Opinion Polls on the Arab–Israel Conflict Since the Six-Day War', *Institute of Jewish Affairs Research Report* (July 1976)

21. LSE FAULDS/3/2/30, Open Door script

22. 'A racist...': LSE FAULDS/3/2/30, Open Door script; 'The best...': LSE FAULDS/3/2/30, Ghada Karmi, correspondence to Andrew Faulds (29 November 1976); 'bombarded...': 'BBC bows to storm over Arab attack', *Jewish Chronicle* (3 December 1976); 'BBC and truth', editorial, *Jewish Chronicle* (3 December 1976)

23. 'National campaigns...': George Mitchell, 'Statement on the Struggle Against Zionism in Britain', *BAZO Info Bulletin* (October 1976); 'Internalised...': Richard Burden, interview (27 June 2012)

24. 'Boundaries': Akiva Orr, in *Matzpen: Anti-Zionist Israelis*, Dir. Eran Torbiner (Israel, 2003), 1:46 http://www.youtube.com/

watch?v=hfcFno2pqJg; 'Became a...': Karmi, *In Search of Fatima*, p.397; 'Acolytes...': Karmi, interview; 'Educators': Tariq Ali, in Torbiner, *Matzpen: Anti-Zionist Israelis*, 24:56

25. 'Arab revolution...': Ran Greenstein, 'A Palestinian Revolutionary: Jabra Nicola and the Radical left', *Jerusalem Quarterly*, 46 (summer 2011): 32–48; 'The outcome...': 'The Palestine Problem and the Israeli–Arab Dispute: May 18, 1967', in *The Other Israel: The Radical Case Against Zionism*, ed. by Arie Bober (New York: Doubleday, 1972), pp.208–13

26. Karmi, interview

27. 'The jumping...': 'Interview with Isaac Deutscher: On the Israeli – Arab War', *New Left Review* 1/44 (July/August 1967): 30–45; 'It's a complete...': Karmi, interview

28. Karmi, interview

29. Leon, *The Jewish Question*

30. 'Among the...': Nathan Weinstock, 'Introduction', in Leon, *The Jewish Question*; 'The theoretical...': Abdullah Schleifer, 'Decline of Dissent?', *Journal of Palestine Studies*, 2/1 (autumn 1972): 128–38; 'Leon's book...': John Rose, 'Karl Marx, Abram Leon and the Jewish Question – a Reappraisal', *International Socialism*, 119 (summer 2008)

Chapter Four: When Anti-Racists Ban Jews

1. Yohanan Manor, *To Right A Wrong: The Revocation of the UN General Assembly Resolution 3379 Defaming Zionism* (New York:

Shengold Publishers, 1996), pp.6–12 & 'Editorial: Israel and the UN The case for expulsion', *Free Palestine* (August/September 1975)

2. 'The world…': 'Palestinians Score Triple Victory', *Free Palestine* (12 December 1975); 'Reeked of…': Daniel Patrick Moynihan and Suzanne Weaver, *A Dangerous Place* (New York: Berkley Books, 1980), p.127; 'Symbolic…': Ambassador Chaim Herzog, 'Statement in the General Assembly by Ambassador Herzog on the item Elimination of all forms of racial discrimination' (10 November 1975) http://mfa.gov.il/MFA/ForeignPolicy/MFA-Documents/Yearbook2/Pages/129%20Statement%20in%20 the%20General%20Assembly%20by%20Ambassado.aspx; 'Do not…': William Korey, 'Soviet Antisemitism at the United Nations: Policy and Propaganda', in *Antisemitism: Threat to Western Civilization*, ed. by Menachem Z. Rosensaft & Yehuda Bauer (Jerusalem: Vidal Sassoon Center for the Study of Antisemitism, 1988), pp.53–107

3. 'British socialism…': Moynihan and Weaver, *A Dangerous Place*, p.74; 'Only regimes…': Moynihan and Weaver, *A Dangerous Place*, p.191

4. *Minutes and Summary of Proceedings*, NUS April Conference, p.79, emphasis in original

5. 'To destroy…': *Minutes and Summary of Proceedings*, NUS April Conference, pp.79–83

6. 'The greatest…': Tim Devlin, 'Student fanaticism "a threat to education"', *The Times* (8 June 1974); 'There are…': John Randall, interview (26 October 2012)

7. Charles Clarke, interview (11 June 2013)

8. 'The issue...': Kate Hoey, 'Palestine: students should not be silent', *Free Palestine* (March 1971); 'To campaign...': MRC National Union of Students Archive (NUS) MSS/280/22/2 *NUS technical colleges conference 1974*, pp.5-6. It is not clear whether the motion was debated or passed; 'Expressing opposition...': London Metropolitan Archives, City of London (LMA), Board of Deputies of British Jews (BDBJ) collection ACC/3121/E/04/0953 Stanley H. Burton to Dr P. P. Newman & Martin Savitt, correspondence (4 & 16 April 1975); 'To expel...': LMA BDBJ ACC/3121/E/04/0953 *NUS April Conference 1975 Agenda* (February 1975), p.72; 'Sanctions...': LMA BDBJ ACC/3121/E/04/0252 Edwin Sicher, 'NUS', *Grassroots* (undated) p.7; 'Will Jewish...': Arnold Wagner, 'Student Threat to Jewish Speakers', *Jewish Telegraph* (17 May 1974)

9. 'Our activities...': Stanley Goldsmith, 'Jewish students get writ to stop Arab "racist" resolution', *Daily Telegraph* (18 March 1977)

10. 'Expelling Jewish...': Judith Judd, 'Jews feel threatened by "college campaign"', *Times Higher Education Supplement* (25 March 1977)

11. Simon Caplan and Alan Elsner, 'Jews at universities', *The Times* (29 March 1977)

12. Sue Slipman, interview (5 January 2010)

13. Nigel Ward, *Zionism – What it is and how to fight it* (International Marxist Group, undated), p.19

14. 'Refuse money...': Assif Shameen, 'SOAS bans Zionists', *Sennet* (19 October 1977) & 'news analysis', *Sennet* (26 October 1977)

15. 'Anti-Jewish student unions under fire', *London Evening Standard* (4 July 1977)

16. David Fletcher, 'Zionist ban at "meeting of hate"', *Daily Telegraph* (3 October 1977)

17. 'In some…': MRC Richard Kuper collection (RK) MSS/250/1/2/8 Andy Durgan 'Fighting Zionism in the colleges', *Socialist Workers Party Bulletin* (May 1977); 'We support…': 'Israel uses torture', *Socialist Worker* (25 June 1977)

18. 'We think…': 'NO to anti-semitism NO to Israel as well', *Socialist Worker* (29 October 1977); 'Physically…': Alex Callinicos, 'Argue with Zionists', *Socialist Worker* (12 November 1977); 'What we…': MRC Alistair Mutch collection (AM) MSS/284/2/3/2 NOISS, *Palestine: fighting for liberation* (undated)

19. 'Policy…': Richard Burden, 'Student perspective in Palestine', *Free Palestine* (March 1978); 'Campaign…': 'BAZO enters third year of campaigning', *Free Palestine* (November 1977)

20. 'The sovereignty…': 'We Say', *Morning Star* (8 October 1973); 'There is…': 'Notes of the Month: Middle East', *International Socialism*, 63 (Mid-October 1973); 'No to…': Alan Adler, 'The Middle East War: Aims and Objectives', *Red Weekly* (26 October 1973)

21. 'Smash…': David Cesarani, interview (11–12 November 2009)

22. Interviews, David Aaronovitch (22 December 2009); Trevor Phillips (14 December 2009); Colin Talbot (12 January 2010); Roger Trask (22 January 2014)

23. 'No limitations…': 'Rights safeguarded', *National Student*

(December 1977); 'Both the…': Paul Infield, 'NUS Conference 1977 – What really happened', *UJS Journal* (December 1977)

24. 'To promote…': On Campus, 'Geordie policy headache for NUS', *Jewish Chronicle* (1 February 1985)

25. Union of Jewish Students, *Right to Organise?*, leaflet (undated)

26. 'The racist…': Keren David '"Racist" slur in poly magazine', *Jewish Chronicle* (29 March 1985)

27. 'And the…': David Osler, interview (11 March 2010); 'Anti-Semitic in…' & 'Zionism is…': CLP Jewish Society, *Stop the J-Soc Banning!*, leaflet, parentheses in the original

28. 'Principled stand…': Cath Christison & Pete Redman, motion, 'Zionism', (14 March 1985)

29. 'Never before…': 'The Lebanon War and Western News Media', *Institute for Jewish Affairs Research Report*, 6 & 7 (July 1984); 'Their fight…': 'Labour Committee on Palestine is formed', *Labour Herald* (16 July 1982); 'Semi-clandestine…': Alex Mitchell, *Come the Revolution: A Memoir* (Sydney: Newsouth, 2011), pp.392–5

30. 'The sole…': *Labour Committee on Palestine Newsletter*, no. 1 (September 1982)

31. 'The Zionist…': H. C. Mullin, 'Zionism and the Holocaust', *Labour Herald* (19 March 1982); 'Blatantly…': D. Rosenburg and N. Nerva, 'Labour Herald review was "anti-Semitic"', *Labour Herald* (7 May 1982)

32. 'Helped form…': Ken Livingstone, *You Can't Say That* (London: Faber & Faber, 2011), pp.219–23

33. Yossi Melman, Interview with Ken Livingstone, *Davar* weekend magazine (30 November 1984)

34. 'Manifestations...': Labour Movement Campaign for Palestine Newsletter, undated; 'Labour Zionism...': Tony Greenstein, 'Labour Zionism', *London Labour Briefing National Supplement* (March 1984); 'To expose...': *Labour Zionism: Socialist or Colonialist?* (London: Labour Movement Campaign for Palestine, 1988)

35. 'It was...': *Labour Movement Campaign for Palestine Newsletter*, no. 2, 1985, emphasis in the original; 'It is Zionism...': *Labour Movement Campaign for Palestine Newsletter*, no. 2, 1986

36. 'A discriminatory...': 'Policy Heading: Palestine', University of York Students' Union (undated); 'Explicit support...' John Izbicki, 'Jewish Society is struck off NUS register at York', *Daily Telegraph* (17 June 1977); 'It should...' & 'We feel...': 'Students' Jewish Society "racialist"', *Yorkshire Evening Press* (16 June 1977)

37. 'To oppose...': Richard Burden and Tim Lunn, motion on Zionism (22 June 1977); 'Totally...': Gill Schiller, interview (11–12 November 2009)

38. 'If I...' & 'People on...': Richard Burden, interview (12 January 2010)

39. Paul Infield, 'NUS Conference 1977'

Chapter Five: The New Alliance: Islamists and the Left

1. 'One of...': Rowena Mason, Kevin Rawlinson & John Harris, 'Jeremy Corbyn praises Stop the War coalition as vital democratic force', *The Guardian* (11 December 2015)

2. Dr Azzam Tamimi, 'Islam and Human Rights', *Inspire* (28 September 2002)

3. 'Their women…': Usama Hasan, 'The lessons of Woolwich', *The Guardian* (23 May 2013), also Event Transcript: 'A Guide to Refuting Jihadism: Critiquing Radical Islamist Claims to Theological Authenticity' (4 February 2014) http:// henryjacksonsociety.org/2014/02/04/a-guide-to-refuting-jihadism-critiquing-radical-islamist-claims-to-theological-authenticity/

4. Ibrahim Hewitt, *Blood on the Holy Land* (Mustaqim, 1988), pp. 20–22

5. 'A breath taking…': *Trends,* vol. 5, issue 4 (undated); 'The Muslim…': 'Around the world with Inayat', *Trends,* vol. 4, issue 4 (undated)

6. 'If I…': 'Tonge sacked over suicide comment', BBC website (23 January 2004) http://news.bbc.co.uk/1/hi/uk_politics/3421669.stm; 'Terrorism…': Ted Honderich, 'Terrorism for Humanity', http://www.ucl.ac.uk/~uctytho/terrforhum.html; 'The ultimate…': Michael Mann, 'Globalization and September 11', *New Left Review* (November/December 2001); 'Heroes…': 'Rachel Corrie, Tom Hurndall and Asif Mohammed Hanif: heroes of the revolutionary youth!', *Spark* (May 2003)

7. 'Legitimate…': Press Release, 'MCB Says "Terrorist List" is ill-conceived' (2 March 2001); 'Finish…': Ahmed Versi, 'Conference agrees intifada the only solution for Palestine', *Muslim News* (undated); 'In the…': Faisal Bodi, 'Bombing for God', *The Guardian* (28 August 2001)

8. 'Do not…': 'Is this a hate speaker?', CST Blog (12

February 2010) https://cst.org.uk/news/blog/2010/02/12/is-this-a-hate-speaker

9. 'The idea ...': Jeremy Corbyn, 'Stop the War Coalition – Meet the Resistance' (30 March 2009) https://www.youtube.com/watch?v=FQLKpY3NdeA; 'Understanding...': Michael J. Totten, 'The Anti-Imperialism of Fools', *World Affairs Journal* (28 August 2012)

10. 'The Covenant of the Islamic Resistance Movement' (18 August 1988) http://avalon.law.yale.edu/20th_century/hamas.asp

11. 'The Covenant of the Islamic Resistance Movement'

12. 'The Palestinian National Charter: Resolutions of the Palestine National Council' (1–17 July 1968) http://avalon.law.yale.edu/20th_century/plocov.asp

13. 'Protest for Lebanon in Central London' (22 July 2006) https://www.youtube.com/watch?v=Iml_fx7RhMM

14. 'From having...': Yair Rosenberg, 'Did Netanyahu Put Anti-Semitic Words in Hezbollah's Mouth?', *Tablet* (9 March 2015)

15. 'From the ...': John Molyneux, 'More than opium: Marxism and religion', *International Socialism*, 119 (24 June 2008)

16. 'The Islamists ...': Chris Harman, 'The prophet and the proletariat', *International Socialism*, 64 (autumn 1994)

17. 'At the...': Martyn Hudson, 'Fight Islamism, not Islam', *Weekly Worker* (19 December 2002); 'It is ...': 'Don't Stop the War Except through Islamic Politics', Hizb ut-Tahrir – Britain (22 Jan 2003)

18. 'I'm in...': Nick Cohen, 'The lesson the left has never learnt', *New Statesman* (21 July 2003); 'Gender-segregated...': Andrew

Murray and Lindsey German, *Stop the War: The story of Britain's biggest mass movement* (London: Bookmarks, 2005), p.62; 'Could overcome…': Richard Phillips, 'Standing together: the Muslim Association of Britain and the anti-war movement', *Race & Class*, vol. 50/2 (2008): 101–13

19. 'Hate-filled…': Reva Klein, Edie Friedman, Francesca Klug, 'Post-march reflections', *The Guardian* (1 October 2002); 'The end…': Azzam Tamimi, 'Zionism must be renounced', *Morning Star* (26 Sept 2003); 'The guiding…': John Pilger, 'John Pilger on the silence over terror in Palestine', *New Statesman* (22 March 2004)

20. 'The Jewish…': Benjamin Franklin [*sic*], 'The Jewish Threat on the American Society', *The New Dawn*, no. 2 (October/November 2000); 'The Zionist…': Press Statement, Action Committee for Al-Quds in Britain (22 October 2000)

21. Jeremy Corbyn, 'Defend the Gaza Protesters Defend the Right to Protest' (15 June 2010) https://www.youtube.com/watch?v=muFKUYPvoNs&feature=youtu.be&a

22. 'End the…': Nahella Ashraf, 'Meeting in Parliament', Stop the War Coalition Website (2 March 2010) http://web.archive.org/web/20100713010420/http://stopwar.org.uk/content/view/1779/27/

23. 'An Islamophobe…': Nick Allen, 'Suicide bombing apologist campaigning for Ken Livingstone in mayoral election', *Daily Telegraph* (16 April 2008)

24. 'Israel…': Mann, 'Globalization and September 11'

25. 'Where else…': Amira Howeidy, 'Our opponents are on the

defensive', *Al-Ahram* (5–11 April 2007); 'Part of...': '2nd Cairo Declaration: With the Palestinian and Iraqi Resistance – Against Capitalist Globalization and US Hegemony', Stop the War Coalition website (14 December 2003) http://web.archive.org/web/20040211223422/ http://www.stopwar.org.uk/article.asp?id=141203

26. 'The anti-war...': 'Lindsey German: Politics for a vibrant new left', *Socialist Worker* (12 July 2003); 'All those...': Victor Kattan interview with George Galloway, Arab Media Watch website (8 June 2004) http://web.archive.org/web/20041119123325/ http://www.arabmediawatch.com/modules.php?name=News &file=article&sid=1669

27. 'Began on...': Andrew Murray, 'Jeremy Corbyn and the Battle for Socialism', 21 Century Manifesto blog (12 February 2016) https://21centurymanifesto.wordpress.com/2016/02/12/ andrew-murray-jeremy-corbyn-and-the-battle-for-socialism/; 'In fighting...': Andrew Murray, *Stop the War! Terror and the New World Order* (London: Communist Party, 2001), p.15

28. 'Anti-imperialism...': Murray and German, *Stop the War*, p.276

Chapter Six: Antisemitism, the Holocaust and the Left

1. 'Let's remember...': Jon Stone, 'Labour anti-Semitism row: Read the Ken Livingstone interview transcripts in full', *The Independent* (28 April 2016)

2. George Galloway, 'Naz Shah, Labour and anti-Semitism', *American Herald Tribune* (27 April 2016)

3. 'Little family quarrels': Fanon, *Black Skin White Masks*, p.87; 'For over forty years ...': Tony Greenstein, 'Holocaust Analogies: Repaying the Mortgage', *Return* (March 1990), pp.14–15

4. Claire Hirshfield, 'The Anglo-Boer War and the Issue of Jewish Culpability', *Journal of Contemporary History*, 15/4 (October 1980): 619–31

5. *Zur Judenfrage* quotes: https://www.marxists.org/archive/marx/works/1844/jewish-question/ & Edmund Silberner, 'Was Marx an Anti-Semite?', in *Essential Papers on Jews and the Left*, ed. by Ezra Mendelsohn (New York: New York University Press, 1997), pp.361/401; 'A nation...': Joseph Stalin, *Marxism and the National and Colonial Question* (London: Lawrence & Wishart, 1941), p.36

6. 'An act...': A. Sivanandan, Liz Fekete and Jenny Bourne, *IRR's Submission To The Labour Party Inquiry Into Anti-Semitism And Other Forms Of Racism* (23 June 2016)

7. 'Is a white...': Fanon, *Black Skin White Masks*, p.87; 'The blackening...': Gil Troy, *Moynihan's Moment: America's Fight Against Zionism as Racism* (Oxford: Oxford University Press, 2013), p.12; 'The guiding hand...': John Pilger, 'John Pilger on the silence over terror in Palestine', *New Statesman* (22 March 2004)

8. 'I refuse...': Jeremy Corbyn, 'Stop the War Coalition – Meet the Resistance'; 'There are some...': Mark Fischer, 'Censorship rally', *Weekly Worker* (23 February 2006)

9. 'It's open season...': India Knight, 'Muslims are the new Jews', *Sunday Times* (15 October 2006); 'Today the new...': Yasmin

Alibhai-Brown, 'Why Muslims must remember the Holocaust', *The Independent* (23 January 2006); 'Islamophobia is…': Kevin Ovenden, 'Racism: The Achilles Heel of Middle Class Liberalism', *Morning Star* (18 January 2016)

10. Tom Mills, Tom Griffin and David Miller, *The Cold War on British Muslims: An examination of Policy Exchange and the Centre for Social Cohesion* (Glasgow: Spinwatch, 2011), p.52; Tom Griffin, Hilary Aked, David Miller and Sarah Marusek, *The Henry Jackson Society and the Degeneration of British Neoconservatism: Liberal interventionism, Islamophobia and the 'war on terror'* (Glasgow: Spinwatch, 2015), p.5

11. 'Donnachie then…': Scottish Council of Jewish Communities, 'St Andrews Student Convicted for Racially Aggravated Attack on Jewish Student' (28 August 2011); 'This is a…': STV website, 'St Andrews student who accused Jewish undergraduate of terrorism found guilty of racism' (23 August 2011)

12. 'Trotsky's theory…': Editor briefing, 'The rise of the Washington "neo-cons"', *The Guardian* (14 April 2003); 'The small and…': 'The War Party', BBC website (18 May 2003) http://news.bbc.co.uk/1/hi/programmes/panorama/3021001.stm, transcript at http://news.bbc.co.uk/nol/shared/spl/hi/programmes/panorama/transcripts/thewarparty.txt; 'Obviously he is…': Paul Foot, 'Worse than Thatcher', *The Guardian* (14 May 2003); 'The Jewish community…': Perry Anderson, 'Scurrying towards Bethlehem', *New Left Review* (July/August 2001)

13. 'It is no...': 'US Zealots prepare for world domination', *Fight Racism! Fight Imperialism!* (June/July 2003); 'There were sixty-three...': William Siret, 'An apology to Palestinians for my role in the British mandate', *Morning Star* (22 November 2006); 'Allow me...': Combat 18 website http://www.skrewdriver.net; 'Certain things...': John Tyndall, 'Conspiracy Unveiled!', *Spearhead* (August 2003)

14. Peter Wilby, 'The *New Statesman* and anti-Semitism', *New Statesman* (11 February 2002)

15. John Pilger, 'War and shopping – the extremism that never speaks its name', *New Statesman* (22 September 2011)

16. Wilby, 'The *New Statesman* and anti-Semitism'

17. 'Paradigmatic victims...': Didi Herman, '"The Wandering Jew has no Nation": Jewishness and Race Relations Law', *Jewish Culture & History*, 12/1–2 (2010): 131–58 (p.140)

18. 'The true heirs...': 'Arabs expelled from the start', *Socialist Worker* (12 June 1982); 'It's funny how...': 'Holocaust Begin style', *Socialist Worker* (26 June 1982); 'Confirms something...': Steve Cedar, 'The road to Beirut', *Socialist Review* (October 1982), pp.20–21

19. 'The spirit...': Amira Hass, 'Nobel Winner: Ramallah Being Turned Into Concentration Camp', *Haaretz* (26 March 2002); 'A hell...': Oona King, 'Israel can halt this now', *The Guardian* (12 June 2003); 'The parallels...': Vanessa Thorpe and Edward Helmore, 'Former Pink Floyd frontman sparks fury by comparing Israelis to Nazis', *The Guardian* (14 December 2013); 'Having visited...': 'Lib Dems condemn MP's criticism of Israel ahead

of Holocaust Memorial Day', BBC website (25 January 2013) http://www.bbc.co.uk/news/uk-politics-21194991; 'In April…': George Galloway, 'Stop Gaza Massacre protest London' (3 January 2009) https://youtube/RFzPm2GWtLA

20. Jim Allen, *Perdition* (London: Ithaca Press, 1987)

21. 'The Zionist lobby': Andrew Bell, 'Court Copout?', *Time Out* (28 January 1987); 'The most lethal…': Steve Grant, 'Trial and Tribulation', *Time Out* (21–28 January 1987); 'I hadn't tangled…': Kathy Hilton, 'A venomous, vicious and unremitting onslaught', *The News Line* (11 April 1987)

22. Caryl Churchill, *Seven Jewish Children: A play for Gaza* (London: Royal Court Theatre, 2009)

23. 'The old stuff…': Howard Jacobson, 'Let's see the "criticism" of Israel for what it really is', *The Independent* (18 February 2009); 'The usual tactic': Letters, Caryl Churchill, 'My play is not anti-Semitic', *The Independent* (21 February 2009); 'While Seven…': Leon Symons, 'Outrage over "demonising" play for Gaza', *Jewish Chronicle* (12 February 2009)

24. 'To "justify"…': Mick Napier, 'Raising the Issues over Holocaust Memorial Day,' *Socialist Worker* (27 January 2007); 'The Zionists…': David T, 'SWP Force Resignation of Member from the Scottish PSC over "Perdition"', Harry's Place Blog (19 January 2007) http://hurryupharry.org/2007/01/19/swp-force-resignation-of-member-from-the-scottish-psc-over-perdition/

25. 'We must…': 'Government announces £2.1 million funding to Auschwitz-Birkenau foundation' (26 May 2011) https://

www.gov.uk/government/news/government-announces-2-1-million-funding-to-auschwitz-birkenau-foundation

26. 'The horror…': David Cameron, 'Speech marking the 25th Anniversary of the Holocaust Educational Trust' (16 September 2013) http://anti-Semitism.org.uk/wp-content/uploads/Cameron-HET-dinner-16th-Sept-2013-1.docx; 'Our work…': Scott Sayare, 'At Holocaust Center, Hollande Confronts Past', *New York Times* (21 September 2012); 'Strengthen mutual…': Declaration by the European Ministers of Education (18 October 2002) https://rm.coe.int/CoERMPublicCommonSearchServices/DisplayDCTMContent?documentId=090000168008da51

27. 'Postwar migration…': Runnymede Trust, 'The Report : Part One – A Vision for Britain' http://www.runnymedetrust.org/reportPartOne.html; 'Frank exposure…': Paul Gilroy, *Postcolonial Melancholia* (New York: Columbia University Press, 2005), iBook edition, pp.20, 141, 149

28. 'Holocaust Commemoration Week Events in Scotland, 2007 Jan 20–28,' Scottish Palestine Solidarity Campaign website http://www.scottishpsc.org.uk/

29. 'Quite rightly…': Jeremy Corbyn, 'Lessons of history: Jeremy Corbyn MP reflects on black history month and the ugly past that is still not being taught to our children', *Morning Star* (23 October 2002); 'A community…': Roey Cohen, 'No laughing matter', *Haaretz* (19 January 2006); 'Seeks to…': 'Genocide Memorial Day 2010 Remembering Man's Inhumanity to Man' (17 January 2010) http://www.inminds.co.uk/genocideday2010.

php#c6; 'Cultural code': Shulamit Volkov, 'Readjusting Cultural Codes: Reflections on Anti-Semitism and Anti-Zionism', in *Anti-Semitism and Anti-Zionism in Historical Perspective*, ed. by Jeffrey Herf (Abingdon: Routledge, 2007), pp.38–49 (pp.41–2)

30. Moira Gray, 'Israel an affront to the anti-fascist heroes', *Morning Star* (27 July 2002)

Chapter Seven: Antisemitism Under Corbyn

1   'Be regarded...': 'The key questions Jeremy Corbyn must answer', *Jewish Chronicle* (12 August 2015)

2   'Sheikh Raed Salah: The Indictments', *CST Blog* (6 July 2011) https://cst.org.uk/news/blog/2011/07/06/sheikh-raed-salah-the-indictments

3   'A suitable way...': Michael Weiss, 'Raed Salah's original 9/11 conspiracy article on Jews and the Twin Towers', *Daily Telegraph* (8 July 2011) http://blogs.telegraph.co.uk/news/michaelweiss/100095918/raed-salahs-original-911-conspiracy-article-on-jews-and-the-twin-towers/; 'Since Salah...': Lahav Harkov, 'Salah arrest an attempt to protect Zionist narrative', *Jerusalem Post* (29 June 2011); 'Israel's British...': MEMO Commentary, 'More extremist than their Israeli paymasters', Middle East Monitor (16 June 2011) http://www.middleeastmonitor.org.uk/resources/commentary-and-analysis/2481-more-extremist-than-their-israeli-paymasters; Press conference quotes from https://youtu.be/JJDPV7hEsdc & https://youtu.be/_KlgQlHGioE

4   'Whether it be…': Baroness Jan Royall, 'Allegations of Anti-Semi-
    tism: Oxford University Labour Club' (2016); 'Zionist stooge': Alex
    Chalmers, 'Anti-Semitism, anti-Zionism, Oxford University, and
    me', *New Statesman* (14 March 2016); 'Cash cow': Naomi Firsht,
    'Extent of claims of antisemitism at Oxford University Labour Club
    revealed in student testimony', *Jewish Chronicle* (7 March 2016)

5   Kirby, Lasharie, Khadim Hussain & Downing: Dave Rich, 'Jew-
    hate: a guide for the perplexed', *Jewish Chronicle* (6 May 2016); Mulla,
    Aziz & Shah Hussain: https://order-order.com/2016/05/02/
    labour-councillor-israel-behind-isis-zionist-jews-are-a-dis-
    grace-to-humanity/, https://order-order.com/2016/05/02/
    another-labour-politician-wants-to-relocate-jews-to-amer-
    ica/ & https://order-order.com/2016/05/02/
    third-labour-councillor-suspended-over-hitler-tweet/

6   Galloway tweets: https://twitter.com/georgegalloway/
    status/587938164368662528 & https://twitter.com/georgegal-
    loway/status/587945160283201537; 'The venal…': Jenn Selby,
    'George Galloway blames "racists and Zionists" for defeat to Naz
    Shah in Bradford West', *The Independent* (8 May 2015)

7   'Subconscious biases': Becky Milligan, 'Naz Shah: My words
    were anti-Semitic', BBC News (18 July 2016)

8   'I've been in…': Matthew Weaver, 'Timeline: events leading to
    Ken Livingstone suspension', *The Guardian* (28 April 2016)

9   'If I had…': 'The Rise of Antisemitism', Hansard, Home Affairs
    Committee Oral Evidence, 14 June 2016, HC 136 Q154–164

10 For a detailed debunking of Livingstone's claims, see Paul

Bogdanor, 'Ken Livingstone and the myth of Zionist "collaboration" with the Nazis', *Fathom* (Spring 2017) http://fathomjournal.org/ken-livingstone-and-the-myth-of-zionist-collaboration-with-the-nazis/

11   Opinion poll: Marcus Dysch, 'Labour support among British Jews collapses to 8.5 per cent', *Jewish Chronicle* (4 May 2016); 'The Labour...': YouGov (9–11 May 2016) https://d25d2506s-fb94s.cloudfront.net/cumulus_uploads/document/1u5r7s2duv/TimesResults_160511_LabourMembers_W.pdf; 'It's such a...': Justin Cohen, 'Exclusive: Labour to reinterview council hopeful who said "Jews reaped rewards of playing victims"', *Jewish News* (14 November 2017); 'Israel was created...': Stephen Oryszczuk, 'Labour councillor suspended for anti-Semitic post', *Jewish News* (13 October 2016); 'It's the super rich...': Lee Harpin, 'Labour removes support from candidate over "Zionist lobby" post', *Jewish Chronicle* (16 November 2017); 'The ZioNazi storm...': Justin Cohen, 'Exclusive: Labour candidate suspended over "ZioNazi storm troopers" posts', *Jewish News* (7 April 2017); 'Powerful Jewish lobby': Tom Peterkin, 'Scottish Labour councillor suspended over anti-semitic allegations', *The Scotsman* (4 May 2016); 'The Zionist powers...': Charlotte Oliver, 'Reinstated Labour councillor attacks "utterly ruthless Zionist powers that be"', *Jewish Chronicle* (11 July 2016); 'Rothschilds' Jewish mafia': Mikey Smith & Nicola Bartlett, 'Labour suspends candidate accused of sharing "question the Holocaust" Facebook posts', *Daily Mirror* (2 April 2018)

12   'The mainstream...': YouGov (25–29 August 2016) https://

d25d2506sfb94s.cloudfront.net/cumulus_uploads/document/
pvxdr2lh73/InternalResults_160830_LabourSelectorate.pdf

13 'Try Russia Today...': Jeremy Corbyn, tweet (26 April 2011)
https://twitter.com/jeremycorbyn/status/62790355829002240;
'historian...': Peter Rushton, 'Israel behind new anti-Iran sce-
nario', Press TV (11 November 2011) https://web.archive.org/
web/20111113180140/http://www.presstv.ir/detail/209518.
html; 'The alleged...': Nicholas Kollerstrom, 'The Walls of
Auschwitz', Press TV (18 May 2008) https://web.archive.org/
web/20111206185527/http://edition.presstv.ir/detail/56287.
html; 'Press TV...': Mark Dankof, 'Empire continues to sweat
over Press TV', Press TV (25 May 2011) https://web.archive.org/
web/20110530174111/http://www.presstv.com/detail/181711.html

14 'We are absolutely...' & 'The way we...': Jim Waterson, 'The
Rise Of The Alt-Left British Media', BuzzFeed (6 May 2017)
https://www.buzzfeed.com/jimwaterson/the-rise-of-the-alt-
left?utm_term=.fjyqax2DM#.bvpmOpMVJ; 'We set up...':
'Establishment Escalating Attacks On Skwawkbox And Other
Left Media', Skwawkbox (20 October 2017) https://skwawkbox.
org/2017/10/20/establishment-escalating-attacks-on-skwaw-
box-and-other-left-media/

15 Opinion polls: Freddie Sayers, '"You may say that I'm a dreamer":
inside the mindset of Jeremy Corbyn's supporters', YouGov
(27 August 2015) https://yougov.co.uk/news/2015/08/27/
you-may-say-im-dreamer-inside-mindset-jeremy-corby/
& YouGov (25–29 August 2016) https://d25d2506sfb94s.

cloudfront.net/cumulus_uploads/document/pvxdr2lh73/ InternalResults_160830_LabourSelectorate.pdf; 'If we put...': 'Richie Debates Canary Editor Kerry-Anne Mendoza On The Futility (Or Not) Of Elections', The Richie Allen Show (5 April 2016) https://youtu.be/qquXnU1JufQ; 'The Myths...': 'Nick Kollerstrom On The Myths And The Realities Of The Holocaust & The British Memorial', The Richie Allen Show (27 January 2016) https://www.youtube.com/watch?v=vqdxGPTsM9Y; 'Media madness...': Ed Sykes, 'The Labour party suspends Ken Livingstone, but Twitter isn't buying it', The Canary (28 April 2016) https://www.thecanary.co/uk/2016/04/28/labour-par- ty-suspends-ken-livingstone-twitter-isnt-buying/; 'Wholly legitimate...': Kerry-Anne Mendoza, 'The inconvenient truths that prove it is not anti-semitic to compare Israel to Nazi Ger- many', The Canary (4 May 2016) https://www.thecanary.co/ uk/2016/05/04/the-inconvenient-truths-that-prove-it-is-not- anti-semitic-to-compare-israel-to-nazi-germany/

16 'Pagan Holocaust...': Marlon Solomon, tweet (18 January 2018) https://twitter.com/supergutman/status/953923757407657985; 'We resolutely...': Labour Party Forum, Position Statement https://www.facebook.com/groups/LabourPartyForum/; 'TLPF membership...': Daniel Allington, '"Hitler had a valid argument against some Jews": Repertoires for the denial of antisemitism in Facebook discussion of a survey of attitudes to Jews and Israel', Discourse, Context & Media (2018), p.6 https:// doi.org/10.1016/j.dcm.2018.03.004

17 All quotes and statistics relating to Palestine Live are from David Collier, Antisemitism Inside Palestine Live Parts 1 & 2 (6 March 2018) http://david-collier.com/wp-content/uploads/2018/03/180305_livereport_part1_FINAL.pdf & http://david-collier.com/wp-content/uploads/2018/03/180305_livereport_part2_FINAL.pdf

18 'Nazi-grade...': 'Palestine Live and Me', Harry's Place blog (10 March 2018) http://hurryupharry.org/2018/03/10/palestine-live-and-me/; 'I replied...': 'Corbyn admits membership of controversial FB group, but denies seeing anti-Semitic posts', *Jewish News* (9 March 2018) http://jewishnews.timesofisrael.com/corbyn-admits-membership-of-controversial-fb-group-but-denies-seeing-anti-semitic-posts/; 'Like a...': Jeremy Corbyn, Facebook comment (2 December 2014) https://www.facebook.com/SybilCock/posts/10152576095948613?comment_id=10152577167213613&comment_tracking=%7B%22tn%22%3A%22R0%22%7D; 'David's problem...': Jeremy Corbyn, Facebook comment (6 March 2011) https://www.facebook.com/soniaklein/posts/10150154219456882?comment_id=15459351&comment_tracking=%7B%22tn%22%3A%22R4%22%7D; 'Hugely profit...': Jeremy Corbyn, Facebook comment (3 March 2011) https://www.facebook.com/permalink.php?story_fbid=1891325450674&id=1467640116&comment_id=1443913&comment_tracking=%7B%22tn%22%3A%22R%22%7D; 'Does the...': Jeremy Corbyn, Facebook comment (28 January 2011) https://www.facebook.com/keith.

flett.90/posts/137143946348415?comment_id=1022511&comment_tracking=%7B%22tn%22%3A%22R8%22%7D

19 'A mural...': MearOneHD, 'Mear One – False Profits', YouTube
    (23 September 2012) https://www.youtube.com/watch?v=b-
    9p8Og6-YcY; 'Jewish and...': Shane Croucher, 'Mear One's Brick
    Lane Street Art: Is Mural Anti-Semitic?', International Business
    Times (4 October 2012)

20 'Whether intentional...': Marcus Dysch, 'Mayor: Tower Hamlets
    mural "to be removed"', Jewish Chronicle (4 October 2012); 'They
    want...': Luciana Berger, tweet (23 March 2018) https://twit-
    ter.com/lucianaberger/status/977183210051338241; 'Responding
    to...': Stephen Pollard, 'There is only one word for Jeremy Cor-
    byn', Jewish Chronicle (24 March 2018)

21 'In the end...': Howard Jacobson, 'Enough is Enough', Jewish
    Chronicle (29 March 2018)

22 'Enough is enough...': Jewish Leadership Council & Board of
    Deputies of British Jews, 'Letter to Jeremy Corbyn' (25 March
    2018) https://www.thejlc.org/letter_to_jeremy_corbyn

23 'Has surfaced...': Jeremy Corbyn, letter to Jonathan Goldstein
    & Jonathan Arkush (26 March 2018) https://www.bod.org.uk/
    wp-content/uploads/2018/03/Jeremy-Corbyn-letter-to-Jon-
    athan-Goldstein-and-Jonathan-Arkush.pdf; 'Accusations
    of...': Momentum, tweet (2 April 2018) https://twitter.com/
    peoplesmomentum/status/980812045162565637?s=11

24 Opinion polls: YouGov (27–29 March 2018) https://d25d2506s-
    fb94s.cloudfront.net/cumulus_uploads/document/a1lnfhilsh/

TimesResults_180329_LabourMembers_W.pdf & Deltapoll
(5–6 April 2018) file:///C:/Users/PC/Downloads/Observer-poll-Apr18.pdf; 'Desperation…': 'Right-Wing Cynicism
Laid Bare: Corbyn Didn't Even Defend the Mural. The "Row"
Hurts Jewish People', Skwawkbox (25 March 2018) https://
skwawkbox.org/2018/03/25/right-wing-cynicism-laid-bare-corbyn-didnt-even-defend-the-mural-the-row-hurts-jewish-people/; 'Explain…': Sarah Ditum, tweet (31 March 2018) https://
twitter.com/sarahditum/status/980074416376827904?s=11;
'When people…': Kevin Schofield, 'Labour MP who attended
anti-Semitism demo "run out" of local party meeting', PoliticsHome (6 April 2018) https://www.politicshome.com/
news/uk/political-parties/labour-party/news/94167/labour-mp-who-attended-anti-semitism-demo-run-out; 'Tackling
antisemitism…': Jennie Formby, tweet (5 April 2018) https://
twitter.com/jenniegensec/status/981991599705088001

25 'right wing…': Christine Morgan, Facebook comment (26
March 2018) https://www.facebook.com/SKWAWKBOX/
posts/1384249288343746; 'More ridiculous…': Emma Baker,
Facebook comment (23 March 2018) https://www.facebook.
com/SKWAWKBOX/posts/1381987191903289; 'Wealthy Jewish…': William Donald Williams, Facebook comment (26
March 2018) https://www.facebook.com/SKWAWKBOX/
posts/1384249288343746; 'The "Friends…"': Ian Burrill, Facebook comment (26 March 2018) https://www.facebook.com/
SKWAWKBOX/posts/1383944255040916; 'This is about…':

Rose Thomas, Facebook comment (26 March 2018) https://
www.facebook.com/SKWAWKBOX/posts/1384698118298863;
'Just more...': Craig Mitchell, Facebook comment (28
March 2018) https://www.facebook.com/TheCanaryUK/
posts/1772740136098105; 'Zionists run...': Mike Letham, Facebook comment (27 March 2018) https://www.facebook.com/
TheCanaryUK/posts/1772278019477650; 'This is what...': Lee
Cockrane, Facebook comment (26 March 2018) https://www.face-
book.com/TheCanaryUK/posts/1771274772911308; 'Maybe...':
Michael Ashall, Facebook comment (26 March 2018) https://
www.facebook.com/TheCanaryUK/posts/1771189562919829;
'Yesterday...': Frances Naggs, Facebook post (27 March 2018)
https://www.facebook.com/groups/WeSupportJeremyCor-
byn/permalink/1007319269429947/; 'An antisemitic...': John
McDonnell, tweet (30 March 2018) https://twitter.com/john-
mcdonnellmp/status/979680801699790854?lang=en; 'Zionist
Jewish...': Gabriel Pogrund, Jon Ungoed-Thomas & Richard
Kerbaj, 'Vitriol and threats of violence: the ugly face of Jeremy
Corbyn's cabal', *Sunday Times* (1 April 2018)

Chapter Eight: Why Chakrabarti Failed

1   'Cultural problem...': Baroness Jan Royall, 'Allega-
    tions of Anti-Semitism: Oxford University Labour Club'
    (2016); 'Disappointment...': Jan Royall, untitled, Jew-
    ish Vanguard blog (17 May 2016) http://www.jlm.org.uk/

baroness_royall_on_her_report_there_is_too_often_a_culture_of_intolerance_where_jews_are_concerned_and_there_are_clear_incidents_of_antisemitism

2   'An honest…': Martin Bright, 'Visceral hostility is not new from loose cannon Ken', *Jewish Chronicle* (5 May 2016); 'Antisemitism and…' and all subsequent quotes from Chakrabarti Report: Shami Chakrabarti, 'Report: The Shami Chakrabarti Inquiry' (30 June 2016)

3   'Institutional…': David Hirsh, 'Submission to the Labour Party Inquiry into Antisemitism' (17 May 2016)

4   'Traitor': Kevin Schofield, 'Jewish Labour MP left in tears at launch of anti-Semitism report', PoliticsHome (30 June 2016) https://www.politicshome.com/news/uk/political-parties/labour-party/news/76781/jewish-labour-mp-left-tears-launch-anti-semitism; 'It was…': Mark Gardner, 'Corbyn and the rent-a-mob: How to wreck an anti-racism event', *Jewish News* (1 July 2016); 'Do you…': Marcus Dysch, 'How the unveiling of Labour's antisemitism report turned into a Corbyn calamity', *Jewish Chronicle* (30 June 2016)

5   'Gold standard…': Jeremy Corbyn, 'My speech at the launch of the Chakrabarti report' http://jeremycorbyn.org.uk/articles/jeremy-corbyn-my-speech-at-the-launch-of-the-chakrabarti-report/; 'I saw…': 'Jeremy Corbyn Accused Of "Catastrophic Failure Of Leadership"' YouTube (2 July 2016) https://www.youtube.com/watch?v=U9aJzuLf1W0; 'Antisemitism at…': 'Video: For Transparency, #MarcWadsworth's Actual Words Re

Ruth Smeeth', Skwawkbox (25 April 2018) https://skwawkbox. org/2018/04/25/video-for-transparency-marcwadsworths-actual-words-re-ruth-smeeth/; 'Make way...': Anoosh Chakelian, 'Jewish Labour MP Ruth Smeeth was reduced to tears at Labour's anti-Semitism inquiry press conference', *New Statesman* (30 June 2016); 'The political...': Marcus Dysch, 'How the unveiling of Labour's antisemitism report turned into a Corbyn calamity', *Jewish Chronicle* (30 June 2016); 'Whitewash...': Rowena Mason, 'Corbyn's offer of peerage to Shami Chakrabarti causes Labour tensions', *The Guardian* (4 August 2016)

6 'Incendiary': BBC *Daily Politics* and *Sunday Politics*, tweet (13 May 2018) https://twitter.com/daily_politics/status/ 995614890269159425?s=11; 'Grossly offensive...': Jeremy Corbyn, tweet (5 April 2017) https://twitter.com/jeremycorbyn/ status/849615483657748480?lang=en; 'Extraordinary...': Stephen Oryszczuk, 'EXCLUSIVE interview with Len McCluskey: "Ken's comments were indefensible"' *Jewish News* (14 December 2017); 'Corbyn: Ken Livingstone...': Hansard, Home Affairs Committee Oral evidence, 4 July 2016, HC 136 Q228, Q315–323

7 'Sad...': Pippa Crerar, 'Ken Livingstone quits Labour after antisemitism claims', *The Guardian* (21 May 2018)

8 'For far...': David Hirsh, 'The Livingstone Formulation', Engage website (5 October 2010) https://engageonline. wordpress.com/2010/ 10/05/david-hirsh-the-livingstone-formulation/; 'Ulterior motives...': 'The Nonsense Of Smeeth's "Name & Shame" Demand', Skwawkbox (2 September 2016)

https://skwawkbox.org/2016/09/02/the-nonsense-of-smeeths-name-shame-demand/; 'The Establishment...': 'Most Dangerous Rule-Change In Years Is In Line For Conference 2017 Vote', Skwawkbox (21 August 2017) https://skwawkbox.org/2017/08/21/most-dangerous-rule-change-in-years-is-in-line-for-conference-2017-vote/; 'The Labour right...': James Wright, 'Jewish voters are done with the bogus antisemitism smears against Jeremy Corbyn', The Canary (26 March 2018) https://www.thecanary.co/uk/analysis/2018/03/26/jewish-voters-are-done-with-the-bogus-antisemitism-smears-against-jeremy-corbyn/; 'Media pundits...': James Wright, 'As the Labour coup falls apart, the media scrapes the bottom of the barrel to smear Corbyn', The Canary (30 June 2016) https://www.thecanary.co/uk/2016/06/30/labour-coup-falls-apart-media-scrapes-bottom-barrel-smear-corbyn/; 'Coordinated effort...': Kerry-Anne Mendoza, 'The sickening campaign to silence Corbyn and the Left by exploiting victims of the Holocaust', The Canary (28 April 2016) https://www.thecanary.co/uk/2016/04/28/how-the-establishment-is-trying-to-silence-corbyn-and-the-left-with-cries-of-anti-semitism/

9   'They're trying...': Ben, tweet (19 April 2018) https://twitter.com/Jamin2g/status/986914500510212096; 'Mood music...': BBC *Newsnight*, 'Labour does not have anti-Semitism issue: Len McCluskey', YouTube (26 September 2017) https://www.youtube.com/watch?v=CzWgwEQNtS8; 'It's a smear...': Rajeev Syal, 'Diane Abbott says claims of antisemitism within Labour

are smear', *The Guardian* (1 May 2016); 'Exaggerated...': Ken Loach, 'Letter: Clarifying My Comments on the Holocaust', *New York Times* (13 October 2017); 'Utterly disgusting...': Vice News, 'Jeremy Corbyn: The Outsider', YouTube (31 May 2016) https://www.youtube.com/watch?v=94ptAcbfKP0; 'No one...': Jonathan Freedland, 'Labour and the left have an antisemitism problem', *The Guardian* (18 March 2016); 'With antisemites...': Jewish Leadership Council & Board of Deputies of British Jews, 'Letter to Jeremy Corbyn' (25 March 2018) https://www.thejlc. org/letter_to_jeremy_corbyn; 'Pain...': Jeremy Corbyn, letter to Jonathan Goldstein & Jonathan Arkush (26 March 2018) https:// www.bod.org.uk/wp-content/uploads/2018/03/Jeremy-Corbyn-letter-to-Jonathan-Goldstein-and-Jonathan-Arkush.pdf

10 'Smeared as...': Paul Mason, 'How Labour can fight back against the British establishment's attempt to destroy it', *New Statesman* (4 April 2018); 'A socially...': David Rosenberg, 'Enough is Enough: What would Mandela have said?', Jewish Voice for Labour website (28 March 2018) http://www.jewishvoiceforlabour.org. uk/antiracism/reflections-on-mondays-events-in-parliament-square/; 'A malicious...': 'Enough is Enough', Jewdas website (29 March 2018) https://www.jewdas.org/enough-is-enough/; 'Corbyn's alarming...': Peter Kirker, 'Enough already with this zionist frenzy', *Morning Star* (4 April 2018)

11 'The smear...': 'Vote anti-racist, vote pro-immigrant – vote Jeremy Corbyn, says David Rosenberg', Jews For Jeremy (31 August 2015) https://jewsforjeremy.org/2015/08/31/

vote-anti-racist-vote-pro-immigrant-vote-jeremy-corbyn-says-david-rosenberg/; 'To counter...': 'About Us', Free Speech on Israel (8 January 2017) http://freespeechonisrael.org.uk/about-us/#sthash.Jo8f8Y3X.dpbs; 'Mischievous...': 'FSOI Submission to Chakrabarti Inquiry', Free Speech on Israel (undated) http://freespeechonisrael.org.uk/shami-chakrabarti-inquiry-remit-make-submission/#sthash.nwh1GpiV.dpbs; 'Lie': 'Free Speech on Israel motions for labour movement and other anti-racist organisations', Free Speech on Israel (undated) http://freespeechonisrael.org.uk/model-motion-on-antisemitism-allegations-for-labour-movement/#sthash.94USIhQR.dpbs; 'False flag...': Daniel Sugarman, 'Leading JVL figure blames "Zionists" for deaths of thousands of Jews in Holocaust', *Jewish Chronicle* (2 May 2018)

12 'Take down': Ian Cobain & Ewen MacAskill, 'Israeli diplomat caught on camera plotting to "take down" UK MPs', *The Guardian* (7 January 2017); 'Improper interference...': Ian Cobain & Ewen MacAskill, 'Labour calls for inquiry into Israeli diplomat's "take down MPs" plot', *The Guardian* (8 January 2017); 'Most senior...': Mike Cushman, 'Al Jazeera Lifts the Lid on the Swamp of Israeli Subversion', Free Speech on Israel (17 January 2017) http://freespeechonisrael.org.uk/al-jazeera-israeli-subversion/#sthash.qS1UtW4O.dpbs; 'Plays no...': Edward Malnick, 'John McDonnell accused of hypocrisy over Labour anti-Semitism', *Sunday Telegraph* (3 June 2018); 'False accusations...': Pete Firmin, 'Defending Ken is

Defending Jeremy', Labour Briefing (10 April 2017) http://labourbriefing.squarespace.com/home/2017/4/10/defending-ken-is-defending-jeremy; 'The Tory…': Mick Brooks, 'Antisemitic Slurs: Time to Fight Back', Labour Representation Committee (28 March 2018) https://labourrep.com/blog/2018/3/28/antisemitic-slurs-time-to-fight-back; 'The malicious…': Welsh Labour Grassroots Momentum, 'On Anti-Semitism in the Labour Party', Labour Representation Committee (29 March 2018) https://labourrep.com/blog/2018/3/30/welsh-labour-grassroots-momentum-statement-on-anti-semitism-in-the-labour-party; 'The baseball…': Jonathan Rosenhead, 'Building an alternative voice', Labour Briefing (24 April 2018) http://labourbriefing.squarespace.com/home/2018/4/24/building-an-alternative-voice; 'Allegations of…': 'Statement from Africans For Jeremy Corbyn Values', Labour Representation Committee (15 June 2016) http://l-r-c.org.uk/news/story/statement-from-africans-for-jeremy-corbyn-values/

13 'Engaging…': Jack Mendel, 'Demands to revoke Jewish Labour Movement award', *Jewish News* (26 September 2017); 'Defenders…': 'What is the Jewish Labour Movement?', Free Speech on Israel (undated) http://freespeechonisrael.org.uk/who-are-jewish-labour-movement/#sthash.zfFZYEPH.dpbs; 'A representative…': 'Who Is The Jewish Labour Movement?', International Jewish Anti-Zionist Network leaflet (undated); 'We have…': Glyn Secker, blog comment (25 March 2018) http://www.jewishvoiceforlabour.org.uk/

jvl/a-jvl-statement-on-the-current-attacks-on-jeremy-cor-byn/#comment-3058

14 'Every time ...': 'Leah Lavane [*sic*] for Hastings & Rye: We remit our rule change, but we ask you to recognise the dangers of the NEC rule change', Jewish Voice for Labour (26 September 2017) http://www.jewishvoiceforlabour.org.uk/labour-party-policy/leah-la-vane-hastings-rye-remit-rule-change-ask-recognise-dangers-nec-rule-change/; 'Conference ...': 'Naomi Wimborne-Idrissi wows Labour Party conference', Jewish Voice for Labour (25 September 2017) http://www.jewishvoiceforlabour.org.uk/labour-party-policy/naomi-wimborne-idrissi-wows-labour-par-ty-conference/; 'This is ...': Matthew Weaver & Jessica Elgot, 'Labour fringe speaker's Holocaust remarks spark new antisem-itism row', *The Guardian* (26 September 2017); 'History is ...': 'Ken Loach on "false" anti-Semitism claims by Labour MPs', BBC News (26 September 2017) http://www.bbc.co.uk/news/av/uk-politics-41404925/ken-loach-on-false-anti-semitism-claims-by-labour-mps; 'I listened ...': Stephen Oryszczuk, 'EXCLUSIVE interview with Len McCluskey: "Ken's comments were inde-fensible"' *Jewish News* (14 December 2017); 'Transforms the ...': 'Len On JVL – "Really Impressed, We'll Be Getting Involved Not Just Endorsing"', Skwawkbox (26 September 2017) https://skwawkbox.org/2017/09/26/len-on-jvl-really-impressed-well-be-getting-involved-not-just-endorsing/

15 'Anti-Zionism does ...': Moshé Machover, 'Anti-Zionism does not equal anti-Semitism', Labour Party Marxists (21 September 2017);

'Anti-Semitism scandal ...': Dave Rich, tweet (18 September 2017) https://twitter.com/daverich1/status/909707321500225536; 'From supporters ...': 'Don't expel Moshé Machover', Free Speech on Israel (13 October 2017) http://freespeechonisrael. org.uk/machover-corbyn/#sthash.mQer1LB6.QV2D1In8.dpbs; 'We are ...': David Shearer, 'Build the momentum', *Weekly Worker* (2 November 2017) & Lucy Lips, 'Moshe Machover Reinstated', Harry's Place blog (31 October 2017)

16 'Good people ...': Justin Cohen, 'Exclusive Jewish News interview with Jeremy Corbyn: "I'm not an anti-Semite in any form"', *Jewish News* (28 March 2018)

17 'What debt ...': Paul Francis, 'Leading Labour activist Jacqueline Walker, of Thanet Momentum, suspended over comments about the holocaust', Kent Online (4 May 2016)

18 'Spurious ...': Labour Representation Committee, 'Lift the suspension of Jackie Walker!' (4 May 2016) https://labourbriefing. squarespace.com/home/2016/5/4/lift-the-suspension-of-jackie-walker; 'Frenzied ...': Jon Lansman, 'A frenzied witch-hunt is not the way to combat anti-Semitism or any form of racism', Left Futures (9 May 2016) http://www.leftfutures.org/2016/05/a-frenzied-witch-hunt-is-not-the-way-to-combat-antisemitism-or-any-form-of-racism/; 'Amongst': Lee Levitt, 'Jackie Walker in Edinburgh: cheers and a standing ovation', *Jewish Chronicle* (6 August 2017); 'increasing convergence ...': Jackie Walker, 'We Must Not Be Silent!' (26 May 2016) http://labourbriefing. squarespace.com/home/2016/5/28/we-mustnot-be-silent

19 'If offence…': Ashley Cowburn, 'Momentum vice chair Jackie
    Walker apologises over "appalling" Holocaust comments', *The
    Independent* (28 September 2016)

20 'Hierarchy of…': Jacqueline Walker, Facebook post (4 April
    2018) https://www.facebook.com/jacqueline.walker.3990/vid-
    eos/10155698255679912/; 'In recent…': Jackie Walker, 'History
    of The Lynching' (undated) https://jackiewalker.org/the-lynch-
    ing-3/history-of-the-lynching/; 'The outrageous…': Labour
    Against the Witch-Hunt, leaflet (January 2018); 'A cynical…':
    Labour Against the Witch-Hunt, 'Anti-Semitism: Open letter
    to Jeremy Corbyn and the left on the NEC' (undated) https://
    www.change.org/p/labour-against-the-witchhunt-anti-sem-
    itism-open-letter-to-jeremy-corbyn-and-the-left-on-the-nec;
    'Ridiculous…': 'Labour's Chris Williamson: "It was a privilege to
    share platform with Jackie Walker"', *Jewish News* (19 March 2018)

21 'It's all…': Jessica Elgot, 'Leaked minutes show Labour at
    odds over antisemitism claims', *The Guardian* (6 April 2018);
    'There is…': Labour Party National Executive Commit-
    tee, 'Recommendations of the NEC Antisemitism Working
    Group' (22 May 2018); 'International Red…': Labour Coun-
    cillors Against Antisemitism, tweet (21 March 2018) https://
    twitter.com/AntisemitismOut/status/976383505100832769;
    'A jew…': Labour Councillors Against Antisemitism, tweet
    (21 March 2018) https://twitter.com/AntisemitismOut/sta-
    tus/976383364432351232; 'Labour Councillors…': Twitter
    account @AntisemitismOut

22   'political reasons...': Sam Coates, tweet (28 March 2018) https://
       twitter.com/SamCoatesTimes/status/979100823836872704;
       'Shenanigans around...': Hurryupharry, tweet (30 March 2018)
       https://twitter.com/hurryupharry/status/979699587005939712;
       'Damaging the...': Richard Ferris & Matthew Mahabadi, 'We
       tried to call out anti-Semitism in our local Labour party – we felt
       ignored', *New Statesman* (28 March 2018)

23   'Nothing you...' and all subsequent quotes from Livingstone dis-
       ciplinary hearing: 'Hearing Before The National Constitutional
       Committee Of The Labour Party In The Matter Of The National
       Executive Committee Of The Labour Party-V-Mr Ken Living-
       stone' (30 March–4 April 2018)

24   'It has...': Andrew Gilligan, 'Jewish councillors expose Cor-
       bynistas' "crude abuse"', *Sunday Times* (18 March 2018);
       'Singling-out'...: Philip Rosenberg, 'The institutional racism in
       my local Labour party', *Jewish News* (23 February 2018); 'Mono-
       mania...': Private conversation with the author (5 June 2018)

25   'Hostile environment...': 'Formal complaint re; Dulwich and
       West Norwood (DAWN) Constituency Labour Party (CLP)'
       (4 February 2018)

Conclusion: Institutional Antisemitism

1   'Detected in...': Sir William MacPherson, 'The Stephen Law-
       rence Inquiry Report' (February 1999)

2   'Has too...': Jeremy Corbyn, letter to Jonathan Goldstein &

Jonathan Arkush (26 March 2018) https://www.bod.org.uk/ wp-content/uploads/2018/03/Jeremy-Corbyn-letter-to-Jonathan-Goldstein-and-Jonathan-Arkush.pdf

3 'The failure…': Home Affairs Committee, Antisemitism in the UK, HC 136, 2016–17

4 'Throughout…': Adam Langleben, 'I was a Jewish Labour councillor in Barnet – and I warned Jeremy Corbyn what was coming', *New Statesman* (9 May 2018)

5 Justin Cohen, 'Jeremy Corbyn tells Chanukah party that three Barnet seats are "within our reach"', *Jewish News* (14 December 2017); 'Jeremy Corbyn: No anti-Semitism was "ever done in my name"', *Jewish News* (19 April 2018)

ABOUT THE AUTHOR

D r Dave Rich is a leading authority on antisemitism, anti-Zionism and political extremism and lectures regularly on these subjects in the UK and overseas. He is head of policy at the Community Security Trust, a UK Jewish charity that advises and represents the UK Jewish community on matters relating to antisemitism, terrorism and extremism, and an associate research fellow at the Pears Institute for the Study of Antisemitism, Birkbeck, University of London, where he completed his PhD in 2015. He has written for newspapers and journals including the *New York Times, Guardian, New States-man, Huffington Post, Standpoint, Ha'aretz, World Affairs Journal, Jewish Chronicle, Israel Journal of Foreign Affairs* and the *Forward*. His academic publications include chapters and articles on hate crime, Islamist extremism, the abuse of Holocaust memory, antisemitism on university campuses and the UK campaign for Soviet Jewry. He tweets at @daverich1 and in his spare time he still dreams about playing for Manchester United.

INDEX

INDEX

Britain
    race relations 205–7
    role in Middle East xix–xx, 2
Britain–Palestine All-Party Parliamentary
    Group 150
British Anti-Zionist Organisation
    (BAZO) 28, 99–100, 143, 145,
    150
    student politics 120, 130, 152–3
British media 24, 50, 91, 164, 213
British National Party (BNP) 145, 198, 215
Brockway, Fenner 13, 67
Brown, Gordon xvii, 239
BSkyB 274
Bull, Alan 322–3, 325
Bunglawala, Inayat 169
Burden, Richard 99, 100, 130, 150–54,
    155–6
Burnham, Andy 299
Burrowes, David 296–8
Bush, George 213
Butler, Judith 175
BuzzFeed News 264
Byers, Lord 57

Cairo, Egypt 50–51
Cairo Anti-war Conference 188–9
Callinicos, Alex 129
Cambridge University 125
Cameron, David 231, 293
Campaign for Nuclear Disarmament
    (CND) 8, 10
Campbell, Bob 249
Canary, The 263–4, 267, 281, 282, 300
capitalism 108, 115, 189, 199–200, 206
    association with Jews 200–202, 217
Carter, Jimmy 32
Cartwright, Russell 325
Cesarani, David 131–2, 223–4
Chakrabarti Inquiry 288–98, 320, 340
Chakrabarti, Shami 287–98, 338
Chalmers, Alex 247, 286
Charlie Hebdo 326
Chaucer, Geoffrey 243
Childers, Erskine 27
Chomsky, Noam 321
chosen people concept 20, 50–51, 114, 226
Christian students' societies 125

Church of England 241
Churchill, Caryl 225–7
City of London Polytechnic 139
City University, London xvii
Clarke, Charles 118, 121
Class Nature of Israeli Society, The 26, 101
class politics 8, 14, 15, 90
Clause 4 Group 154
Cliff, Tony 24
Collier, David 269, 271
colonialism
    British xx, 78, 205–8
    Israel xviii, 19–20, 25, 49, 104–5,
    111–13, 188, 199–200
Combat 18 group 214
communism 115
Communist Party 6, 12, 131, 152, 190, 191
Communist states 112–13
Conservative Party 142, 240, 246, 294, 300
conspiracy theories
    antisemitic 21, 27, 52–3, 106,
    200–201, 212–16, 330, 335
    Zionist xxiii, 21, 55–6, 189, 214–16,
    250–51
Corbyn, Jeremy 10, 84, 239, 262, 264–6,
    281–2, 296, 299, 313, 321, 328–9
    anti-Zionism xv, 147–50
    British colonialism xix–xx, 235
    Chakrabarti Inquiry response 293–9
    Labour Party leadership 191–2, 240,
    250, 261–2, 285, 293, 305, 319, 320,
    332, 336, 338, 346, 349–50
    Stop the War Coalition 189–90, 209
    support for Palestinians xviii, 142,
    160–62, 172, 174–5, 185–6, 188–9,
    209, 240–2, 269, 314–16
    support for Raed Salah 242, 244–7
    views on antisemitism 196–9, 272–80,
    288, 292, 348–50
    views on Israel xx, 34, 72–3, 247
Corrie, Rachel 171
Couchman, Terry 260
Council for the Advancement of Arab-
    British Understanding (CAABU) 28,
    81, 98
Council of Europe 232
Cox, Jox 293
cricket tours 43–8, 57

401

attitude to Israel 73, 220–21
British Anti-Zionist Organisation
(BAZO) 100, 153
support for Palestinians 144, 161, 177–8
Gardner, Mark 294
Gates Jr, Henry Louis 244
Gaza Strip xix, xxiv, 7, 33, 72, 141, 184–5,
220–21, 225–7, 267
General Union of Arab Students (GUPS)
27, 81, 139, 140, 155
National Union of Students (NUS)
119–20, 133–5, 137
genocides 199–200, 218, 230–31, 255
Genovese, Eugene D. 244
German, Lindsey 161, 181–2, 190, 193
Germany 201
Ghana 13
Ghannouchi, Sheikh Rached 161
Gilbert, Mads 274
Gilbert, Martin 224
Gilroy, Paul 232–3
Global South see also third world 188
globalisation 191, 232
Golan Heights xix, 33
Goldberg, Joe 331
Gratrex, Tony 270
Greater London Authority 187
Greater London Council 144–5, 146–7
Greaves, Bernard 40
Greaves, Tony 61
Green, Elleanne 270, 273–4, 315
green line 33, 36–8
Greenstein, Tony 100, 143, 148, 200,
314–15, 320, 349
Gromyko, Andrei 3, 4
Gruenwald, Malchiel 222
Guardian, The xviii, 32, 92–3, 95, 109,
136, 172–3, 183, 186, 213, 301
offices 44
guerrilla fighters 16, 75–6
Guevara, Che 23, 170
Guido Fawkes 252

Haavara Agreement 258
Hain, Peter 42–5, 56, 64, 68, 86, 88, 93–4,
96–7
Hall, Stuart 18
Halliday, Fred 74

Hamas 241
British support xxiv, 17, 160, 169–75,
179, 187, 189, 193, 242
Corbyn, Jeremy xv, 174–5, 279
Covenant 175–7
suicide bombings 159, 164–5, 174
Hammami, Sa'id 91, 93, 97
Hanegbi, Haim 101
Hanif, Asif Mohammed 171, 173, 174
Harakat-ul-Mujahideen (HUM) 172
Hardie, Keir 203
Harman, Chris 85, 180
Hasan, Usama 168
Hasbara 268
Hawatmeh, Nayef 82
Healy, Gerry 143
Helbawy, Kamal 160–61
Hellyer, Peter 40–42, 47–8, 50–53, 62, 65,
68, 80, 83–4, 96
Herzog, Chaim 114
Heydrich, Reinhard 312
Hezbollah
British support xxiv, 17, 161, 177–8, 189
Corbyn, Jeremy xv, 174–5, 279
policies 172
Hirsh, David 290, 299
Histadrut, Israel 5
Hitler, Adolf 195–6, 254–8, 270, 296,
297, 325, 329, 333
Hizb ut-Tahrir 168, 173, 181
Hoey, Kate 119
Hollande, François 231–2
Holocaust 184, 244, 257, 263, 303–4,
312, 315, 316, 326, 330
commemoration 228–36, 318
denial xvi, 106, 145, 209, 241, 261,
265, 267–71, 311, 322, 333–4, 343
modern comparisons 220–25, 251
re-evaluation 199–200, 218–19, 236,
335
survivors 4, 105, 234
Holocaust and the Liberal Imagination,
The 228
Holocaust Educational Trust 230–31, 297
Holocaust Memorial Day 228, 232, 235,
267, 318, 332
Home Affairs Select Committee 256,
296, 342

INDEX